T0270983

Reconsidering Central Bank Independence

Central bank independence has become one of the most widely accepted tenets of modern monetary policy. According to this view, the main role of independent central banks is to maintain price stability through the adjustment of short-term interest rates. *Reconsidering Central Bank Independence* argues that the global financial crisis has undermined confidence in this view as central banks increasingly have to address concerns other than price stability, such as financial stability, the need for output recovery and other broader policy goals. Large balance-sheet expansion by central banks followed the global financial crisis, which overlapped considerably with the financial policy of their respective governments. Exploring the consequences of this shift to a more diverse set of policy challenges, this book calls for a return to the consensus role for central banks and analyses what this might mean for their future independence.

STAN DU PLESSIS IS Professor of Macroeconomics at Stellenbosch University, where he is Chief Operating Officer and formerly Dean. A past president of the Economic Society of South Africa, he studied at the University of Cambridge, Stellenbosch University and the Wharton Business School, and is a member of the Academy of Science of South Africa.

ANDREAS FREYTAG is Professor of Economics at the Friedrich Schiller University Jena, where he heads the Schumpeter Center for Research on Socio-Economic Change, and Honorary Professor at the University of Stellenbosch. He is associated with many international education organisations and think tanks.

DAWIE VAN LILL is a Senior Macroprudential Specialist at the South African Reserve Bank and teaches macroeconomics at Stellenbosch University. His research spans time series methods and machine learning, with a particular interest in monetary policy. Recently, he has been exploring the development of macroeconomic models to assess the distributional effects of government policies.

Reconsidering Central Bank Independence

STAN DU PLESSIS
Stellenbosch University

ANDREAS FREYTAG
Friedrich Schiller University Jena

DAWIE VAN LILL
Stellenbosch University

CAMBRIDGE
UNIVERSITY PRESS

Shaftesbury Road, Cambridge CB2 8EA, United Kingdom

One Liberty Plaza, 20th Floor, New York, NY 10006, USA

477 Williamstown Road, Port Melbourne, VIC 3207, Australia

314–321, 3rd Floor, Plot 3, Splendor Forum, Jasola District Centre, New Delhi – 110025, India

103 Penang Road, #05–06/07, Visioncrest Commercial, Singapore 238467

Cambridge University Press is part of Cambridge University Press & Assessment, a department of the University of Cambridge.

We share the University's mission to contribute to society through the pursuit of education, learning and research at the highest international levels of excellence.

www.cambridge.org
Information on this title: www.cambridge.org/9781108493291

DOI: 10.1017/9781108681186

© Cambridge University Press & Assessment 2024

First published 2024

A catalogue record for this publication is available from the British Library

A Cataloging-in-Publication data record for this book is available from the Library of Congress

ISBN 978-1-108-49329-1 Hardback

Contents

Illustrations

Preface

Until recently, and for a generation, inflation had been dispelled from the developed world and from much of the developing world too. This benign era followed periods of high inflation all over the world, often leading to chronically high inflation in many developing countries. But inflation returned in the wake of the COVID-19 pandemic and the Russian invasion of Ukraine, reaching levels not seen in the developed world for forty years. The precise causes of this latest inflation remain to be determined at the time of writing in September 2023.

Fifteen years ago, the world economy was rocked by the Great Recession, the most significant peacetime disruption of economic activity internationally since the Great Depression of the 1930s. Pierre Siklos (2017), in his book *Central Banks to the Breach*, gives a very detailed and highly readable account of the monetary policy that led to the Great Recession as well as the policy responses to the crisis. It is at this point that we pick up the thread. We tell the story of monetary policy decisions following the Great Recession by focussing on the rules of conduct for monetary policy, or what economists call the institutions of monetary policy. This narrative is complemented by consideration of various theoretical approaches to the role for central banks as well as the extensive empirical evidence of the consequences of different institutional arrangements.

We place the concept of central bank independence (CBI) at the centre of the analysis, as this institutional development was decisive for the benign outcomes of monetary policy, including low inflation, in the early 1990s. By contrast, the relationship between central banks and governments has evolved over the past fifteen years, endangering the independence of central banks, as central banks have become increasingly drawn into a broader policy agenda. It is the contention of this book that the current surge in inflation is related to this deterioration in the independence of central banks and the associated confusion of their policy mandate.

With the benefit of hindsight, central banks appear to have been complacent in the run-up to the Great Recession, contributing to the asset bubbles (notably, but not exclusively, in US residential property) through excessively accommodative monetary policy. Having contributed inadvertently to the asset bubble, central banks came to the rescue of the faltering international system when the bubble burst. They did so by conventional means, that is, by lowering their policy interest rates as well as by unconventional means through the use of their powerful balance sheets.

The European Central Bank (ECB) was called on to do even more within a few years of the Great Recession as fears of fiscal collapse threatened the integrity of the single currency. And just more than a decade after the onset of the Great Recession, a global pandemic asked for yet greater policy intervention to mitigate the consequences of a massive international demand shock together with unprecedented disruption to the international supply system. In this decade and a half, monetary policy has become overburdened with policy objectives. Central banks have been called on to help stimulate real economic activity and job creation, finance the state, secure price stability as well as financial stability, and even ease the transition to greener economies. In the course of this process, central bank balance sheets enlarged, and distortions in asset markets again resulted in banks assuming more risky activities, as materialised in the problems of two major banks in the United States (Silicon Valley Bank and the First Republic Bank) and in Switzerland at Credit Suisse in March 2023.

On the one hand, this evolution gave central banks more power, as they are responsible for a wide array of topics. During the last fifteen years, observers got the impression that central banks were increasingly responsible for the economic success of the EUROZONE or the United States. Central bankers became political superstars. On the other hand, this prominence made central bankers more dependent on political events and decisions. With government finances under severe strain in many countries, pressure for monetary accommodation of fiscal policy mounted, and it became harder for central banks to move away from the extremely low interest rates of the last decade and more. This policy evolution was encouraged by what was presented as new theoretical ideas in monetary economics, which offered intellectual cover for a permissive monetary policy to finance higher public deficits. Such a free lunch would indeed be a startling discovery in economics.

The consequences of these developments in monetary policy are far-reaching. Observing economic stagnation, governments may see the need for economic reforms, but are well aware of the political costs of a reform process, with the cost of economic disruption at the start of the reform process and the sought-after improvement only in the subsequent years, a trajectory economists call the J-curve. As this process may last too long for a potential re-election in the coming general elections, governments in democracies may prefer the apparently easy option to lean on public spending in support of short-run output gains. Since the Great Recession, this extra spending has been financed through public debt that carried barely any interest cost on account of the central bank's interest rate and balance sheet policies.

These low interest costs along the yield curve may, in addition, repress structural change via commercial banks, whose profits shrink through lower and lower interest earnings. In these circumstances, banks prolong their support for ailing companies that would find it hard to secure finance in more normal circumstances. At the same time, banks become reluctant to lend to more risky new enterprises. The combined effect is that the banking sector supports less dynamic enterprise, lowering the prospects for productivity growth in the economy as a whole. This may be particularly difficult in ageing societies, in which people want to invest in secure assets, but see no interest-bearing supply. If low-income savers do not pursue an aggressive investment strategy in more risky assets, they face the prospect of inadequate retirement provision.

It is an oversimplification to trace the evolution of central bank conduct to the central bankers alone. Against this background, we analyse the politico-economic trends that have emerged in the past decades to understand the dynamics of the relation between central banks and other political actors in industrialised countries.

The book consists of three parts, with three chapters in each. In Part I, we lay the 'Theoretical Foundations'. We start it with a brief historical overview of the emergence of independent central banks (Chapter 1). In Chapter 2, we briefly discuss the causes and consequences of inflation to lay the foundation for a detailed analysis of the relation between monetary policy and other policy fields in Chapter 3. We show that different schools of thought (Chicago, Virginia, Freiburg) come to similar conclusions, although their methodological starting points are very different.

Part II analyses and relates 'Balance Sheet Operations in Different Times and CBI'. Chapter 4 is dedicated to the more recent history of monetary policy in the period labelled the Great Moderation. We focus on the Federal Reserve Board (Fed), the Bank of England (BoE), the Bundesbank and its successor, the ECB, as well as the South African Reserve Bank, which offers an interesting and contrasting perspective. Chapter 5 offers a description and an interpretation of the policy responses of four leading central banks (Fed, ECB, BoE and the Bank of Japan) to the Great Recession. This is followed by a more general analysis of balance sheet operations of central banks against the background of CBI in Chapter 6.

Finally, Part III changes the focus to the 'Political Economy of CBI in the Real Economy'. Chapter 7 takes an Olsonian perspective. We ask what drives central bank balance sheet policies in democracies. This development is understood from the perspective of Mancur Olson's groundbreaking theory of the 'rise and decline of nations', which accounts for the increasing difficulty of reform as distributional coalitions impose the slavery of the rent-seeking society (as according to the framework of the former chief economist of the General Agreement on Tariffs and Trade, Jan Tumlir) on democratic societies. In light of these considerations, the factual degree of CBI might be lower than it appears at first glance. Chapter 8 adds to a clarification of this confusion by discussing the need for transparency and accountability in light of a growing literature – mainly driven by political science – on the perceived democratic deficit of technocratic policy solutions. We show that this literature overlooks important aspects of CBI. In the final chapter (Chapter 9), we discuss the latest reactions of central banks to the rise of inflation, which can be interpreted as an attempt to safeguard their independence against governments. We consequently argue for a return to a division of labour in line with the Tinbergen rule of economic policy, which can be translated as one objective, one instrument, one agency. This shift would place much more responsibility for broader economic outcomes on the shoulders of governments, leaving central banks to tend to the narrower agenda of monetary stability.

Acknowledgements

The plans for this book began in 2014 when Stan and Andreas presented a few ideas for a policy-oriented study at the Monetary Policy Group of the Economics Department at Stellenbosch University. We received so many interesting questions and comments that we sat down for a coffee directly afterwards, almost overwhelmed. As a consequence, we decided to think about a book. For this impulse, we like to thank our colleagues in Stellenbosch. Over the coming years, we repeatedly met these colleagues to discuss our progress. In particular, we would like to mention Monique Reid and Hylton Hollander. We also want to thank a number of – partly unknown – colleagues in many places with whom we discussed the topic on various occasions: academic conferences, policy-oriented workshops or arbitrary meetings over a meal or coffee.

Despite this head start, the progress we made in the following years was modest, not least because of significant career developments Stan experienced. When Dawie finished his PhD on a related topic and joined the Economics Department in Stellenbosch, the two original authors invited him to team up with them – with much benefit for the book. Stan and Andreas are well aware of the challenge that a book project represents for a young scholar who needs to settle and find his place in the academic world.

When we were almost finished with the manuscript, the COVID-19 crisis hit and demanded much energy for teaching. In addition, it did not allow for personal meetings between the authors for almost two years. That said, these are all cheap excuses. The main responsibility for the long production process is ours.

We, nevertheless, see some benefit in the delay. Had we finished the book in 2019 it would have been outdated within a couple of months, as the most interesting and decisive developments in monetary policy were still unknown then. With the benefit of hindsight, we are happy to have experienced the delay. In fact, while the multiple crises went on, we did not see the need to hurry. The events were too exciting!

This is the time to thank Phil Good and his team at Cambridge University Press who without any complaints accepted our repeated requests for more time. Their endless patience always served as encouragement. We hope the final product can justify our slow speed and their patience. In Jena, Friederike Karl and Henri Bisch-Chandaroff supported us with editorial work, the value of which cannot be overestimated.

Abbreviations

APF	Asset Purchase Facility
APP	Asset Purchase Program
BIS	Bank for International Settlements
BoE	Bank of England
BoJ	Bank of Japan
BVAR	Bayesian vector autoregression
BVG	German Constitutional Court of Justice
BWS	Bretton Woods System
CA	current account
CBI	central bank independence
CBPP	Covered Bond Purchase Program
CBS	currency board system
CEO	chief executive officer
CME	comprehensive monetary easing
CPFF	Commercial Paper Funding Facility
CPI	consumer price index
DSGE	dynamic stochastic general equilibrium
DWF	Discount Window Facility
EAPP	Extended Asset Purchase Programme
ECB	European Central Bank
ECS	Enhanced Credit Support
EEC	European Economic Community
ELTRs	extended collateral long-term repos
EME	emerging economy
EMS	European Monetary System
EMU	(European) Economic and Monetary Union
ERM	II European Exchange Rate Mechanism II
ESCB	European System of Central Banks
ESFS	European System of Financial Supervision

ESM	European Stability Mechanism
EU	European Union
Fed	Federal Reserve Board
FDI	foreign direct investment
FLS	Funds for Lending Scheme
FOMC	Federal Reserve Open Market Committee
FRFA	Fixed Rate Procedure with Full Allotment
FROs	fixed rate operations
GDP	gross domestic product
GFC	global financial crisis
GMT	Grilli, Masciandaro, Tabellini
GSE	government sponsored enterprise
GVCs	global value chains
HBOS	Halifax Bank of Scotland
IMF	International Monetary Fund
IPCC	Intergovernmental Panel on Climate Change
JGB	Japanese Government Bond
KfW	German Kreditanstalt für Wiederaufbau
LLR	lender of last resort
LSAP	large-scale asset purchase
LTRO	longer term refinancing operation
Mo	balance sheet of a central bank
MBS	mortgage-backed securities
MEP	Maturity Extension Program
MMT	Modern Monetary Theory
MROs	main refinancing operations
N	employment
NGO	non-governmental organisation
OECD	Organisation for Economic Co-operation and Development
OMT	Outright Monetary Transaction
PAP	principal–agent problem
PDCF	Primary Dealer Credit Facility
PEPP	Pandemic Emergency Purchase Programme

PSPP	Public Sector Purchase Programme
QE	quantitative easing
QE1, 2, 3	first, second and third quantitative easing, respectively
QEP	quantitative easing programme
QQE	quantitative and qualitative monetary easing
QVAR	Qual VAR
R&D	research and development
S	seigniorage
SARB	South African Reserve Bank
SFSO	Special Funds-Supplying Operations to Facilitate Corporate Financing
SGP	Stability and Growth Pact
SLS	Special Liquidity Scheme
SMF	Sterling Monetary Framework
SMP	Securities Markets Programme
SOE	state-owned enterprise
SVAR	structural VAR
TAF	Term Auction Facility
TALF	Term Asset-Backed Securities Loan Facility
TLTRO	targeted LTRO
TSLF	Term Securities Lending Facility
TVP-VAR	time-varying parameter vector autoregression
VAR	vector autoregressive model
ZIRP	zero interest rate policy
ZLB	zero lower bound

PART I The Theoretical Foundations

I History of Central Banking

In a modern economy, markets are incomplete, information is both scarce and requires resources to discover and unlock, and transactions are costly. For these reasons, assets, liabilities and balance sheets matter and create a pivotal role for the financial sector that can help us to manage a portfolio of assets and even allocate resources to the future.

Banks and other financial intermediaries offer a range of services: they lower the information cost associated with investment and saving, and they provide insurance. But their most important function is the process we call intermediation, whereby banks match the needs of investors (retail deposits and wholesale lending) with borrowers who wish to finance consumption, investment or other business activities. From our current vantage point, a central bank appears to be a necessary component of a financial sector, and not just a component, but pre-eminent among the banks and assigned the responsibility to regulate the conduct of other banks and financial institutions as well as given a mandate to implement policy with far-reaching consequences. This was not always so.

A central bank with its modern roles and responsibilities emerged as a complete package only during the first decades of the twentieth century. These key functions are: (i) to be a banker to the government, (ii) to have a monopoly over the issuance of notes and coins, and to (iii) be regulator of and (iv) a lender of last resort to the financial sector (Capie et al., 1994). The forerunners of banks with one or more of these functions reach back hundreds of years, with the Sverige Riksbank of Sweden, founded in 1668, recognised as the oldest. The Bank of England (BoE) followed in 1694; then there was a long gap before the Banque de France was established in 1800. By the beginning of the twentieth century there were eighteen central banks internationally, a number that grew to fifty-nine by the middle of that century and has reached 179 at the time of writing (2022).[1]

The purpose of this chapter is to trace the evolution of central banking prior to the emergence of modern central banking in the twentieth century as well as the developments of that century until the disruption brought by the global financial crisis (GFC) of 2008/2009, followed by the crisis of the EUROZONE, the COVID-19 pandemic and the Russian invasion of Ukraine, starting February 2022, in slightly more than the subsequent decade. It is a dramatic story: the functions that define a modern central bank are inherently in tension, as will be evident from the post-war history of these institutions and their policy frameworks. The drama came to a head by the late 1970s, and the former Chair of the Federal Reserve Board (Fed) in the United States described it as follows at the time:

> One of the time-honored functions of a central bank is to protect the integrity of is nation's currency, both domestically and internationally. In monetary policy central bankers have a potent means for fostering stability of the general price level. By training, if not also by temperament, they are inclined to lay great stress on price stability, and their abhorrence of inflation is continually reinforced by contacts with one another and with like-minded members of the private financial community. And yet, despite their antipathy to inflation and the powerful weapons they could wield against it, central bankers have failed so utterly in this mission in recent years. In this paradox lies the anguish of central banking. (Burns, 1979, p. 7)

From that crisis in the 1970s emerged a widely shared modern framework for monetary policy as well as an institutional framework shared by many central banks. This consensus has been challenged

---

[1] The dates and numbers of central banks in the past were taken from Tables 1.1 and 1.2 in Capie et al. (1994) and the latest count of central banks from the website of the Bank for International Settlements (www.bis.org).

fundamentally in the aftermath of the GFC. This book concerns one important dimension of that consensus, the independence of central banks, which has lately been under severe pressure.

1.1 A BANK FOR THE GOVERNMENT

Towards the end of the thirteenth century, Marco Polo learnt of the paper money issued for Kublai Khan at the mint of Kanbala. The colourful account is worth quoting at some length:

> In this city of Kanbala is the mint of the Great Khan, who may truly be said to possess the secret of the alchemists, as he has the art of producing money by the following process.
>
> ...[T]he coinage of this paper money is authenticated with as much form and ceremony as if it were actually pure gold or silver; for to each note a number of officers, specially appointed, not only subscribe their names, but affix their seals also ... in this way it receives full authenticity as current money, and the act of counterfeiting it is punished as a capital offence. When thus coined in large quantities this paper currency is circulated in every part of the Great Khan's dominions; nor dares any person, at the peril of his life, refuse to accept it in payment.
>
> All his Majesty's armies are paid with this currency, which is to them the same value as if it were gold or silver. Upon these grounds, it may be certainly affirmed that the Great Khan has a more extensive command of treasure than any other sovereign in the universe. (Polo, 1930, p. 159)

The Venetian's metaphor was more penetrating than he could have intended in an era when alchemy retained an air of respectability. Ultimately, however, the treasure of the Khan's mint, like the alchemist's prize, proved ephemeral. Because the Mongol Empire's revenue was indeed vast, the abuse of seigniorage was not, initially, extreme and the subsequent inflation contained; but over time, the balance of revenue and expenses turned ever less favourable and inflation rose. As the value of money declined in the succeeding states, trust eroded and paper money was eventually abandoned to restore stability in exchange (Tullock and McKenzie, 1985; Kasper and Streit, 1998).

As for the Great Khan, it was government's continuous desire not just for finance, but for the management of government debt on favourable terms that motivated the establishment of some of the earliest central banks. The Nine Years War (1688–1697), and especially the need to rebuild the English fleet after the disastrous naval battle of Beachy Head (1690), prompted the government of William III (William of Orange) to establish the BoE as a limited liability company with the exclusive right to act as the government's banker, manage government debt and issue bank notes. Similar considerations motivated the establishment of the Banque de France, the Iberian central banks and the first two Banks of the United States in the nineteenth century (Capie et al., 1994, p. 7).

Governments' interest in cheap finance created an inherent tension with a bank that was at the same time a major investor in government bonds, the value of which would be eroded if the value of the currency was undermined. This tension, as well as the associated threat to the independence of the central bank, will take centre stage in our discussion of the monopoly central banks gained over the issuance of currency. Meanwhile Adam Smith had little doubt that 'in every country in the world ... the avarice and injustice of princes and sovereign states, abusing the confidence of their subjects, have by degrees diminished the real quantity of metal, which had been originally contained in their coins' (Smith, 1981 [1776], p. 43). The diminution in the real quantity of metal, as Smith described it, is the modern phenomenon of inflation.

In a number of post-Westphalian states, the motivation for the foundation of a central bank included explicitly the desire to develop the commercial banking sector. These included the central banks of the Netherlands, Denmark, Sweden, Norway and Austria–Hungary (Capie et al., 1994, p. 4). In many cases these were initially the only commercial bank in the respective country and did not need to be given *de jure* monopoly status on the issuance of currency.

Over time, the corporate financial sector developed in these countries and business rivalry emerged between the private sector banks and the central banks. At this point, the central bank took its place among the rest of the banking sector, albeit with notable privileges as banker to the government. These central banks did not yet enjoy a monopoly on the issuance of currency, nor did they function as lender of last resort, let alone determine interest rate policy, features now regarded as the necessary functions of a modern central bank. The competitive tension between a privileged central bank and the developing commercial banking sector was resolved in most countries only during the early twentieth century with the withdrawal by central banks from commercial banking, while the 'commercial banks voluntarily accepted the central bank's leadership – even by such informal mechanism as the Governor's eyebrows', in the words of Capie et al. (1994, p. 3).

I.2   A MONOPOLY OVER THE ISSUANCE OF NOTES AND COINS

It was in the course of the nineteenth century that central banks gained the monopoly over the issuance of local currency now associated with these institutions. During that century's early decades, the convertibility of central bank currency into gold and/or silver made it redundant to also require legal status for the central bank's currency. But that legal status was nevertheless valuable, and over the course of the second half of the century provided a pre-eminence to currency issued by the central bank. By the beginning of the twentieth century, it was expected in countries with a central bank that the latter would enjoy a monopoly to issue the means of payment.

I.3   A LENDER OF LAST RESORT

On the occasion of Milton Friedman's ninetieth birthday, Ben Bernanke, then Chair of the Fed, reviewed the evidence presented by Friedman and Schwartz (1963) in *A Monetary History of the United States* and concluded that they were right to assign much blame for the Great Depression on the failure of the Fed to support the banking sector. As Chair of the Fed, Bernanke said: 'We're very sorry. But thanks to you, we won't do it again.' The Fed would not neglect its lender of last resort duty again and in 2008, with Bernanke at the helm, the Fed had to make good on its promise. It did so, expanding the lender of last resort function of the modern central bank mightily not only to support illiquid banks, but also to prevent the entire financial system from collapsing in an extraordinary moment of crisis. In the process, they deployed concepts such as forward guidance and quantitative easing (QE) to justify a vast expansion of the central bank's balance sheet.

The idea that the central bank should use its balance sheet to provide temporary support to illiquid, though solvent, banks was not clearly understood until Bagehot's *Lombard Street* in 1873 (Bagehot, 1873). The logic behind the lender of last resort is that, under fractional reserve banking, a solvent bank can be forced into closure by even temporary liquidity pressure, the extreme form of which is a run on the bank. More disconcertingly still, such a panic could spill over to other banks, none of whom will be able to meet the liquidity requirements of a full-scale run on the banks. A central bank that steps in to provide temporary liquidity for a bank in such an embarrassing position will prevent the bank's collapse and restore public confidence in the banking system as a whole. If it is known that the central bank stands ready to perform this function credibly, then the public's confidence in the entire banking sector is strengthened and the risk of bank runs is reduced, if not avoided completely.

By 1913, the four main functions of a modern central bank could be recognised in the major central banks of the era, although the United States was to some extent an exception. Capie and his co-authors summarise this pre-war consensus as follows: the central banks enjoyed considerable independence from government and had, as its main objective, the maintenance of the gold standard (Capie et al., 1994, p. 15). To this end, the main policy instrument was interest rate control, the effectiveness of which was ensured by using discounting bills and open market operations. The central bank was the government's bank and no longer operated in competition with commercial banks. At this time, central banks had not yet been given a regulatory or supervisory role in the financial sector, but often exercised leadership and co-ordination to rescue financial institutions under the evolving lender of last resort principle.

1.4 THE DEVELOPMENT OF MACROECONOMIC POLICY AND THE EMERGENCE OF THE MODERN CONSENSUS

The Great War ended not just the European empires, but also fiscal prudence and the sound monetary management associated with the gold standard. Continental governments, especially the former central powers and Russia, had nowhere to turn but the printing press in an ultimately futile attempt to match their expenditure with a dramatically diminished tax base. As the allies were increasing the pressures on the German fiscus at Versailles, Keynes left the peace negotiations to write *The Economic Consequences of the Peace* (Keynes, 1924), wherein he predicted not just the ensuing hyperinflation, but also the disintegration of industrial society that follows the destruction of its money.[2] These predictions proved distressingly accurate, and as inflation accelerated on the continent, Keynes rose to the front rank of economists.

The 1920s brought a brief respite, but the mis-priced return to the gold standard was ill-fated in Britain. Costly deflation ensued during the Great Depression; indeed, some – most famously Friedman and Schwartz (1963) – argued that the Great Depression was the result of monetary mismanagement, which allowed a recession to spiral into a depression.

Normal economic relations were suspended during the Second World War as price controls were combined with a dramatic expansion of the productive state. Towards the end of the war, however, a return to monetary order internationally

---

[2] 'Lenin was certainly right', Keynes (1924, p. 220) argued: 'there is no subtler, no surer means of overturning the existing basis of society than to debauch the currency'.

was fundamental to the negotiations at Bretton Woods, New Hampshire. Though the ensuing international monetary system was anchored to gold via the dollar, the system failed to restrain either the Fed, or other central banks, in the expansionary policies that followed the adoption of full employment and active stabilisation as goals for macroeconomic policy (Bordo and Schwartz, 1999). Monetary stability with fiat money required different institutions, and these were slow to emerge.

The first post-war effort to create such institutions was the remarkable attempt that culminated at Bretton Woods at the end of the Second World War with an agreement on fixed (but adjustable) exchange rates among the signatories of the agreement. In this system the US dollar was anchored to gold and the other currencies pegged to the US dollar. The partner countries had to secure the bilateral exchange rates, which created the problem of the nth currency, describing the incentive for the United States to determine the inflation rate for the whole Bretton Woods System (BWS). During the 1960s and part of the 1970s, the US government had to finance the Vietnam War, and urged the Fed to provide the loans for these expenditures. These easy monetary conditions resulted in pressure on the US dollar to depreciate and capital to flow to partner countries. These foreign central banks then had to buy dollars to support the system, which meant they expanded their balance sheets and imported inflation.[3]

The system collapsed when the US government closed the gold window in August 1971, which unanchored the entire system, ushering in the era of floating exchange rates. Therefore, the full BWS lasted only from January 1959 (when the European currencies became fully convertible) to August 1971; in practice, the exchange rate used for transactions was much less stable than appears from the official rates (Reinhart and Rogoff, 2002).

---

[3] Former German Chancellor Helmut Schmidt, an economist by training and then economics minister, was cited in the press as announcing that 'every dollar will be shot at the border in the future'.

There are many differences between the institutional arrangements of the BWS and modern monetary policy regimes. A number of differences are listed by Rose (2007), including that the BWS was a deliberately designed system while modern floating exchange rates are not, and that gold had a central role in the BWS yet has none in the modern system. In his list of contrasts, the most important for this book is that central banks were politically dependent under BWS, in contrast with their largely independent modern successors. A major obstacle to central bank independence (CBI) was that the exchange rates in the BWS were a political decision: the central banks had to maintain the respective exchange rate of the national currency to the dollar. Therefore, they were not in full control of the monetary base, although they still tried to sterilise dollar inflows. In this respect, during the BWS, monetary policy was decided in cabinets to a certain degree.

The 1970s, following the collapse of Bretton Woods at the start of that decade, and the disturbances of the oil shocks, underlined the inability of the then existing monetary policy regimes to maintain monetary stability. Indeed, Figure 1.1 shows just how poorly a selection of prominent central banks fared in protecting the purchasing power of their respective currencies. The figure shows the extent to which the purchasing power (in 1960 terms) of 100 currency units in 1960 had been eroded by the end of the year 2020, for a selection of developed and developing countries.

The graph in Figure 1.1 should be interpreted as follows: each bar shows the percentage of 100 units of local 1960 purchasing power that remained after sixty years. It is the process of inflation that causes the bar to decline over time; absent inflation, the bars would have remained at 100 over time. For example, the cumulative impact of inflation in the United States since 1960 eroded the 100 units of local purchasing power in US dollar terms to 10.2 by 2020. Germany fared better, but still lost a cumulative 80 per cent of the purchasing power of the local currency over six decades, while the other countries on the graph did worse – and the entire purchasing power of the Turkish lira was, to some decimal places, wiped out over these decades.

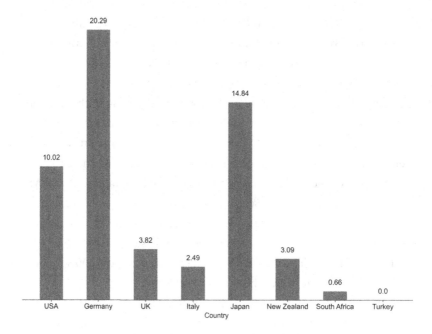

FIGURE 1.1 The purchasing power at the end of 2020 of 100 units of
local currency units in 1960
Source: Data from OECD statistics

Post-Bretton Woods, the international financial system adopted
a comprehensive fiat money regime for the first time; and for the first
time there was no automatic centralised check on the discretion of
modern monetary authorities.[4] Recently, Kydland and Wynne (2002)
argued that there is now a consensus on the need for careful institutional design as the 'best' guarantee of monetary stability under a fiat
money regime; and a nominal anchor is one important aspect of such
institutional design. (See Mishkin and Savastano (2002) for the same
conclusion with respect to emerging market economies.)

Kydland and Wynne's (2002) interpretation of the literature cor-
responds with former head of the International Monetary Fund (IMF)
Michel Camdessus' use of the term 'policy standard' to describe a

---

[4] Meanwhile, the industrialised world adopted floating exchange rates, which were
required for retaining independence for monetary policy decisions, in the light of
increasing capital flows.

fiat money system. The value of fiat money is ultimately determined by the institutional design of the system and the policies encouraged by these institutions. Or as Michael Woodford (2003, p. 1) argued: 'We now live in a world of pure "fiat" units of account, the value of each of which depends solely upon the policies of the particular central bank with responsibility for it.'

A nominal anchor is what economists call an 'institution', that is, a rule for the conduct of the policy authorities that links the nominal objectives with the stance of their policy tools. More formally, institutions are 'a set of constraints on behaviour in the form of rules and regulations; a set of procedures to detect deviations from the rules and regulations; and, finally, a set of moral, ethical behavioural norms which define the contours that constrain the way in which the rules and regulations are specified and enforcement is carried out' (North, 1984, p. 8), or, in game-theoretic terms, the institutions are the 'rules of the game' of social interaction (North 1990). A nominal anchor is that part of the institutional design that provides the 'rules of the game' for the central bank.

The gold standard was a notably strict form of a nominal anchor. Absent such strict limitation on the discretion of the central bank, there is no check on the amount of money that the central bank can issue and, consequently, no automatic check to inflation. That is to say, without deliberate design a modern fiat money system lacks a nominal anchor (Bernanke et al., 1999). Indeed, that is what Arthur Burns experienced practically as the anguish of a central banker in the post-Bretton Woods era, when even the weak anchor of that system fell away.[5]

During that same period, Milton Friedman (1977) used his Nobel Prize acceptance lecture to argue that the then prevailing mix of macroeconomic policies and institutions could not last, as it entailed incentives that would encourage either a drift to higher inflation or

---

[5] Arthur Burns was Chair of the Board of Governors of the Federal Reserve System in the United States from 1970 until 1978, that is during a period of high inflation and high unemployment.

to institutional changes that would encourage lower inflation outcomes. He was predicting a return to more explicit nominal anchors,
and that is indeed what emerged from the 1980s onwards.

But Friedman (1977) maintained that it was not the task of
monetary policy alone to ensure favourable inflation outcomes in
a fiat money system. Fiscal and exchange rate policies have significant influence on the money supply too. Such influence is generated,
for example, through the financial policy of the government used in
financing its exhaustive expenditure and through the impact of the
balance of payments on the stock of domestic money. It follows that
any comprehensive account of discretion on monetary policy requires
a limit on the discretion of exchange rate and fiscal policies too.

If the government commits to an explicit nominal anchor for
monetary policy, a double commitment is, in effect, made as Mishkin
(2000) has argued: first, that fiscal policy will not dominate monetary
policy; and second, that monetary policy *will* dominate fiscal policy.
The independence of central banks to set their instruments without
regard for the implications thereof for fiscal policy was a major step to
rebalance the power within the mix of macroeconomic policy. Or, in
the three-point summary of the modern approach given by Svensson
et al. (2002): define a clear goal for monetary policy; grant operational
independence to the central bank in the pursuit of that target; and
hold the monetary authorities accountable for their performance.

Friedman predicted that the institutions of macroeconomic policy would have to change if monetary order was to return. The core
of his prediction is that fiat money requires a nominal anchor; and,
in step with his prediction, central banks have increasingly adopted
explicit nominal anchors since the early 1980s. Various forces have
contributed to the changes that Friedman predicted. Among these,
the inadequate monetary management of the 1970s was a primary
factor; governments learn, or are forced to learn, via the ballot box.
Globalisation – broadly defined as the increasing interdependence of
economies owing to expanding international trade, capital flows and
migration – has also played an important role.

Towards the end of the twentieth century, one nominal anchor, the then novel idea of 'inflation targeting', emerged as a serious rival to alternative anchors such as nominal exchange rate targets, money supply growth targets or even the theoretically attractive nominal gross domestic product (GDP) targets that were highly favoured by the early 1990s (e.g. Hall and Mankiw, 1994) but only ever tried implicitly in one case – in South Africa from 1986 to 1989 (see also Section 4.4).

The practical result of the focus on nominal anchors since the 1970s, and the success of explicit and implicit inflation targeting regimes, generated a very different outcome from that which led to Burns' anguish and Friedman's Nobel in 1976. Since then, inflation has been brought under control in the industrialised world and in much of the developing world; the internal average inflation rate declined from 14.8 per cent for the first five years of the 1980s to 3.2 per cent for the five years that ended in 2020, according to the IMF's World Economic Outlook Database. Inflation not only declined but also became more stable until 2021. In 2022, inflation reappeared. This sanguine era of low and stable inflation has, for the time being, ended.

By the end of the twentieth century, these changes had already become so widespread that global inflation declined to 6.6 per cent for the last five years of the century (IMF World Economic Outlook Database). Indeed, for the Nobel Laureate Robert Mundell (2000, p. 327), 'the clue to the twentieth century lies in the link between its first and last decades', as he traced the profound economic and even political consequences of the initial success and subsequent mismanagement of the gold standard, followed by the contradictory system of Bretton Woods and the re-emergence of prudent money, when central banks had learnt how to implement nominal anchors for fiat money with flexible exchange rates.

1.5 RULES AND DISCRETION IN THE HISTORY OF CENTRAL BANKING

Prior to the 1970s, the debate on rules versus discretion divided economists into a camp favouring an active role for policymakers in achieving the goals of macroeconomic policy and a camp that argued that such goals were best achieved by tying the hands of policymakers. In this dichotomy, rules are passive, while discretion is allowed to policymakers, who may take an active response to the state of the economy. The debate turned on whether there was both the need and the technique for economists to interfere benevolently, or whether prudence combined with science to suggest that despite economic pathologies, policymakers should shun activism as their knowledge and instruments lacked the requisite precision to correct market failures.

Friedman (1968) famously argued that the knowledge limitations of policymakers favours rules over discretion, especially in monetary policy. Policymakers, he argued, were not so ignorant that policy instruments would be perversely adjusted in the wrong direction, given the state of the economy. Rather, policymakers could not incorporate the long and variable lags of the transmission mechanism in their optimisation problem, with the result that policy adjustments were, generally, 'too late and too much'.

To Friedman's case for rules was added the powerful argument that monetary authorities had been trying to set the instruments of policy based on incorrect models of the economy – models where long-run trade-off existed between inflation and unemployment. With a correct model of the economy, the scope for beneficial discretion is greatly undermined, as shown famously by Kydland and Prescott (1977).

The next important step in the debate was taken by Barro and Gordon (1983a, p. 607) with the argument, in their words, that 'discretion amounts to disallowing a set of long-term arrangements between the policymaker and the public'. Subsequently, the central aspect of a rule has come to be recognised as the commitment by policymakers to future behaviour, not the presumed permanence of parameters in the policy rule.

This modern understanding of a policy rule is what Taylor has called a contingency plan, that is, '[a] plan that specifies as clearly as possible the circumstance under which a central bank should change the *instruments* of monetary policy.... Implicit in this definition, is that the policy rule will in fact be used, and expected to be used, *for many periods into the future'* (Taylor, 2000, p. 3, emphasis in the original). In the words of Stephen Cecchetti (1998, p. 1), 'a policy rule [is] ... a systematic rule for adjusting the quantity that the Central Bank controls as the state of the economy fluctuates'. Though it is a rule, such a contingent plan responds to the state of the economy and is hence properly called an 'activist rule'.

A rule, understood as a contingency plan, is clearly not the mechanistic standard of earlier Friedman vintage that implied a 'fixed setting for the instruments of monetary policy' (Taylor, 1993, p. 196). Rather, the broader understanding of rules provides a way of thinking about monetary policy that implies a distinction between the 'policy' and the 'stance of policy'. Consequently, the evaluation of monetary policy proceeds along two axes, with respect to the policy (rule) on the one hand, and with respect to the day-to-day implementation of the policy (the stance of policy) on the other. And great care has to be taken to design the incentives facing the monetary authorities in both policy and implementation. This modern understanding of policy rules that respond to the state of the economy, especially the projected state of the economy, is assumed in the remainder of this book.

1.6 SUMMARY

The rise of the modern monetary policy consensus by the late twentieth century created an awkward problem. Monetary authorities, constrained by a nominal anchor, gained the power formerly yielded by elected governments to manage the instruments of monetary policy. The solution does not tell us what checks there will be on the authority of the technocrats at the central banks, though. Whereas economists may be convinced, technically, of a nominal anchor such as inflation targeting, there are broader political issues at stake, including the accountability of an independent inflation targeting central bank in a democratic society and the rationale for limiting the discretion of a powerful policymaking institution.

These are familiar questions from the literature on political science: (i) who should rule, and (ii) how do we prevent the authorities from causing too much harm?

The first of these questions has been answered both theoretically and empirically over the course of the last half-century with the modern consensus on modern monetary policy as described in this chapter. The second question has been more vexed. As the modern consensus was emerging, Stanley Fischer (1995, p. 4) already observed that the 'potentially enormous power' of an independent central bank remains undefined. And as Charles Freedman observed at about the same time, 'on the surface, at least, there can be a "tension" between the mechanisms needed to ensure the accountability of the central bank to government or parliament and the ability of the central bank to carry out its responsibility as an institution somewhat apart from government' (Freedman, 1993, p. 92). This tension has elsewhere been called the 'democratic deficit' of independent central banks (Briault et al., 1996, p. 7).[6]

This tension between the need for independence by the central bank and the desire for society to hold the same bank accountable in a democratic setting runs through this book. Nevertheless, that is no longer *the* major objection to the modern conception of an independent central bank with an explicit nominal anchor. Since the GFC, we have seen political pressure on central banks assume a very different role: to acquire vast portfolios of government debt and to try and generate sustained economic growth by supporting the most expansionary fiscal policies on record. The combined effect of such fiscal activism and the monetary accommodation thereof is that the relationship between governments and central banks changes fundamentally. It is the central theme of this book that this change will prove frustrating for policymakers. Abandoning monetary prudence will undermine the modest but important contribution that sound money can make to modern society.

---

[6] The debate on potential democratic deficits will be illustrated in some detail in Chapter 8.

2 Focus on Inflation

The Rationale for CBI since Ancient Days

MANAGEMENT CONSULTANT: *Um, listen, if we could, er, for a moment move on to the subject of fiscal policy –*

FORD: *Fiscal policy?!*

MANAGEMENT CONSULTANT: *Yes.*

FORD: *How can you have money if none of you actually produce anything? It doesn't grow on trees, you know!*

MANAGEMENT CONSULTANT: *You know, if you would allow me to continue!*

CAPTAIN: *Yes, let him continue.*

MANAGEMENT CONSULTANT: *Since we decided a few weeks ago to adopt leaves as legal tender, we have, of course, all become immensely rich.*

FORD: *No, really? Really?*

CROWD MEMBERS: *Yes, very good move...*

MANAGEMENT CONSULTANT: *But we have also run into a small inflation problem on account of the high level of leaf availability. Which means that I gather the current going rate has something like three major deciduous forests buying one ship's peanut. So, um, in order to obviate this problem and effectively revalue the leaf, we are about to embark on an extensive defoliation campaign, and, um, burn down all the forests. I think that's a sensible move, don't you?*

MARKETING GIRL: *That makes economic sense...*[1]

2.1 INTRODUCTION

That inflation is a social pathology is clear, even in science fiction. Because of the persistence of inflationary problems and the permanent

---

[1] Douglas Adams, *The Hitchhiker's Guide to the Galaxy*, BBC Radio 4, 12 April 1978.

threat of inflation to the welfare of societies,[2] monetary policy in the twentieth century evolved to focus on securing price stability or the close cousin thereof: fighting inflation. This has been a central part of the development of macroeconomic policy since the 1930s (Hansen, 1941; Friedman, 1948). Experience over the century and theoretical developments in macroeconomics combined to encourage this focus on securing low inflation as the policy objective for monetary policy.

Inflation is a serious economic pathology, but not only an economic problem; it also has a strong political connotation. In Keynes' *The Economic Consequences of the Peace*, referred to in Chapter 1, he attributes to the communist revolutionary Lenin the argument that inflation provides the best way to destroy capitalist society (Keynes, 1924). While the provenance of the quote is doubtful (Fetter, 1977), this claim highlights the severely disruptive effect of especially high and variable inflation in a market economy. The predictable rise of inflation and the associated subsequent political turmoil in the former Central Powers following the Versailles peace demonstrated Keynes' argument powerfully. In the early 2020s, we are again seeing rising inflation in Western democracies, where it has risen to the top of the political agenda.

The second aspect that is addressed by the Adams quote that introduces this chapter is that inflation is a monetary phenomenon; although this may not be so 'always and everywhere' (Friedman, 1970). Let's start with the conceptual level. In the words of Laidler and Parkin, inflation is 'a process of continuously rising prices, or equivalently, of continuously falling value of money' (Laidler and Parkin, 1975: 741). The effects of inflation have been observed for thousands of years (Schwartz, 1973) and though the term 'inflation' in its original usage referred to an expansion in the supply of money (Hazlitt, 1964), by the middle of the nineteenth century, Jevons (1863) linked it in the now familiar manner with an 'inflation of

---

[2] The German Minister of Economic Affairs in the late 1960s and early 1970s, Karl Schiller, has been quoted as comparing inflation with a rusty nail in a wooden house: never dead and always labouring.

prices'. But Jevons was equally aware that inflation as described is never observed, since a simple aggregation of observed prices yields a mixture of absolute and relative price changes. His suggestion was to use a geometric mean of all prices to identify the monetary component of prices changes, or what he called the price changes 'due to a change on the part of gold' (Jevons, 1865, 296).

Lately, inflation has invariably been associated with changes in some aggregate price index, usually a consumer price index (CPI). These are typically cost-of-living indices with weights determined by the observed pattern of household expenditure, giving the indices a grounding in welfare economics (Cecchetti and Wynne, 2003). Not designed to measure inflation in the first instance, CPIs suffer from a number of well-known problems when employed to that end, including:

1. Substitution bias: Consumption patterns are not fixed, but evolve in response to inter alia relative price changes. This substitution effect results in an over-estimation of inflation by fixed weight CPIs, which tends to exaggerate the influence of components that have experienced large relative price increases.
2. Quality bias: It is difficult to account for improvement in the quality of goods and services, and failing to account for these improvements will overstate the inflation rate.
3. New goods bias: It is difficult for a CPI to account for new goods, and failing to do so causes another upward bias in the estimation of inflation as these goods are often subject to rapid price declines once introduced. (Cecchetti and Wynne, 2003: Box 1)

The gap between the concept and the measurement of inflation also drives a wedge between money supply growth and measured inflation. Despite the widespread use of CPI to proxy inflation, it is important to remember that such proxies mix both the effect of inflation as well as relative price changes, which can make a material difference at any point in time.

Be that as it may, it is difficult to overlook the tight relation between a high growth rate of money (measured in leaves earlier) and the subsequent surge in inflation encountered all too frequently.[3] Since central banks have gained a monopoly over the issuance of legal tender from the nineteenth century onwards, their control over legal tender has also become relevant for the control of inflation.

Therefore, central banks have always placed much emphasis on controlling the quantity of money. By the same token, money growth and the central banks' balance sheets have always been prominently placed on the radar of observers from politics to the media and academia. The German Bundesbank, for example, has raised much concern and criticism by regularly missing its money growth target (Gischer et al., 2005).[4]

This chapter discusses briefly and concisely the broad causes and stylised costs of high and chronic inflation. We then move on to a solution to the problem of inflation, which has been identified as a separation of responsibilities so that every policy objective is assigned to one policy tool, also known as the Tinbergen rule (Tinbergen, 1952). We start, however, with a brief historical sketch outlining the long history of inflation, which was already a problem in the Roman Empire.

2.2 A SHORT HISTORICAL SKETCH OF INFLATION

Inflation is probably as old as the use of money. Emperors and politicians have, throughout the ages, seen the short-term advantages of issuing money to gain seigniorage revenue.[5] For the issuing authority money is a liability, which can be used to acquire assets. For the users, however, it is only a credible storage of value and instrument of payment if it can be changed into a real asset whenever

---

[3] As we see later (Section 4.3), the developments in the last decades put this relation into question.

[4] In fact, between 1974, when it introduced a money target, and 1999, when the European Central Bank became responsible for monetary policy, the Bundesbank missed its own objectives in about half of the years.

[5] Seigniorage in general is defined as the income a central bank can generate when emitting money. It is the difference between the face value of a currency and the cost of producing it. Since the holder of the currency trusts that she gets the face value in resources, it is more accurate to define the social benefits of this difference over time as seigniorage.

required. Therefore, one way of increasing seigniorage is devaluing circulating currency, preferably without letting those that are using it know.

In the Roman Empire, it was quite common practice for politicians to campaign expensively and thus accumulate high levels of debt before taking office. This created a strong incentive to devalue the currency once they were in power. Nero (AD 54–68) is reported to be the first Roman emperor who debased the silver coins by slowly reducing the silver share of coins. His successors further reduced the silver share, culminating in hyperinflation during the crisis of the third century (He, 2017). This period was characterised by civil war, social unrest and chaos. Diocletian (AD 284–305) was able to stabilise the Roman currency, and returned to a system relatively close to the gold standard that was applied in the late nineteenth and early twentieth centuries (Gaettens, 1955).

Since the Roman inflation, there have been several periods of high and chronic inflation. In Spain, there was the Vello-inflation in the first half of the seventeenth century. France experienced a similar inflationary episode after the death of Louis XIV in 1715 and during the French Revolution (1789–1799). In addition, Prussia was subject to inflationary pressure during the Seven Years War (1756–1763). Warfare is generally associated with high inflation, as government finances are strained and the tax base compromised (Gaettens, 1955). At the same time, the willingness of international and domestic investors to finance wars is limited, so that governments regularly used the printing press.

The twentieth century witnessed many periods of high and chronic inflation, sometimes even hyperinflation (see Table 2.1), and numerous attempts to counteract these (Freytag, 2005). With respect to monetary policy, the century after the successful and stable period of the gold standard can be roughly divided into four phases. The Great War and the 1920s and 1930s were characterised by economic instability. Until 1924, the main problem was high inflation, particularly in Europe (Sargent, 2017). This changed dramatically during

Table 2.1 *Hyperinflation in different times*

Location	Time	Month with highest inflation rate	Highest monthly inflation rate	Equivalent daily inflation rate
Hungary	Aug 1945–Jul 1946	Jul 1946	4.19×10^{16}%	207%
Zimbabwe	Mar 2007–Mid-Nov 2008	Mid-Nov 2008	7.96×10^{10}%	98.0%
Yugoslavia	Apr 1992–Jan 1994	Jan 1994	313,000,000%	64.6%
Germany	Aug 1922–Dec 1923	Oct 1923	29,500%	20.9%
Greece	May 1941–Dec 1945	Oct 1944	13,800%	17.9%
China	Oct 1947–Mid-May 1949	Apr 1949	5,070%	14.1%
Free City of Danzig	Aug 1992–Mid-Oct 1923	Sep 1923	2,440%	11.4%
Venezuela	End 2016		475.8%	
Armenia	Oct 1993–Dec 1994	Nov 1993	438%	5.77%
Turkmenistan	Jan 1992–Nov 1993	Nov 1993	429%	5.71%
Taiwan	Aug 1945–Sep 1945	Aug 1945	399%	5.50%
Peru	Jul 1990–Aug 1990	Aug 1990	397%	5.49%
Bosnia and Herzegovina	Apr 1992–Jun 1993	Jun 1992	322%	4.92%
France	May 1795–Nov 1796	Mid-Aug 1796	304%	4.77%
China	Jul 1943–Aug 1945	Jun 1945	302%	4.75%
Ukraine	Jan 1992–Nov 1994	Jan 1992	285%	4.60%
Poland	Jan 1923–Jan 1924	Oct 1923	275%	4.50%
Congo (Zaire)	Nov 1993–Sep 1994	Nov 1993	250%	4.26%
Russia	Jan 1992	Jan 1992	245%	4.22%
Russia/USSR	Jan 1922–Feb 1924	Feb 1924	212%	3.86%
Tajikistan	Jan 1992–Oct 1993	Jan 1992	201%	3.74%
Argentina	May 1989–May 1990	Jul 1989	197%	3.69%
Bolivia	Apr 1984–Sep 1985	Feb 1985	183%	3.53%

Country				
Belarus	Jan 1992–Feb 1992	Jan 1992	159%	3.22%
Kyrgyzstan	Jan 1992	Jan 1992	157%	3.20%
Kazakhstan	Jan 1992	Jan 1992	141%	2.97%
Austria	Oct 1921–Sep 1922	Aug 1922	129%	2.80%
Uzbekistan	Jan 1992–Feb 1992	Jan 1992	118%	2.64%
Azerbaijan	Jan 1992–Dec 1994	Jan 1992	118%	2.63%
Congo (Zaire)	Oct 1991–Sep 1992	Nov 1991	114%	2.57%
Peru	Sep 1988	Sep 1988	114%	2.57%
Taiwan	Oct 1948–May 1949	Oct 1948	108%	2.46%
Hungary	Mar 1923–Feb 1924	Jul 1923	97.9%	2.30%
Chile	Oct 1973	Oct 1973	87.6%	2.12%
Estonia	Jan 1992–Feb 1992	Jan 1992	87.2%	2.11%
Angola	Dec 1994–Jan 1997	May 1996	84.1%	2.06%
Brazil	Dec 1989–Mar 1990	Mar 1990	82.4%	2.02%
Democratic Republic of Congo	Aug 1998	Aug 1998	78.5%	1.95%
Poland	Oct 1989–Jan 1990	Jan 1990	77.3%	1.93%
Armenia	Jan 1992–Feb 1992	Jan 1992	73.1%	1.85%
Tajikistan	Oct 1995–Nov 1995	Nov 1995	65.2%	1.69%
Latvia	Jan 1992	Jan 1992	64.4%	1.67%
Turkmenistan	Nov 1995–Jan 1996	Jan 1996	62.5%	1.63%
Yugoslavia	Sep 1989–Dec 1989	Dec 1989	59.7%	1.57%
Germany	Jan 1920	Jan 1920	56.9%	1.51%
Kazakhstan	Nov 1992	Nov 1993	55.5%	1.48%
Lithuania	Jan 1992	Jan 1992	54.0%	1.45%
Belarus	Aug 1994	Aug 1994	53.4%	1.44%
Taiwan	Feb 1947	Feb 1947	50.8%	1.38%

Source: Own compilation based on He (2017).

the next decade, with low, and sometimes even negative, inflation as the world was hit by the Great Depression. This was partly due to repressed prices, which lasted during World War II. Directly after the war, inflation rates in many of the countries most damaged by the war rose again to high levels.

The second phase began with the establishment of the Bretton Woods System (BWS). In its era there was, in general, relative macro-economic stability world-wide, with only very few examples of high inflation. The year 1973 marked the end of this phase when the BWS was finally abandoned. One central reason was the aforementioned problem of the nth currency. This problem occurred because of the different tasks of the members of the exchange rate regime. The United States as country n guaranteed a gold price ($35 per ounce). All other members except for the United States had the obligation to maintain the exchange rates in the BWS with $n-1$ exchange rates towards the US dollar. When the United States resorted to expansive monetary policy to ease the fiscal burden of the Vietnam War, the constantly growing supply of US dollars caused capital exports from the United States and devaluation pressure on the dollar. The need for all other $(n-1)$ countries to purchase dollars to keep the exchange rate stable led them to imported inflation. This contributed to dissatisfaction with the exchange rate regime, particularly in Germany (James, 1996).[6]

The following two decades can be seen as the third phase, characterised by exchange rate volatilities and severe monetary instability, in particular in developing countries. In some Latin American countries hyperinflation occurred, while others, such as Israel, had to deal with chronic inflation for many years. In addition, industrialised countries also suffered from annual inflation rates that were higher than usual, even in the double digits.

---

[6] James (1996, pp. 197f.) also argues that part of the inflationary process in Japan and Germany was due to faster growth in these countries as compared with the United States leading to an increase in the price of non-tradables with subsequent inflation (Balassa-Samuelson effect).

The period since the early-1990s (the fourth phase) can be defined as a decade of disinflation. Not only industrialised countries, but also parts of the developing world have been very successful in this respect. To give a few examples, many countries in transition, for instance the Czech Republic, Slovakia, Hungary and Poland, as well as some Latin American economies, including Brazil and Argentina, managed to reduce inflation remarkably. In the enthusiasm of the moment, some observers even described a 'New Economy' in the early 2000s characterised by persistently high real growth rates, very limited fluctuations and low inflation rates (Freytag, 2002).

In the event, the optimism was not justified, and was punctured by the crises in 2001 and, more seriously, 2008.[7] However, in contrast with many recessions of the twentieth century, these crises were not associated with high and chronic inflation.

Not everyone escaped inflation, though, even in this benign period. Argentina experienced renewed chronic inflation after the country's currency board collapsed in 2000, followed by a debt default, which removed access to the international capital markets for a decade. However, the subsequent return to the world capital markets lasted only briefly. In spring 2020, Argentina defaulted again, on a number of government bonds, and inflation reached over 40 per cent. Even worse, Venezuela has experienced hyperinflation since 2018; in 2023, the IMF expected 500 per cent. During 2018, inflation in Venezuela hit over 65,000 per cent (IMF World Economic Outlook Database); such high rates were only reached in Zimbabwe in the late 2000s. These unfortunate economic developments occurred while both of these countries formally meet the criteria of democracies. This is a salutary lesson that government delegated to serve the public interests may end up harming it through poor monetary policy, or, more precisely, by forcing their central bank into poor monetary policy.

---

[7] It seems adequate to interpret the period since 2008 as a new phase in monetary policy. None of the regularities observed until the GFC seem to hold since; the COVID 19 crisis and the Russian aggression contributed further to this. We discuss this issue in subsequent chapters.

2.3   CAUSES OF INFLATION

In a monetary system where the value of the currency is not definitively fixed, such as a completely hard gold standard, there is always scope for inflation (or deflation). This is true of all modern monetary systems too, which are typically called fiat money systems. As mentioned earlier, in the late twentieth century, Michel Camdessus (formerly head of the IMF) used the term 'policy standard' to describe a fiat money system. The value of fiat money, so he argued, is ultimately determined by the institutional design of the system and the policies encouraged by these institutions. Should these policy decisions allow monetary growth to outstrip the demand for money, it is likely that the value of money will decline consistently, which is the process of inflation.

In general, the causes of excessive money growth are deficiencies in other policy fields. Mainly fiscal problems and labour market distortions contribute to the pressure on monetary policymakers to raise the money supply as a means to eliminate these difficulties. Since money is an asset, and the prices of assets are often determined in a forward-looking manner, it is often the expected conduct of monetary (and fiscal) authorities that influence even current inflationary outcomes. Hence the importance of inflation expectations in modern monetary policy practice.

2.3.1   Budget Deficits and Hyperinflation

The literature on high inflation provides a stark message: it is highly correlated with unsustainable government budget deficits. This is particularly true for hyperinflation (Fischer et al. 2002). But even at more moderate levels, inflation can be related to a number of fiscal biases. The fiscal bias towards inflation revolves around the idea of inflation taxes and seigniorage revenue, unindexed tax brackets, and a lowering of the real cost of the national debt in the case of unanticipated inflation (Fischer, 1995).

As long as the central bank is part of the consolidated public sector, the government has access to seigniorage as a source of revenue, where seigniorage is defined as the real resources that the government can appropriate through the act of base money creation. A government with a monopoly over money can always acquire real resources to the extent that base money expands more rapidly than inflation, or, as Keynes (1923, p. 37) observed on the eve of the Continental hyperinflation following the peace of Versailles: 'A government can live for a long time ... by printing paper money. That is to say, it can by this means secure the command over real resources, resources just as real as those obtained by taxation. The method is condemned, but its efficacy, up to a point, must be admitted....' The desire to obtain seigniorage is, historically, one of the chief reasons for the state's monopoly on the issuance of money.

The central reason for policymakers to increase the money supply is their inability to ensure a sustainable public sector budget.[8] Such fiscal difficulties often arise from the following causes: too many inefficient public enterprises, high-risk premia on capital markets, an excessive public expenditure, including on an unsustainable welfare system, and an inefficient tax system. At the same time, the government is unable or unwilling to cut expenditure elsewhere.

The first reason is that governments have engaged in business activities that, from an economic point of view, are mainly private activities. For instance, the state often runs a variety of enterprises. Especially utilities such as electricity, transport and telecommunication have been, or still are, state-run in many countries. Although there is no economic reason why these enterprises should automatically produce losses in a competitive environment, as domestic monopolists they have normally done so, among other reasons since the state has tried to realise social objectives via price policies; that is, by keeping energy prices below costs. Moreover, they have not been forced to work efficiently, that is X-inefficiency, in other words,

[8] Here we consolidate the central bank and the general government for the sake of the argument, namely that monetary policy has been used for other objectives than price stability. In reality, central banks are state agencies but separated from government – exactly for the reasons laid out in this chapter.

inefficient behaviour of actors not fully controlled by competition has occurred. The main economic problems related to such state activities on markets for goods and services are manifold. Domestic relative prices are distorted. This hampers economic dynamics and structural change. The South African case with its catastrophically loss-making electricity utility (that also plunges the country into hours of darkness daily) is an extreme one that demonstrates the more general point.

Owing to losses from state-owned enterprises, expenditure is higher than economically necessary. Consequently, tax revenues are lower than economically possible. Another aspect of such governmental business activities relates to the multiple crisis of the younger past. Governments in Europe bought shares of vulnerable but systemic companies (such as energy suppliers) and faced losses, which need to be financed through new bonds, which the European Central Bank (ECB) purchased.

Second, the countries in question have trouble sustaining access to capital markets. Domestic as well as foreign investors are not happy to grant governments of these countries credit. Hence, borrowing is either impossible or very costly: the risk premia are very high. In these circumstances there is evidence that inflation tax is a preferred (or perhaps the only) source of revenue, especially in countries suffering heavily from the results of a war. The public, in turn, shifts resources to current consumption, which is to be preferred over future consumption. If, as in the German case of 1922/1923, the burden of reparation amounts to a manifold of GDP, there might even be consensus that inflation tax is to be preferred over bond financing, even if possible and affordable (Cukierman, 1995).

Third, in many countries the welfare state has gone beyond economic necessities and fiscal limits. The fiscal burden associated with this development also contributes to the budget deficit. Although it is impossible, *ceteris paribus*, that it will lead to hyperinflation, a permanent pressure on the government to obtain fresh funds exists. Moreover, the distortions caused by an exaggerated welfare state contribute to future budgetary problems.

The fourth reason for high and persistent budget deficits is an inefficient tax system. The administration is not able to enforce tax collection properly. Tax avoidance is high. As a consequence, tax (and tariff) revenues are by far insufficient to cover all expenditures. Governments then prefer inflation over regular taxation (Brennan and Buchanan, 1981).

Yet it is only to the extent that the private sector holds and uses the money issued by the central bank that the latter is able to obtain real resources by creating more money balances. Since seigniorage, which leads to inflation, erodes the value of the money balances held by the private sector, seigniorage functions as a tax on the domestic money balances of the private sector.

But as Keynes hinted, the efficacy of seigniorage is limited, and it is limited precisely by the inflationary consequences of seigniorage (Cagan, 1956). Since inflation diminishes the value of local currency, the demand for that currency declines as inflation rises. We see this process in the extreme when local populations switch to other currencies, such as the US dollar, when their own currency collapses under hyperinflation. This means that a government's attempt to command extra real resources via the seigniorage (and the inflation tax) become counter-productive when pushed too high. From the empirical evidence of a cross-section of developing countries, Agénor (2000) shows that even fairly modest rates of seigniorage, above 3 or 4 per cent of GDP, can initiate this counter-productive spiral of higher inflation, lower demand for money balances and a lower inflationary tax revenue.

2.3.2 *Money Growth and Limited Inflation*

Whereas the relation between money growth and inflation is strong in cases of high inflation rates, it is less clear in low-inflation periods. Benati (2009) shows that after the disinflation period in most Western countries in the 1980s, shocks in the velocity of money were also responsible for inflation surges. This result is consistent with the observed data since 2009. Despite the unprecedented growth of

Western central banks' balance sheet, notably the Fed, the ECB, the BoE and the Bank of Japan (BoJ), inflation rates did not increase, at least not until early 2021. On the contrary, especially in the EUROZONE, inflation was extremely moderate.

That said, public debt cannot be assigned so clearly to less severe inflation episodes. Inflation in such periods can nevertheless be attributed to governmental calculus. Although the Phillips curve trade-off is no longer seen as being relevant in academic literature, there is still the problem of political business cycles, as first discussed in the 1970s (Nordhaus, 1975; Hibbs, 1977). According to their theories, governments facing elections increase public demand to initiate an employment boom in the short run, which is financed through a central bank loan to the government. This demand shift is planned to be effective prior to election day. Since the monetary impulse only leads to inflation with a time lag, in the medium or long run (in other words after the election) they create inflation by this policy, because the increased demand is not met by an according increase in supply. The public is seen as myopic in this setting: it takes the boom for real and does not anticipate the inflation shock after the election.

2.4   THE ECONOMIC COSTS OF INFLATION

For an analysis of the costs of inflation, it is worthwhile distinguishing two typical patterns of the course of inflation: chronic inflation and hyperinflation. Chronic inflation persists for years with medium to high, at any rate volatile, annual inflation rates. The annual rates vary between 10 per cent and several hundred per cent (Végh, 1995, p. 38). The definition of hyperinflation sees it as an inflation rate of equal to or more than 50 per cent per month (Cagan, 1956). Normally, hyperinflation does not last as long as chronic inflation. But its costs in the short run are much higher than in cases of chronic inflation (especially when wages, taxes and so on are indexed). Hyperinflations are characterised by decreasing real balances, increasing dollarisation, an enormous public budget deficit, partly caused by the hyperinflation itself

(Oliveira–Tanzi effect), an undervaluation of the domestic currency on the foreign exchange markets and a bad reputation for the government (Bernholz, 1995). These properties also make hyperinflation very costly.

2.4.1   Theoretical Considerations

Even if inflation is fully anticipated, there are costs, which can be generalised as follows. First, inflation can be interpreted as a tax on cash holdings, which causes welfare losses – in other words, there is an excess burden (Bailey, 1956); second, the holding of cash balance is not optimal; third, there are menu costs; and fourth, if marginal tax rates are progressive, the real tax burden rises. Inflation causes particularly high costs if it is chronic or in the case of hyperinflation. In this case, it can only be imperfectly anticipated. The most important costs are associated with inefficient allocation of factors and distortions in the use of resources and with the distribution of wealth and income. In the following, we briefly remind the reader of the costs associated with high and/or chronic inflation (Freytag, 2002).

First, there are information problems. The informational content of prices is reduced or destroyed by inflation. An increase in prices cannot be traced back unambiguously to changing scarcities. The reason could also be inflation. Prices no longer function as signals indicating new entrepreneurial chances. Resources will not be allocated to their best use. In addition, information about scarcities becomes obsolete faster than in times of stability. Economic agents then have to use resources to obtain the correct information, which is costly (Murphy et al., 1990).

Second, redistribution takes place. The real interest rate can become negative if the inflation rate has been underestimated at the time when a contract on a credit has been signed or a bond has been purchased. Money loses its function as a storage of value. This has negative distributive consequences. The borrower gains at the expense of the lender. However, if the inflation rate has been overestimated leading to too high nominal interest rates, the real interest rate is rather high. Then, the is exactly the opposite: the lender gains at the expense of the borrower.

Third, this experience causes people to avoid investment at home (Keynes, 1924). They either purchase durable goods or they invest abroad. Inflation can cause capital flight. In the long run, intertemporal markets lose their importance and are eventually abandoned completely. This deters foreign direct investment (FDI). Lower real investment reduces employment and growth. Both will *ceteris paribus* be lower than in the case of long-term monetary stability.

Fourth, high and volatile inflation diminishes savings. If individuals cannot ensure that they keep the real value of capital plus an adequate rate of return for holding savings, they will spend their income on consumption. This also has negative consequences on growth and employment.

Fifth, it is even unclear whether the public budget can be improved when the government monetises its deficits. On the one hand, bonds held by the central bank and the public devalue regularly. The real value of the bonds is lower at the time of repayment than at the time of issuing. The government gains from this devaluing. On the other hand, inflation reduces real tax revenues since the tax payment can be delayed. However, if marginal tax rates are progressive with respect to nominal income or capital and tax deductions are limited to a nominal value, the real value of tax revenues increases. To sum up, the net effect on the real public budget is a priori not clear. Only if the government is able to force the public to buy its bonds will it certainly gain from inflation tax. Moreover, nominal seigniorage is higher if the government systematically varies the inflation rate (Johnson, 1977). There is an incentive for the government to be dishonest.

Sixth, the pattern of consumption is not constant when inflation is extremely volatile. If this period persists, firms are unable to predict the potential turnover (in terms of volume). Their success becomes arbitrary and does not depend on properties such as product quality and entrepreneurial abilities.

Finally, inflation reduces the social consensus within a society if certain groups systematically lose whereas others win. For instance, wage negotiations become more controversial since the future inflation rate is not predicable.[9] It will only be obvious a posteriori whether the real income has risen or fallen. Either employees or employers will be discontented with the result: if real wages have fallen, unions will put in another demand for higher salaries; if real wages have risen, people will be fired, and the social climate suffers from inflation.

Naturally, these costs are lowest if the inflation rate is moderate and stable over a long period. People are then able to successfully adjust to inflation by indexing their contracts or by concentrating on the conclusion of short-term contracts. Similarly, costs of inflation are highest if inflation rates are very high and volatile. In other words, the higher the costs of inflation, the less people are able to anticipate them.

2.4.2   Some Empirical Evidence

In this subsection, we briefly assess empirically how inflation affects other macroeconomic variables such as employment, growth and investment. The evidence is relatively unambiguous as regards inflation and economic growth. Countries with high inflation grow slower than countries with stable price levels. Estimating a sample of over 100 countries from 1960 to 1990, Robert Barro comes to the conclusion that this negative correlation is particularly high when inflation rates are higher than 10 per cent: an increase in average inflation by ten percentage points leads to a loss of growth by approximately 0.2 to 0.3 per cent. However, in the long run the loss in real output is remarkable. He also shows that investment is negatively correlated with inflation (Barro, 1995).

---

[9] It is never exactly predictable, but the mean variation of the prediction reaches a considerable value in case of high and volatile inflation rates.

Similar results are estimated by other authors (Grimes, 1991; De Gregorio, 1992; Fry et al., 1996). The latter analyses the correlation of inflation and growth for Latin America and the BoE Group. Again, the results are stronger for countries with high inflation rates. Nevertheless, it has been shown that even very low inflation rates are very likely to reduce economic growth rates (Grimes, 1991; Ghosh and Phillips, 1998). Robert Lucas, on the other hand, reports the absence of a relationship between economic growth and inflation and concludes that inflation and unemployment are not associated (Lucas, 1996).

We also find that other theoretical considerations can be confirmed by the history of hyperinflations. During the German hyperinflation of 1922/1923, the government had enormous difficulties in collecting enough taxes to cover its expenditure. He (2017) shows that the German budget was in deficit during the inflation period. This led to changes in tax policy: the relative importance of direct taxes diminished whereas indirect taxes gained importance, especially by shifting the tax base from volumes to values. At the same time, banks did not wish to open small accounts. Savings, therefore, declined sharply. Not only did consumption increase relatively, but also the pattern of consumption changed, with the added complication that inflation measurement via the CPI became difficult. Finally, unemployment increased during the latter stages of hyperinflation to levels as high as 25 per cent. Moreover, it seems that a special group, namely the membership of unions, was especially hit by unemployment. Furthermore, the distributive effects were extremely unjust: a few people gained at the expense of the majority. The last two points indicate that inflation increases social tensions (Kiehling, 2004). This evidence is backed by Easterly and Fischer, who show the adverse impact of inflation on inequality and perceived fairness (Easterly and Fischer, 2001).

2.5 FIRST POLICY CONCLUSION

The history of inflation suggests that it is almost never by pure accident that inflation is high or volatile. It seems inadequate to blame such processes on ignorance or error, at least in the long run. Rather, governments use monetary policy for more than one purpose; they deviate from the Tinbergen rule.

This leads to a range of policy conclusions. First, different times and different countries have experienced a variety of forms of inflation and their origins. Thus, there is no one-size-fits-all solution for monetary policy. That said, second, there is nevertheless one lesson, namely that it is important to find a way to enable governments to finance their budget without resorting to the printing press. Third, it is not enough to find such a policy mixture. In order to be effective, the public must be informed and must also believe that the government will refrain from monetisation.

The central lesson is that if governments want to ensure that the public is informed it should commit to a low inflation policy in a credible, that is, enforceable form. From the 1970s onwards, economists have built an enormous stock of knowledge about credible commitment mechanisms under different institutional frameworks, among them the strict separation of fiscal and monetary policy, with the latter being conducted by a central bank that is independent from the political process. Chapter 3 discusses the theoretical foundations and practical implications of CBI.

3 The Political Economy of CBI

3.1 INTRODUCTION: THE FUNDAMENTAL PROBLEM
OF MONETARY POLICY

Central bank independence (CBI) is a relatively new institutional occurrence,[1] but rules to constraint central bank discretion have been discussed in both academic quarters and governments much longer. The observation that governments are prone to misuse their access to legal tender to meet short term objectives other than price stability is old, is at least as old as David Hume (Hume, 1777). When this leads the inflation, the explicit (or often implicit) trade-off is between inflation and these other short-run objectives.

As we clearly state in Chapters 1 and 2, inflation is a monetary policy outcome over the long term.[2] The inflation rate is the outcome of a complex transmission process, which the central bank may know well and be able to steer relatively safely, but not perfectly so. We also assume that in general, societies prefer low inflation over higher inflation. Given the costs of inflation (Laidler and Parkin, 1975),[3] this judgement seems justified.

Nevertheless, CBI is not an exclusively economic issue. Rather it has its roots and gains its relevance from the political process. Since Herbert Simons' seminal paper (Simons; 1936) in the economics literature and similar analyses on the European continent, the case has been made that a market economy needs policy rules (which some observers rather call institutions) to function properly. With the emergence of behavioural and institutional economics, this has also

---

[1] See also Section 1.5.

[2] In reality, this is a too simple assumption since the central bank can fully control the monetary base (its balance sheet) or the interest rate for assets it buys.

[3] See also Section 2.4.

been widely accepted in economic policy circles. A special subset of such rules deals with monetary policy, as Simons argues.

While some authors consolidate the central bank with the government in practice, a separation of tasks has become standard in most economies; at least there is no major country without a distinct institution called the central bank that is responsible for monetary policy. The main reason for this separation of tasks is the theoretical intuition associated with the name of Jan Tinbergen, namely the assignment of one policy instrument per distinct objective (Tinbergen, 1952). Tinbergen argues that for each policy objective, policymakers need a distinct instrument and based his argument on a formal theoretical model that avoided over- or under-determination if the governments assigned one instrument to the achievement of each policy objective. According to the Tinbergen rule, monetary policy – here interpreted as the setting of a policy interest rate – should concentrate on the objective of price stability, but no other objectives. This assignment problem also seems best addressed if there is a special agency for every policy objective, so that the agency does not face conflicting incentives or trade-offs and can exclusively concentrate on the assigned objective. It also protects the agencies from being exposed to too many pressure groups.

That implies that the central bank does not have several departments that each use an individual policy instrument to meet different objectives, such as price stability and employment. The latter is assigned to a specialised agency to the extent that it is a coherent policy objective, whereas the central bank is exclusively responsible for price stability. This restriction allows for clear-cut responsibilities and avoids conflicts of interest within the dedicated policy agency. It also increases the credibility of policy announcements. However, this assignment does allow for co-ordination of policies and interaction between agencies, despite some concern that such co-ordination always suffers (Stiglitz, 1998). It is surely in line with the Tinbergen rule if central banks are assigned price stability as their main objective, but are also obliged to support the general economic policymaking of the government, as it is found in many central bank laws.

3.1.1 The Underlying Principal–Agent Problem

This logic does not imply, however, that governments, or leading policymakers in practice do not interfere, or try to interfere, in monetary policy.[4] Governments may see an advantage in using monetary policy for more than the objective of price stability. The less transparently the policy mix is communicated, the less the public (or the electorate) may be able to assign policy measures individually to certain outcomes.

Economic theorists have found it useful to analyse this situation with a two-stage principal–agent problem (PAP). A PAP is generally defined by a relatively poorly informed principal who is commissioning a task to a better-informed agent. The principal cannot observe either the properties/characteristics or the actions of the agent, only the outcomes.[5]

In the first of the two stages of the analysis, the public is described as the sovereign or principal (at least in democracies) and is unable to fully observe and understand both the motives (ex-ante) and actions (ex-post) of the government, which is their agent. The government may not share the public's interest in stable prices, for example. Instead, the government may benefit from a certain degree of inflation, depending first on the level of public debt, second on the potential to tax the public via regular taxes and third on the government's degree of time preference (or time horizon). Therefore, the government may be tempted to use monetary policy for other objectives than price stability. The electorate does not have the tools to assess the causal effects in this matter.

In the second stage of the analysis, the government, in turn, is the principal and assigns the task of monetary policy to a central

---

[4] Recently, political leaders have been the ones who tend to interfere; one may think of President Trump's berating of the Fed whenever they even entertained the possibility of contractionary policy. Social media influence has given political leaders a new channel to communicate with the populace without necessarily suffering the consequences of their actions.

[5] Depending on the nature of the problem, ex-ante PAPs are distinguished from ex-post PAPs. The former refer to asymmetrical information about properties of agents or products, the latter to actions of the agent.

bank as agent. Again, neither the central bankers' attitudes (ex-ante PAP) nor their actions (ex-post PAP) are fully observable for the government, which has to live with this lack of information with respect to details of central banking. Government cannot control the central bank fully.[6] In the literature, often the second PAP is interpreted as the relevant problem (e.g. Walsh, 1995). This, however, may be questioned: as long as the government has the incentive to use monetary policy to meet objectives other than price stability, the government itself has to be interpreted as the agent and the first PAP comes into play. In this version society is the principal, for it has an interest in price stability, as opposed to the government, which has more than one objective and sometimes faces a lack of policy instruments.

That said, any commitment to price stability always means commitment by the government via constructing an adequate monetary policy regime, thereby addressing both PAPs. We will subsequently show that the first PAP is more important for price stability and thus for the economic welfare of a society.

3.1.2   Asymmetrical Information and Credible Policy Announcements

The PAP leads to another fundamental challenge for policymakers, namely to ensure that their policy announcements are credible. The concept of credibility is of utmost importance for policy announcement in all fields, but has been particularly relevant in monetary policy. In the literature, however, the concept is not always clear; it is often confused with reputation. We refer to credibility as a concept applicable for policy measures. It is also important to distinguish between ex-post and ex-ante credibility. In order to stabilise expectations, a policy measure should be credible ex-ante. Whether or not

---

[6] In a branch of the literature characterised as 'revolving doors' literature, a third principal, namely a potential future employer of the central bankers, has influence on the behaviour of the central bank. However, the empirical evidence does not support this model.

the measure was credible, can be measured ex-post. These two concepts demand different indicators to measure them.[7]

Blinder (2000a) offers a working definition of 'credibility' as: 'a central bank is credible if people believe it will do what it says'. Stanley Fischer's (1995) definition is more technical, and though it conveys largely the same message, it adds an important detail: 'a policy is credible when the private sector believes it will be carried out, and when it is correspondingly in the interest of the public sector to carry out the policy once the private sector has acted on its beliefs' (1995, p. 1422). Fischer's emphasis on the effect of the incentives for policymakers when they try to commit credibly to a policy is a recurring theme in the modern literature on central banking, which is discussed later as time inconsistency.

In a survey conducted by Blinder (1996), the economists and central bankers disagreed on the exact content of the concept of credibility. Nevertheless, there appears to be little disagreement on the importance for central banks of gaining credibility. A list of the benefits of credibility that cause it to be so sought after include (Svensson, 1999; Paulin, 2000): first, by anchoring inflation expectations, credible monetary policy eliminates unsettled expectations as an important monetary shock to the economy. Second, the trade-off between inflation variability and output-gap variability can become more favourable for the same reason. Third, stable inflation expectations imply a more direct route through the monetary transmission mechanism for changes to the stance of monetary policy. Finally, since improved credibility implies expectations consistent with the long-run goals of policy, building credibility also means limiting the need for policy intervention as Don Brash (former Governor of the Reserve Bank of New Zealand) argues:

> One useful consequence of this approach to the operation of monetary policy is that we rarely actually do anything other than publish inflation projections, and occasionally comment on the

---

[7] Ideally, the term credibility should be reserved for policy actions, whereas the policy-maker can build up reputation.

evolution of market conditions relative to those assumed in our projections. So long as market participants understand our policy reaction function, believe that we will act consistently with that reaction function, and accept that we have the capacity to inflict some bottom-line pain when taking action, then their incentives are to anticipate the monetary conditions consistent with our inflation target, and trade accordingly ... the fact that financial markets very largely implement policy for us is demonstrative of the power of that transparency. (Brash, 1996, p. 138)

Both the central bankers and the economists in Blinder's (1996) survey associated the credibility of monetary policy closely with the honest and transparent dedication of the central bank to fighting inflation. Ben Friedman (2002) analyses the historical and theoretical context within which credibility has come to assume such prominence and traced the effect of that context on the use of the term 'credibility' in the academic debate and in the practice of monetary policy. Accordingly, he argues that it was the literature on dynamic inconsistency that gave impetus to this concern with credibility. In that literature, credibility means not just that the authorities are able to commit to some target, but more specifically that the authorities are able to commit to a low inflation target.

Furthermore, inflation expectations can in this context be used (and often misused) as an empirical measure of the central bank's credibility. This ready measure of credibility is one of the forces working in favour of the adoption of explicit nominal anchors, such as inflation targets (Svensson, 1999).

3.1.3   An Overview of this Chapter

Chapter 3 presents the basic theoretic concepts that lead to CBI as well as some empirical aspects. The remainder of this chapter deals with several ways in which to address the two-stage PAP. Generations of scholars have dealt with the definition and solutions of this type of problem – without necessarily basing their argument explicitly on a

PAP, though the essence is the same. In Section 3.2, we introduce the 'old' rules versus discretion discussion starting in the 1930s and comprising scholars such as Herbert Simons, Milton Friedman, Friedrich August von Hayek, Walter Eucken and James Buchanan. This literature has a normative basis. In the third section, we briefly discuss the literature on time inconsistency, that is, the problem that an initially optimal policy strategy becomes suboptimal in a dynamic setting where the public can anticipate the policymaker's decisions. Section 3.4 analyses in principle the solutions to the PAP presented in the literature as well as the problems related to independent agencies taking care of monetary policy, with a focus on CBI. Section 3.5 shows the measurement of CBI and its problems. In Section 3.6, we present the empirical evidence, making a strong argument for CBI. Thereafter, we take up a narrow perspective of the political economy of CBI, looking at the circumstances that led to making central banks independent from daily politics as well as those that might reverse this process.

3.2   RULES VERSUS DISCRETION I: SIMONS AND FRIEDMAN, EUCKEN AND COLLEAGUES, BRENNAN AND BUCHANAN, SMITH AND HAYEK

Monetary policy rules have featured large in macroeconomic policy discussion for at least the last century (see Chapter 1). They are present in a number of different schools: the Chicago School, the Freiburg School of Law and Economics, the Virginia Public Choice School and New Institutional Economics. Already in 1936, Henry Simons (1936) suggested that the discretionary power of the monetary authority should be restricted to reduce the potential to surprise the public. His paper was written in the context of the Great Depression and the controversy about the policy conduct of the then young Federal Reserve Board. It has become a very influential paper and a stimulus to the debate on rules versus discretion. Milton Friedman (1968) later built on these foundations with his proposal to establish rules for macroeconomic policy; first, for example, in Friedman (1948), with a hard budget rule to prevent fiscal pressure on monetary policy and later with a policy rule that became renowned as the 'k-percent rule', suggesting that the central bank should increase a predefined monetary aggregate by k-percent every year to prevent fiscal pressure from forcing the central bank to finance the government's deficit.[8]

In parallel with Friedman's work on monetary rules, the approach of the Freiburg School of Law and Economics emphasised the importance of rules in economic policy.[9] Its proponents – notably Walter Eucken (1923, 1955) – distinguish between the rules of the game and the game itself. Eucken, however, did not formulate a defined rule; rather, he formulated principles of economic policy. Central in the canon of such principles was a stable currency. In combination with the neoclassical assignment, to avoid trade-offs between two policy objectives as confirmed by Tinbergen (1952), Eucken's followers later focussed on an independent central bank such as the German Bundesbank. Following the ordo-liberal approach of the Freiburg School of Law and Economics, rules are important for the design of monetary policy.

A slightly different but related perspective has been taken by institutional economists (North, 1990). With respect to monetary policy, institutions play a major role in the work by Brennan and Buchanan (1981), who suggest constitutional restrictions for monetary policymakers to minimise their discretionary leeway. According to White (1999), the consequence is either an independent monetary authority with limited delegated powers or the privatisation of the provision of legal tender to sever the connection between the monetary and fiscal authorities on the integrated public sector balance sheet. It was the fact that in most modern economies the central bank's balance sheet is integrated with the public sector balance sheet that led Friedman to propose stabilising rules either for the fiscal or monetary side to prevent pressure from spilling over from the government finances to monetary

[8] In both Simon's and Friedman's argumentation, it was the central bank that should be constrained by rules. White (1999) argues that technical requirements to the rule make it quite complex.
[9] This approach has been labelled ORDO, as it is focussing on the economic order and its relation to the political order. It is rooted not only in economics, but also in social sciences and religious studies.

instability. This logic falls away if you sever the link between the central bank's balance sheet and the public sector balance.

This latter possibility introduces the perspective of free-banking, which we only briefly pick up here. The basic study on free-banking is Smith (1936/1990) arguing in favour of private competition in providing legal tender. Her starting point is the observation that most central banks have been founded because of government's need for a financier, which is also in a generalised manner the starting point of this book.[10] The argument for free-banking is the following: fierce competition among banks issuing legal tender forces them to deliver price stability. Thus, the free-banking alternative is superior (see also Hayek, 1990). However, as Klein (1974) as well as later authors show, private issuers may well have an interest in going bankrupt and creating hyperinflation. Therefore, and for political reasons, the free-banking alternative has never been reinstalled.

That said, the discussion about central-bank independence and rule-bound monetary policy has a long tradition and has been seen in very different methodological environments. Monetarists, representatives of institutional and constitutional economics as well as the German-based ordo-liberals have argued in a very similar manner and come to similar conclusions.[11] Interestingly, these schools arrived at the conclusion to support rules without a sophisticated formal apparatus. This changed with the rising importance of expectations building for economic, in particular monetary, policy as prevalent in the neo-classical analysis of the time inconsistency phenomenon.

3.3   RULES VERSUS DISCRETION II: TIME INCONSISTENCY

Whereas until the early 1970s, macroeconomic theory mainly used to model policymakers as being benevolent dictators who tried to

---

[10] See Chapter 1.

[11] This is another proof that the German policy model was not unique, in that it could only be applied in Germany during the immediate post-war era, as some observers constantly claim.

maximise an aggregate welfare function, this has changed. Monetary policymakers are seen as individuals with personal interests (Persson and Tabellini, 1999).[12] These interests are incorporated in a monetary policymakers' objective function of the following general form: $W = f(\pi, N, S, CA, \ldots)$. W denotes the utility of the policymaker (and economic welfare), π the rate of inflation (entering the policymakers' utility negatively), N stands for employment, S for seigniorage and CA denotes the balance of the current account, all three affecting W positively. The policymaker is assumed to maximise W with respect to π. The arguments in the objective function can be interpreted as proxies for public welfare from the perspective of the utility of the policymaker in charge. Her/his personal utility may also depend on being in office or on the preferences of her/his constituencies (Alesina and Tabellini, 1988). Choosing the arguments in the objective function has the advantage that they are observable; it also avoids tautologies.

Against this background, it can be taken for granted that, in most cases, inflation is created deliberately or at least accepted by governments who use monetary policy to achieve other than monetary objectives, which are a part of W. Obviously, in such cases, policymakers lack policy instruments or face distortions so that these objectives cannot be met without the help of monetary policy.

3.3.1   Time Inconsistency and the Philipps Curve

The possibility of time-inconsistent monetary policy was first demonstrated by Kydland and Prescott (1977). It is built on a presumed relationship between inflation and unemployment that was highly influential in the third quarter of the twentieth century, This relationship, called the Phillips curve, after the graph plotted by A. W. Phillips (1950) of an inverse long-run association between the rate of unemployment and wage inflation in the United Kingdom. There was no great leap required

---

[12] The term personal interests is a bit misleading. These interests are part of the objective function and may well cover economic policy objectives, which in turn may help the policymakers to meet personal objectives such as re-election or ideology. Again, for the sake of the argument, we assume that central banks are part of the general government.

between an association of wage inflation and the rate of unemployment, and an association of inflation per se with the unemployment rate; nor between a statistical curiosum and a menu offering policymakers the choice between a permanently lower unemployment rate at the cost of a permanently higher level of inflation (and vice versa).

These two leaps occurred to some extent despite the knowledge that the theoretical underpinnings of the Phillips curve were weak (or even absent) and the caution by its early proponents – for example, Samuelson and Solow (1960) – that the short-run trade-off was unlikely to persist in the long run. The 1960s and 1970s demonstrated that there was indeed no long-run relationship between these important magnitudes, but policy models of the era nevertheless embedded a short-run trade-off between inflation and unemployment as a core macroeconomic relationship. It is this relationship that Kydland and Prescott used to demonstrate what has since become known as the time inconsistency of discretionary monetary policy.

In their model, the central bank is benign and commits to low inflation, causing the private sector to have low inflation expectations. At the same time, the monetary authorities have an incentive to use the short-run trade-off between inflation and unemployment once the private sector has believed and acted upon the policymaker's initial commitment to low inflation.

The underlying reason is that the monetary authorities value both low inflation and high employment, and will pursue the latter if the former has apparently been achieved. However, the private sector will soon figure out that the monetary authorities are reneging on their commitment to low inflation. Once the central bank's lack of credibility has been exposed in this way, private sector inflation expectations will rise. Higher actual inflation will not be far behind, leaving the economy with higher inflation and no gain in employment. It turns out that the initial commitment to low inflation was inconsistent, and not because the central bank was incompetent or malevolent. On the contrary, the inconsistency arose from the central bank's desire to do the best for the economy.

Larry Summer's (1991, p. 629) analogy for dynamic inconsistency appeals to the academic taste: 'it always looks good ex post to cancel your exams so that you don't have to grade them; the students have already studied. Likewise, it always looks good to inflate a little more than people expect.'

A central bank with discretion will, in this model, leave the economy with higher inflation and no sustained gain in employment. By contrast, a central bank that adopted a simple rule to enforce low inflation, and eschew the Phillips curve, would achieve the clearly better outcome of lower inflation at the same level of employment.

The reason for the counter-intuitive result that a rule beats informed discretion is due to the non-neutrality of money in the short run, but neutrality in the long run. Neutrality implies that the monetary authorities cannot, in the long run, gain from other goals apart from price stability. However, the short-run trade-off between output and inflation means that an ex ante commitment by the monetary authorities to price level stability lacks credibility; that is, the authorities have an incentive to renege on their commitment and exploit the short run trade-off, ex post. Accordingly, the private sector will learn, rationally, that the commitment is not credible ex ante, causing suboptimally high inflation throughout. For Fischer (1995), this tension between the desire for low inflation, and the incentive to use the short-run trade-off with unemployment through unexpected inflation, lay at the heart of the study of both modern central banking and monetary economics.

That said, it is obvious that expectation formation is central to this topic. Inflation on grounds of the employment motive of policy-makers can lead to more employment only through adaptive expectations; that is, the public forms its expectation only by considering the past, or even naïve expectations, assuming no changes at all. If the government raises inflation every year, the public will never be able to anticipate the inflation rate of the following year properly. Thus, employment will remain above its natural level. Especially before a general election, it sometimes seems attractive to use monetary expansion to create a political business cycle. It has been suggested that much of the inflation from the 1960s to the 1980s can be explained by the widespread belief among politicians in the negatively sloped Phillips curve (McCallum, 1995).

Since the 1990s, theoretical analyses and empirical observations suggest that monetary policy is an inappropriate means to raise employment permanently. The long-run Phillips curve is not negatively sloped (e.g. Friedman, 1987; Broaddus, 1995). The adaptive expectation hypothesis only has limited explanatory power. It presumes that individuals are not able and/or willing to learn from past experience. This is an unrealistic assumption. Therefore, modern macroeconomics has resorted to the concept of rational expectations. Under this assumption, the public understands the logic of the policy model and consequently will not be misguided by time-inconsistent policies. The public does not have perfect foresight (Sheffrin, 1983). Its reaction may well be biased because of uncertainty and stochastic shocks. In other words: the public is neither systematically right nor systematically not right, but understands general patterns. Individuals will be correct on average over a longer time period since they are not systematically wrong. Shocks will be buffeted in the longer run; this holds even if we assume bounded rationality (Simon, 1966). Assuming rational expectations thus changes the calculus. The public adjusts to the inflation, and there is no change in unemployment owing to a surprise inflation; W changes into an objective function focusing on inflation. The result will be an optimal inflation that equals expected inflation and is positive:

3.3.2 Extensions to the Time Inconsistency Model

The theoretical literature about the problem of time inconsistency has assessed a number of major complications of the basic model, of which we think three are of interest for our argument. First, there may be a situation when the need for rules is less strict, namely in cases of repeated interactions (Barro and Gordon, 1983b). In such a case, the central bank can build up reputation. This setting is modelled as an infinite strategic game between the central bank and the public. The central bank (or the government) announces an optimal inflation; let us assume that it announces $\pi = 0$. The central bank maximises an objective function, where the future welfare is discounted with a discount factor r. At each point in time, the central bank compares the sum of the current welfare and the discounted future welfare for a situation with the announced zero inflation and a positive surprise inflation respectively; the past does not matter. The positive inflation would then be chosen for the future, given rational expectations.

This decision-making situation is called a trigger mechanism. It is based on the weight λ that the central bank gives to employment objective and its time preference. The higher the central bank's time preference, the more likely is a surprise inflation. In addition, the rate of time preference r that allows the central bank to stick to announcement is negatively dependent on λ. In this setting, there is no need for a formal rule; the central bank can build up reputation, and its announcements are credible because of the trigger mechanism.

The second situation when – even under rational expectations – it cannot be excluded that the public is misled by the announcement, since it assumes that the policymaker has private information about the economic environment and/or about her/his own attitude and properties that the public does not have. In this case, it may be possible to betray the public, at least in the short run.

In the models by Backus and Driffill (1985) as well as Cukierman (2000), the public is uncertain about the type of central banker. There are two types of central bankers who differ with respect to the importance of the arguments in the objective function possible, and the public does not know the type of the officeholder. She may either be a falcon with a rather low preference for the employment motive,[13] implying a zero weight λ or a dove with an accordingly positive weight λ for employment. In a two stage model, the optimal inflation for a falcon is zero and positive for a dove for both periods. If the central banker is a dove and creates a positive inflation in the

---

[13] Alternatively, this type is also called a hawk; the expressions are interchangeable.

first period, the public can be certain that there will also be a positive inflation in the second period.

However, the public cannot tell whether zero inflation in the first period is a reliable predictor for the same outcome in the second period. This is only the case when the central banker is a hawk. If the central banker is a dove with a high rate of time preference, there may be an incentive for the dove to mimic a falcon. Then a pooling equilibrium in the first period occurs instead of a separating equilibrium. By surprising the public in the second period, the dove may generate a higher welfare.

A third extension, which adds to public uncertainty about the type of central banker, deals with the problem that there are stochastic shocks (Cukierman, 2000). Then the public has two problems: it cannot identify the central banker's type in the first period and is unable to assign the realised inflation rate to the actions of the central bank. Inflation may well be the result of a shock. In this case, the model has a slightly different outcome. Welfare under a flexible rule (taking the shocks into account) may be higher than both welfare under a fixed rule and under discretion, because the central bank can react to shocks in order to increase employment without creating higher inflation expectations.

This has an important lesson for policymakers: in the presence of stochastic shocks, they have more flexibility without hurting zero-inflation expectations. As mentioned in Section 2.1, the Bundesbank was regularly criticised for missing its monetary targets, but in most instances had good explanations, which mostly were characterised as external shocks. Its reputation has remained high to date.

3.3.3 Seigniorage and the Current Account as Motives for Inflation

The literature distinguishes two further motives for governments to increase inflation. As already indicated in Chapter 2, an important reason for policymakers to increase the money supply is need for fresh public funds. In the objective function mentioned earlier, employment (N) as an argument in the objective function is replaced by seigniorage (S). To reduce the value of public debt, positive inflation is in the interest of the central bank (government). However, it is almost impossible to maximise seigniorage because the optimal inflation rate would be infinite (Cagan, 1956; Cukierman and Webb, 1995).

Finally, money growth may be seen as a tool to balance the current account (CA) if it is in persistent deficit, which can be reduced through monetary expansion; in the objective function, the CA is the main argument in this case. Money growth with subsequent inflation will cause the domestic currency to devalue (in nominal terms) compared with foreign currencies (in a regime of flexible exchange rates). In theory and provided a normal reaction of trade flows, if the Marshall–Lerner condition holds, the devaluation is designed to stimulate exports and to repress imports.[14] However, the Marshall–Lerner condition is dependent on the very unrealistic absence of capital flows. That said, the effect of inflation on the CA also depends on the reaction of capital flows on the depreciation. Therefore, this theory does not explain the CA.

Modern balance-of-payment theory is based on the Austrian capital theory (Böhm-Bawerk, 1914), and interprets the balance of payments as the result of intertemporal decision-making of internationally acting domestic and foreign savers and investors (Obstfeld and Rogoff, 1994). If capital flows do not alter after the depreciation, the subsequent surge in demand for exports and the decreasing demand for imports will finally – at least partly – reverse the depreciation (Dluhosch et al., 1996). Accordingly, those countries that tried to improve on their CA via inflation regularly failed. However, recent mercantilist impulses such as in the United States after the election of President Trump have not resulted in excessive inflation. The Trump administration mainly used trade policy instruments to reduce the deficit, and did not refer to exchange rate policies;

[14] The Marshall–Lerner condition explains the conditions on the supply and demand sides, respectively, under which a depreciation of the domestic currency can activate the trade balance.

thus it did not use monetary policy tools. Trade policy measures increase prices of imported goods, but these price increases can be contained if the money supply does not increase accordingly. This does not exclude welfare losses as trade theory predicts. In addition, the intertemporal approach to the balance of payments shows that trade policy instruments also do not have the potential to reduce a trade deficit.[15]

3.3.4 Interim Conclusions

The theoretical Sections 3.2 and 3.3 have made clear that the PAP in combination with the time inconsistency policy requires a solution. Given the high welfare costs and distributional unfairness of inflation, and given that the public understands the logic of the model (i.e. has rational expectations), it seems clearly plausible to formulate an inflation target relatively close to zero (price stability), which can be credible. Based on the time inconsistency literature, but also already discussed in the old literature, there are many suggestions for policy solutions, that is, rules for monetary policy, of which most will be discussed briefly in Section 3.4, before we concentrate on independent central banks.

3.4 RULES RATHER THAN DISCRETION: CBI

3.4.1 Selection of Monetary Rules

The traditional policy rule that is not only restricting the government, but also considers the second-stage-PAP between the government and the central bank, is Friedman's monetarist k-rule, suggesting that the monetary base grows at an annual rate of k-percent, which takes all discretionary leeway from the central, and therefore frees the central bank from all political pressure whatsoever. Some authors suggest that this rule should be given legal status (Scheide, 1993). In this case, the central bank's objective function is very simple; it minimises inflation.

---

[15] See Griswold and Freytag (2023) for a nuanced discussion.

Kenneth Rogoff proposes the hiring of a so-called conservative central banker, known to be a falcon, to solve the uncertainty of the public with respect to her type (Rogoff, 1985). However, it may be impossible to identify the type of a central banker, as the theoretical considerations in Section 3.3.2 also show.[16] Moreover, the political pressure on a central banker might be too high to maintain a conservative position as a falcon without a legal or contractarian framework; Karl Popper has already addressed this problem.[17]

Another proposal suggests that the government agrees on contracts with central bankers, thereby for instance limiting their personal income (up to dismissal) in case they miss a certain politically given inflation target (Walsh, 1995).[18] However, contracts for central bankers are only effective if the government itself is committed to stability. Hence, the potential problem is not solved by a contract, but only relocated (McCallum, 1995).

In some cases, it seems impossible to commit to stability exclusively domestically. Then it is sensible to use a hard foreign currency as nominal anchor or even as legal tender to import stability. The weakest form of fixing the exchange rate is a crawling peg, which fixes the domestic currency to the foreign currency with a predefined path of depreciation of the domestic currency. Next would be a fixed exchange rate without the potential to depreciate. The BWS has been such a system since the second World War; it gained relevance again in the 1980s and 1990s when developing and emerging countries pegged their currencies to the US dollar or the Deutschmark.

An even stronger and popular option of the 1990s has been a currency board system (CBS), which does not allow the monetary authority to issue base money without the purchase of

---

[16] The history of central bankers shows that governments often miss the correct type of central bankers. Admittedly, this error has more often happened with an alleged dove who turns out to be a falcon.

[17] In addition, it seems undemocratic to base monetary policy on the preferences of a single person. Therefore, the proposal has its academic credentials, but no practical relevance.

[18] Such a contract was introduced in New Zealand in 1992. See Kirchgässner (1996).

foreign currencies or gold. The domestic currency is pegged to a hard currency and the board has the obligation to accept domestic currency in exchange for the hard currency in the fixed relation. In fact, money supply then is endogenous and depends on the CA. In the 1980s and 1990s, the CBS was quite popular: Hong Kong, Argentina, Estonia, Lithuania and Bulgaria relied relatively successfully on it (Freytag, 2002). Some countries even completely rely on the use of foreign currency, such as Panama, which has dollarised the economy.

These policy options have in common that they bring about a trade-off, the so-called Mundell trilemma or impossibility trinity: in a world of unrestricted capital flows and fixed exchange rate, a domestically determined monetary policy is impossible. The role of the central bank is restricted. The alternative is to strengthen the policy space of central banks under a given objective and a strict legal framework.

3.4.2   Principles of Central Bank Independence

The standard form of monetary commitment to stability since the 1990s has been to grant CBI. First, CBI itself is generally defined relatively simply and clearly as instrument independence and not as goal independence. Independence does not mean that the central bank is free to choose its policy objective. This is not formulated by the central bank, but by a democratically legitimate body, mostly the national parliament. The policy objective is given for the central bank (Debelle and Fischer, 1994). The central bank acts within a legal framework that gives it instrument-independence. This logic can be interpreted as an attempt of the government to solve the first stage of the PAP by committing to a policy assignment that follows Tinbergen and values price stability highly.

To understand the logic of CBI and its effects, second de-facto CBI has to be distinguished from *de-jure* CBI. De-facto CBI describes the effective independence and can only be measured ex-post, for example, by assessing the turnover-rate of central bank governors (Vuletin and Zhu, 2011). *De jure* CBI is best defined as the aggregate of all legal restrictions of the central bank and the government with respect to monetary policy as well as the relation between central bank and government. To assess how CBI determines macroeconomic performance, it is necessary to concentrate on the legal aspects, that is, *de-jure* CBI. If de facto CBI was used to explain policy outcomes, for example, inflation rates, it would be possible for both to be determined by the same exogenous variable. The results would be distorted. This can be avoided by using legal foundations as explanans.

That said, it is important to note that any concept of commitment is not necessarily identical to the credibility of the monetary policy (Freytag, 2005; Siklos, 2008) It may be insufficient to legally introduce CBI in order to achieve low inflation. For a similar reasoning see Forder, who questions statute reading as a method to measure CBI in principle (Forder, 1998). We follow this discussion when introducing the measurement of CBI and the empirical evidence.

3.4.3   *Core Elements of* de jure *CBI*

In this section, the elements defining an independent central bank are discussed in more detail. An independent central bank is characterised by a clearly defined (set of) objective(s), ideally with a strong focus on price stability. In addition, the legal locus of CBI should be as high as possible, for example, constitutional or – as in the European case – in an international treaty. Governmental interference in monetary policy should be minimised, and clear rules about the appointment and dismissal of its governor and directorate are necessary. Most importantly, the central bank's role as financier of the government has to be restricted, as the main cause for high and volatile inflation in history has been debt monetisation. In addition, external obligations may support or distort monetary policy. Finally, the issue of transparency and accountability is adding to the independence of central banks. In detail, the following aspects are crucial:

- A clear definition of the objective of monetary policy in the legal foundation of the monetary regime, namely price stability, makes it easier to refuse the demands of politicians and interest groups. Thus, CBI varies with the kind and number of legally prescribed objectives. It is highest when the monetary authorities are obliged by law to only consider price level stability. The obligation to support the economic policy of the government or to take employment into account as well as stability results in much less commitment. It is lowest if no objective is defined.
- The commitment to stability has to be put into a legal framework. This can be fixed on different constitutional levels. At the upper end of the scale, monetary policy can be integrated into the constitution, which can only be changed by a qualified majority in parliament or by a referendum. At the lower end of the scale, the monetary regime can be implemented by a governmental decree, which of course can be changed much more easily than the constitution. In the latter case, the government is a great deal less committed to stability than in the first. The more difficult a change of the regime is for the government, the higher is CBI.
- The freedom of interventions by the government reflects the choice of instruments as well as the timing and magnitude of their use to meet the given monetary policy objective(s). The more the government keeps control over instruments such as interest rates and open market policy, the lower is CBI.
- The rules for the appointment and dismissal of the central bank's staff have been discussed controversially for a long time, in particular with respect to their independence from politics. In general, two aspects are of interest (Cukierman, 1992). First are the criteria for being appointed as chief executive officer (CEO). The higher the demanded expertise of the CEO in monetary policy, the higher the CBI. Second, how is a potential dismissal organised? For instance, if a dismissal is possible after a change of government or even of certain ministers (Cukierman and Webb, 1995), legal monetary commitment and the independence of the central bank are low. It is also possible that only severe violation of her/his duty leads to the dismissal of the CEO. The latter is correlated with a high level of CBI.
- Monetisation of budget deficits by monetary expansion has always been and still is the main reason for hyperinflation wherever it happened. Public budget deficits per se are not a threat to stability, as long as they are financed on the (international) capital market and used sustainably.

However, public deficits being financed by emitting fresh money has to be avoided, as in the long run it might lead to inflation. Thus, an important factor determining the level of legal commitments is a provision on lending fresh money to the government. Hence, the highest commitment is given when the central bank is allowed to buy government bonds neither on the primary nor the secondary market. Even central bank holdings of government bonds purchased on the secondary market have fiscal effects as long as the seigniorage is added to public revenues. Moreover, if the central bank is not allowed to buy government bonds' on the primary market but may still purchase them on the secondary market, it is rather easy to circumvent this regulation, as the example of the ECB clearly demonstrates (see Chapters 4 and 6). Thus, the lower the level of commitment, the easier it is for the government to borrow money from the monetary institution.

- It is possible to take external obligations. These raise the level of commitment compared with a situation without these obligations. First, the government can *ex-ante* fix the exchange rate towards an international currency such as the US-dollar, the EURO or the Swiss franc. It illustrates that the government is willing to keep the exchange rate stable, that is, to import stability. This is particularly important after a period of high and volatile inflation. However, there may be a downside, as already expressed in the so-called impossibility trinity: if the government fixes the exchange rate towards a foreign currency (or a basket), the central bank loses policy space and needs to use monetary policy to maintain the exchange rate. If the domestic currency is not under pressure to depreciate (and lose stability), but to appreciate, the problem of imported inflation may occur. Second, the government can grant convertibility, which offers an alternative to the domestic currency for the citizens and puts pressure on the central bank to deliver stable money.

- The correlation of CBI to stability and the accountability and transparency of the central bank to the government or parliament is not clear. On the one hand, the central bank has to create transparency (Bini Smaghi, 1998); an informed public is more likely to form realistic expectations than an uninformed one. On the other hand, accountability must not lead to the right of the government or parliament to participate in monetary policy. The higher the level of commitment, the better the public is informed about monetary policy. The highest level is given when the public has to be informed by at least quarterly reports of the central bank (or via a detailed website). It is the least when no information is required.[19]

To summarise, CBI is higher the more of these elements are considered. However, legal commitment does not imply a guarantee for the behaviour of governments and central banks. Although commitment is a device to make monetary policy more transparent, acceptable and stability oriented, it may not be possible to cover all possibilities in an Act of Parliament such as a central bank law. It remains incomplete. Governments and central banks still may have an informational advantage over the citizens. This is an advantage they may wish to explore. Legal commitment to an independent central bank is a way to prevent such a behaviour. In the following, various measures of CBI are introduced.

3.5 MEASURING CBI

After defining the constitutive elements of CBI, the measurement of CBI must be discussed. This measurement is needed for several reasons. First, an indicator of CBI is a tool to compare governments' formal commitment to stability. Thereby, it exerts some – probably relatively mild – pressure on governments to grant its national central bank instrument independence. Second, it is a tool to measure the influence of CBI on macroeconomic variables, first and foremost inflation. In order to allow for unbiased estimations, the chosen indicator of CBI must not contain results of the political process. For this purpose, *de-jure* CBI is the adequate concept.

As mentioned earlier, de-facto CBI is measured as a political action by the government, namely to replace the central bank's CEO (turnover rate). The higher this rate is, the less independent the central bank is. As for *de-jure* CBI, there are a number of indicators of CBI, which are mainly based on two approaches; a relatively

[19] See Section 8.3.

comprehensive survey is offered by Marco Arnone and his co-authors (Arnone, 2006a; Arnone, 2006b). Either CBI is measured as the simple sum of 0-1-statements regarding the various properties of central bank legislation (Parkin, 1978; Grilli et al., 1991), labelled the Grilli, Masciandaro, Tabellini (GMT)-method, or as a weighted or unweighted average of these properties, measured in a Likert-scale (Cukierman, 1992), labelled the Cukierman-method.

CBI is generally measured by assessing the central bank law with respect to the ability of the central bankers to pursue a stability oriented monetary policy free of political influence, with reference to the core elements of CBI presented earlier. Thus, certain criteria are introduced and given numerical values, which are either added up (GMT-method) or averaged in weighted or unweighted form (Cukierman-method). The measures of CBI in general have similar components, which can be differentiated into five groups (Directorate, Policy formulation, Policy objective, Lending to the government, External obligations). Not all measures consider all aspects mentioned in the following. The index constructed by Grilli et al. is divided into political and economic independence. The measure is based on a set of questions, which are answered by yes and no (0 or 1 respectively). The higher the score, the higher is CBI. No weighting takes place (Grilli et al., 1991).

The alternative method was developed by Cukierman (Cukierman, 1992). It is applied in a number of papers (Dvorsky, 2000; Freytag, 2001; Cukierman et al., 2002) Cukierman's original index of CBI is measured by sixteen components, which are normed between 0 and 1 with equidistant codings (Cukierman, 1992). The higher the value, the higher is CBI. The advantage of the latter method is that the outcome is more differentiated than with the GMT method.

This procedure of statute reading has been subject to severe criticism. Forder (1996) argues that the concept is methodologically flawed, as it gives no credit to informal rules and to actual behaviour. For instance, the central bank's ability to conduct monetary policy may be limited despite a high degree of CBI owing to exchange rate regimes set up by the government. He also claims that statute of a central bank does not allow an assessment of the government's commitment to stability.

Another criticism is that a single indicator may not be adequate for all countries, in other words: a one-size-fits-all-solution leads to distortions (Siklos, 2008). Less fundamentally, and accepting the concept of CBI in general, Posen (1998) argues that the financial sector is able both to influence the degree of CBI and inflation; its dislike of inflation causes both. Similarly, Hayo (1998) as well as de Jong (2002) argue that cultural aspects can exert pressure on the government to grant CBI and to keep inflation low. In other words, as *de-jure* CBI is endogenous, it may be difficult to use it as an exogenous variable for policy outcome.

One consequence of these criticisms would be to apply different commitment mechanisms (Hayo and Hefeker, 2002) as a means to guarantee price stability. However, other mechanisms such as contracts for central bankers (Walsh; 1995) or appointing a conservative central banker (Rogoff, 1985) have even stronger flaws, as they do not provide a solution to the fundamental PAP between the public and the government. Theoretically, CBI or a similar commitment mechanism can be seen as the least problematic way to solve it. However, we need empirical evidence. In the next section, we discuss this: Is high CBI really contributing to low inflation?

3.6 EMPIRICAL EVIDENCE: CBI AND INFLATION

The relation between CBI and inflation has frequently been investigated empirically. Most studies use an indicator for *de-jure* CBI and a variety of control variables to test the hypothesis that CBI causes low inflation. The general results support this basic hypothesis. On average, independent central banks deliver lower inflation than dependent ones.

Despite these empirical investigations, three general problems must be addressed on this topic. First, correlation does not necessarily imply causality (Berger et al., 2001). This holds particularly as the degree of CBI is not exogenously given, but depends on historical experience. Granting CBI may also neglect accountability and leave too much room for central banks' discretion. In addition, central banks' behaviour can be directed at securing their high degree of independence (Forder, 2005). Thus, a clear direction of causality is difficult to maintain. Second, cross-section studies compare different countries at the same time and do not cover developments over time. Therefore, pooled regressions are preferable (Arnone and Romelli, 2013). Third, it seems that heterogeneity with respect to the development level of countries plays a major role. In those countries where the rule of law is generally accepted, the legal status of the central bank is decisive for the success of its policy. In other countries, the correlation between legal status and inflation is rather arbitrary.

Consequently, the empirical evidence is less clear than the analysis would theoretically claim. In cross-country studies, the empirical relation between legal indicators of CBI and price stability is positive, at least for a sample of industrialised countries and increasingly for transition economies. With respect to industrialised countries, all legal measures applied are negatively correlated with inflation. By contrast, for developing and transition countries, this relation is not that robust (Klomp and de Haan, 2010). Legal measures of CBI do not display a strong impact on inflation. However, Christopher Crowe and Ellen Meade show that CBI as measured by the indicators presented here increased until the GFC hit the world economy in 2008, and that there is a positive influence of this trend on inflation rates (Crowe and Meade, 2007; Crowe and Meade, 2008). In addition, a significant negative correlation can be found between de-facto CBI measured as turnover rate of central banks' CEOs and inflation; this holds especially when the fired central banker is replaced with a government ally (Vuletin and Zhu, 2011).

One important conclusion of these results is that CBI must not be confused with credibility (Freytag, 2005). Credibility of a policy is only given if the public has trust in the respective legislation. It obviously heavily depends on an enforcement mechanism. Such a mechanism could be that the entire economic order is stability friendly. Therefore, a number of studies have been conducted that use CBI in combination with other policy measures or institutional aspects. Pierre Siklos argues that stature reading alone does not measure CBI correctly, but claims that a mixture of four *de-jure* (mandate, decision-making process, autonomy and appointment procedure) and de-facto (economic freedom, exchange rate regime type, inflation target and accumulated inflation forecast errors) core elements of CBI can explain inflation. In fact, there is a significant negative correlation between CBI and inflation, in particular at the tails of the distribution (Siklos, 2008). This procedure is in part problematic as its de facto core elements are partly *de jure* elements (exchange rate regime), partly policy outcome (forecast errors), and thus also results of the policymaking process and partly elements of the economic order (economic freedom).

To overcome such problems, an estimation strategy would be to separate CBI from institutional variables that mirror the economic order and let both interact. In a cross-country study, Kai Hielscher and Gunther Markwardt show the positive influence of CBI on inflation being contingent on good institutional quality (Hielscher and Markwardt, 2012). A similar study on democracies since the Bretton Woods era shows that the effect of CBI on inflation is dependent on other policies too (Franzese, 1999).

In an own panel study over five decades for the Organisation for Economic Co-operation and Development (OECD), we can show a similar result. If the degree of economic freedom is high, CBI is causing stability (Belke et al., 2014). These results have further been supported with studies analysing the effects of monetary reform on stability. Only if other elements of the economic order are favourable is a monetary reform (i.e. the commitment to stability) successful; we tested for labour market flexibility, fiscal soundness and economic freedom (Freytag 2002, 2005).

In sum, the empirical literature supports the theoretical analyses discussed in Sections 3.2 and 3.3. and shows that independent central banks have a better prospect to guarantee price stability than dependent ones. This result is contingent on institutions favourable to economic prosperity. So it is fair to say that CBI as a concept gathered large support in the two decades before the global financial and economic crisis. Today, after four serious global crises,[20] this support seems less strong; this trend will be discussed in subsequent chapters, in particular in Part II. Against this background, it may be sensible to analyse the political economy of CBI from a theoretical perspective more closely.

3.7 THE POLITICAL ECONOMY OF (GRANTING AND TAKING) CBI?

After the global financial and economic crisis, central banks started to engage in huge balance sheet operations and to purchase government bonds; during the COVID-19 crisis, they have proceeded along this avenue, which has become even broader since the Russian invasion into Ukraine and its consequences for energy prices in the European Union (EU). This policy is regularly criticised as a sort of surrender of central banks, which respond to treasurers' demands. We will discuss this allegation later. However, to understand the current situation of central banks, it is necessary to take a step back and to analyse the incentives of politicians to interact with central banks. As it is correct to see the central bank as part of the government, its independence separates it from the cabinet and allows for its own judgements of the economic and political situations and according decisions. This analysis comprises three steps. The first is to ask for the drivers of granting CBI. In other words, why do politicians decide to delegate (Crowe, 2006)? The second is to briefly discuss the relations of the central bank to parliament and government in general against the background of the allegation that central bankers have become powerful technocrats without a democratic

---

[20] These are the Lehman crisis (2008), the Eurocrisis (2010), the COVID 19 crisis (2020) and the Russian aggression against Ukraine (2022).

mandate (Tucker, 2018). Third, we look at the incentives to reduce the independence of central banks. This political economy analysis is of enormous importance if one wants to understand the threats that independent central banks face.

3.7.1 Why Do Governments Delegate?

The positive theoretical literature about CBI is relatively limited. It uses game theory to simulate the interaction between governments and central banks when it comes to delegation of tasks to the central bank (Crowe, 2006; Weymark, 2007). In addition, the normative theoretical analysis has clearly shown that granting CBI as a rule-bound policy framework is welfare enhancing when compared with discretionary monetary policy. Therefore, it is fair to assume that welfare-maximising governments have an interest in low inflation; they also may be aware of the problematic incentive structure that is emerging if they do not separate monetary policy from other policy fields. This explanation is in line with the textbook version of a benevolent dictator who is pursuing policies in the best interests of society. In the field of monetary policy, it may have some explanatory power, as many countries changed their central bank laws during the late 1980s and early 1990s. The academic literature, in particular the first seminal papers, introduced in this chapter may have had a considerable influence.

A second approach is based on political economy reasoning. In reality, often policy reform towards strict rules is triggered through crisis. After the Second World War, the German Reichsbank was dissolved by the Allies. In March 1948, the predecessor of the German Bundesbank, the Bank deutscher Länder, was founded. It already enjoyed a relatively high degree of independence (at least from German authorities, not from the Allied Banking Commission), which was extended with the foundation of the Bundesbank in 1957. The effect of this high independence was that politicians learned from past experience and did not want to interfere into the central bank's business (Marsh, 1992). Similarly, the Reserve Bank of New Zealand was given a new statute in the course of the comprehensive economic policy reform of the 1980s. Until 1989, the Reserve Bank was dependent on the government and followed multiple goals set by the government; the economy was highly protected and inefficient. In the new structure, the Reserve Bank was given a distinct policy objective (price stability) and granted independence – with the exception that the bank had to negotiate and publish a so-called Policy Target Agreement with the government (Capie and Wood, 2013). Freytag discusses a range of about thirty monetary reforms in the twentieth century; those that were successful are characterised by binding rules and high institutional quality (Freytag, 2002, 2005).

A third driver, in combination with the second one, may be peer pressure. In the 1980s, when inflation in many countries became increasingly unbearable, governments all over the world started to grant their central banks independence. Similarly, academic research published measures of and data on CBI, which was quickly picked up in central banks themselves. This process was supported by the traditionally close relation between monetary policymaking and academia, which is much closer than in other fields of economic policy. Successful independent central banks increased the pressure on governments in other countries. This process was institutionalised with the founding of Economic and Monetary Union (EMU). The Treaty of Maastricht made it obligatory for potential member countries to grant their CBI. In the course of the 1990s, for instance, the Banque de France became politically independent. The same happened to the BoE, although the United Kingdom never intended to join the EMU.

3.7.2 Permanent Tensions between Central Banks and Politicians

Needless to say, the relation between the central bank and governments and/or parliaments are not always free of conflict. In particular when governments are in need of additional funds, they exert pressure on central banks. A prominent example is the conflict between the German Minister of Finance Theo Waigel and the German Bundesbank in 1997, which became publicly known as

Operation Goldfinger. Waigel foresaw difficulties for Germany in meeting the 3 per cent public deficit Maastricht criterion prior to entering the EMU and urged the Bundesbank to revalue its gold and foreign exchange reserves, which the Bundesbank traditionally kept in its balance to the lowest historical value. A revaluation would have meant an extra profit for the German Treasury of about 20 to 30 billion Deutschmarks. With this increased Bundesbank profit, Germany would have met the criterion. The German public, notoriously fond of the Bundesbank, took the side of the bank. The minister was unable to force the Bundesbank into this action (Scholtes, 2019). Similar clashes have taken place in other countries.

In addition, central banks are often accused of misusing power and behaving undemocratically. A regular claim is that central bankers are unelected technocrats who are not accountable to the public (Tucker, 2018). Parliamentarians and non-governmental organisations (NGOs) regularly demand to have a say in monetary policy, and argue that this participation would increase the democratic legitimacy of monetary policy. Hetzel counters this prediction, and argues that vested interests would gain influence on monetary policy if it was decided in parliament (Hetzel, 1997).[21]

In any case, as long as the decision to grant CBI is a democratic decision of an elected body and can be reversed if a majority of delegates and voters is in favour of the reversal, there is no reason to doubt the democratic legitimacy of the delegation of competence to the central bank. This holds in particular as long as CBI is restricted to instrument independence.

3.7.3   Is Independence Here to Stay?

Although in the last thirty years the track record of independent central banks has been positive, with low inflation, while at the same time growth rates in many countries have been solid, CBI is not set in stone. In a crisis, central banks may be forced to react and to take

---

[21] See Chapter 8 for a thorough discussion of the democratic legitimacy of CBI.

unconventional measures. Therefore, CBI might not be secured during crisis (Capie and Wood, 2013).

New macroeconomic thinking such as the hypotheses of secular stagnation and savings glut (obviously related), modern money theory (MMT) has already led to policy suggestions, which consider the consolidation of central banks with treasuries. Ideas such as zero interest, or even negative interest rates, as a non-constraint for public debt are obviously contradicting the idea of a central bank responsible mainly for price stability and conducting monetary policy in accordance with but not dependent on or even obedient to governments.

This leads to the question of whether CBI has a future, which is particularly relevant against the background of the crisis-ridden decade the world has experienced since the Great Recession. During this period, the presence, activities and perception of central banks in the public changed. Whether this change is also a herald of declining independence of central banks is an open question. We try to shed light on it in the following Parts II and III.

PART II Balance Sheet Operations in Different Times and CBI

4 Central Banks and the Great Moderation

4.1 INTRODUCTION

4.1.1 The Great Moderation

The political division of labour as described in Chapter 3 was maintained in the Western world after World War II until the GFC. Based on experience and theoretical developments in macroeconomics (such as the time inconsistency literature), an increasing number of central banks worked consistent with the Tinbergen rule to implement stability oriented monetary policy successfully and more or less independently from the political process. In Germany and Switzerland, CBI was already high in the 1950s, while other countries followed later. By the 1990s, policymakers finally supported or at least accepted CBI in almost all OECD countries. In the subsequent twenty years, many emerging markets and developing countries followed suit.

The associated monetary stability was the backdrop for a period of stable and prosperous advance in developed economies from the mid-1980s onwards, gathering pace with the end of the Cold War, and only halted by the GFC. Real GDP growth in the world economy was stable – and in some countries such as China or India remarkably high: inflation was low and output volatility decreased after the end of the 1970s. This period of remarkable macroeconomic stability has been called the Great Moderation (Bernanke, 2004; Davis and James, 2008).

Three general themes dominate the literature on the possible causes of the Great Moderation. They are: (i) microeconomic factors such as technological and managerial innovations, (ii) improvements in monetary policy and (iii) good luck (Bernanke, 2004).

It is unsurprising that many central bankers emphasise the role of good policy since the Volcker era (Bernanke, 2004), and there is an influential academic literature to back this claim (Clarida et al., 2000; Bernanke, 2004). Others assign more weight to the microeconomic factors, claiming that monetary policy in advanced economies was generally directed at low inflation from the 1950s onwards, with the notable exception of the late 1960s and the 1970s, when the United States financed the Vietnam War with expansionary fiscal policy, when oil price shocks disrupted the international economy and the world had to adapt to floating exchange rates. In this view, the stability oriented monetary policy since the early 1980s was rather a return to normality (Davis and James, 2008).

This book is written from the perspective that central banks in the 1980s and beyond contributed to the Great Moderation through improved monetary policy. However, in the run-up to the GFC, the same central banks may have been insensitive to the impact of their policy decisions on assets prices, notably in the housing market. Together with housing subsidies in the United States during the Clinton and Bush administrations, monetary policy contributed the environment that created the GFC, which started as a collapse of the subprime mortgage market.

4.1.2 An Overview of this Chapter

This chapter focusses on the experiences of two prominent central banks in the developed world and one emerging market economy: we start with the Federal Reserve Board, then move on to Europe, to look at the Bundesbank and its legal successor, the ECB. In the final section of this chapter, we consider an emerging market economy and the South African Reserve Bank.

4.2 GREENSPAN'S FED

It was Paul Volcker who turned the Federal Reserve Board and the United States back towards stability. His actions were instrumental to the set of principles later applied by his successors, of whom

Alan Greenspan was the most significant for this particular story. Volcker broke the stubborn inflation expectations that had plagued his predecessor, Arthur Burns, and caused much misery in the American economy. Once he had anchored inflation expectations at more appropriate levels, the Fed could proceed in what was a remarkably rule-like manner, even though no formal policy-rule had been adopted.

Over this period, inflation targeting emerged elsewhere as an experimental framework for monetary policy, and, with the demonstrable success of some early adopters, became a widespread and robust system (Rose, 2007).

Central banks in the developed world and those in the developing world were moving towards a system that could maintain monetary stability in the wake of the collapse of the Bretton Woods system in the early 1970s. Central bankers in the developed world incorporated the results of the academic debate together with their experience, and by the turn of the century four trends in the theory of monetary policy had emerged that would be central to the story of the Great Moderation (Fischer, 1995; Sterne, 1999; Friedman, 2000). These four trends are: (i) emphasis on the importance of credibility to the success of monetary policy; (ii) the increasing use of explicit policy targets; (iii) CBI; and (iv) the use of feedback rules. The trends towards credibility and explicit targets, and feedback rules are most relevant to the presumed connection between monetary policy and the Great Moderation, and are the theme of this section. CBI is a theme of the entire book and is not discussed in detail in the next few paragraphs.

4.2.1 Credibility

One of the most important effects of the theoretical advances since the 1950s and practical experience with monetary policy has been an increasing recognition that the credibility of monetary policy is a crucial precondition for its success. Accordingly, the pursuit of credibility has risen to the first order of priorities at central banks.

At the end of the twentieth century, Alan Blinder reported on an interesting survey of central bankers and monetary/macroeconomists relating to the issue of monetary policy credibility. As mentioned earlier, he (2000a, p. 1422) defines 'credibility' as 'a central bank is credible if people believe it will do what it says'.[1] This is the heart of the matter: credibility is about acting consistently with expected policy behaviour. It implies that the policymaker is able to articulate a clear commitment to a particular policy and then to honour that commitment.[2]

A list of the expected benefits of credibility include (e.g. Svensson, 1999): first, by anchoring inflation expectations, credible monetary policy eliminates unsettled expectations as an important monetary shock to the economy. Second, the trade-off between inflation variability and output-gap variability can become more favourable for the same reason. Third, stable inflation expectations imply a more direct impact on monetary policy adjustments to economic magnitudes such as inflation. Finally, since improved credibility implies expectations consistent with the long-run goals of policy, building credibility also means limiting the need for policy intervention (Brash, 1996).

The Blinder survey did not yield agreement on how credibility is established. However, the respondents ranked the factors contributing to credibility in the following order: living up to your word; independence for the central bank; history of fighting inflation; openness and transparency; and the ability to withstand fiscal pressure (Blinder, 2000a). There do not appear to be any shortcuts to credibility; rather, as Blinder (2000a, p. 1431) concludes, 'central banks get their credibility the old-fashioned way; they earn it by building a track record for honesty and inflation aversion (in that order

---

[1] Again, we see that the term credibility is used for an actor, not for a policy measure. Blinder talks of reputation.

[2] This definition comes close to the definition we offer in Chapter 3, namely that credibility is a function of the compatibility of the monetary commitment with the other elements of economic order.

of importance)'. Alan Greenspan's tenure was the exemplar of such credibility in which he was widely trusted, supported by an extraordinary track record – despite many crises – and a clear commitment to the independence of the Fed.

That said, CBI is at the heart of the Fed's policy stance. Its formal independence from politics as measured by the indicators introduced in Section 3.5 is lower than that of the Swiss National Bank, the Bundesbank or the ECB. Nevertheless, the Fed has worked relatively undisturbed by politics in the times after Volcker, and even later attempts to intervene by politicians, President Trump for example, have been unsuccessful (see Chapter 8).

4.2.2   Explicit Targets and Feedback Rules

Though the Fed did not, during the Greenspan period, adopt explicit numerical targets to guide its policy, analogous to the inflation targets adopted elsewhere, it nevertheless acted in a rule-like manner. John Taylor (1993), showed in the early 1990s how the Fed had operated systematically since the Volcker period, as if it had adopted a formal policy rule.

This modern understanding of a policy rule is what Taylor has called a contingency plan, '[a] plan that specifies as clearly as possible the circumstance under which a central bank should change the instruments of monetary policy ... [and] Implicit in this definition, is that the policy rule will in fact be used, and expected to be used, for many periods into the future' (Taylor, 2000, p. 3), or, in the words of Stephen Cecchetti, 'a policy rule [is] ... a systematic rule for adjusting the quantity that the Central Bank controls as the state of the economy fluctuates' (Cecchetti, 1998, p. 1).

A rule understood as a contingency plan is clearly not the mechanistic standard of the earlier Milton Friedman. The implementation of this kind of contingency plan is closely associated with the observations about credibility made earlier, as Michael Woodford observed at the time this consensus was gaining strength in the early 2000s:

> In my view, rules are important not because central bankers can't
> be relied upon to take the public interest to heart, or because they
> don't know what they're doing, but because the effects of monetary
> policy depend critically upon what the private sector expects about
> future policy, and hence about the future course of the economy.
> Thus effective monetary policy depends more on the management
> of *expectations* than on any direct consequences of the current
> level of interest rate ... the best way to do this is by being explicit
> about the *rule* that guides its decision making. The central bank
> also needs to establish a reputation for actually following the rule.
> (Woodford in Parkin (2002, Part 9), emphasis in the original)

Of course, the rule (and hence the expectations of its continued implementation) is itself contingent on the central bank's understanding of
the economy represented by its suite of economic models. And there
is no threat to the credibility of the authorities' commitment to a
rule if the specification of the rule is updated periodically, as knowledge of the economic system improves, provided that this knowledge
is disseminated transparently.

It is the systematic nature, not the supposedly fixed parameters, of policy rules that is important in modern normative policy
analysis. Or, as Alan Greenspan described the use of policy rules at
the Federal Reserve Board, 'we try to develop as best we can a stable
conceptual framework, so policy actions are as regular and predictable as possible – that is, governed by systematic behaviour but open
to evidence of structural macroeconomic changes that require policy
to adapt' (Greenspan, 1997, no page).

It is to this systematic and stabilising behaviour of the Fed,
which gained such credibility under the leadership of Alan Greenspan,
that researchers point when they attribute a significant role in the
Great Moderation to improved monetary policy.

4.3 FROM DEUTSCHMARK TO EURO

European monetary policy, as conducted by the ECB, was shaped
by the German Bundesbank from the beginning of the European

integration. Therefore, an account of the Great Moderation in Europe requires significant emphasis on the Bundesbank's contribution. The Bundesbank was the leading central bank in Europe until the introduction of the European Monetary System (EMS) in 1979 and beyond. The latter was a multilateral adjustable exchange rate system implemented by most member states of the erstwhile European Economic Community (EEC), with Britain always something of an exception.[3]

As mentioned earlier, the Bundesbank's degree of CBI is among the highest in the world. Within the group of developed countries, no other central bank enjoyed independence during the 1980s comparable to that of the Bundesbank, as measured by Cukierman's early index (Cukierman, 1992). Their policy objective was clearly defined, lending to the government was prohibited, and the bank decided autonomously about money growth and its discount rate. The German government was not entitled to override the Bundesbank's decisions on monetary policy, but was responsible for exchange rate policy. The Bundesbank followed a strategy to announce a growth corridor every year from 1974 for the money supply, which it did not meet in about half of the years until 1998. Nevertheless, its reputation grew over the course of its existence from 1957 (and is still high in Germany at the time of writing). Inflation was moderate in Germany, except for a few years during the BWS and in the aftermath of the first oil crisis in 1973.

Exchange rate policy in Europe was shaped by the BWS. However, already in the early 1970s, policymakers developed a plan for a European Currency Union, the Werner-Plan, which was quickly abandoned again (Willgerodt et al., 1972). Towards the end of the BWS, the EEC introduced a currency system known as snake, which also did not work as planned. Finally, the EMS was established in 1979. It was a system of fixed but adjustable exchange rates between the member countries. By contrast with the BWS, the EMS

---

[3] There was a short period between October 1990 and September 1992 when the United Kingdom was part of the EMS. It had to leave, and later also opted out of the EMU.

was designed with a symmetrical system of central bank interventions, which required all member countries' central banks to intervene should pressure mount on one of the member currencies. The EMS worked quite successfully and delivered the circumstances for low inflation and stable exchange rates in most of its members. Where the 1980s and 1990s are concerned, it is therefore reasonable to attribute to monetary policy framework associated with the EMS a significant role in the benign macroeconomic outcomes – inflation and output stability – of that period.

The EMS was also the foundation for EMU, which started its existence as the European System of Central Banks in 1999. The ECB became responsible for monetary policy in the EMU on 1 January 1999 and started its work as a visible central bank with bank notes and coins on 1 January 2002. The statute of the ECB was laid down in the Treaty of Maastricht negotiated in December 1991 and signed in February 1992. This grants the ECB a high degree of CBI. Indeed, the independence of the ECB even exceeds the Bundesbank's CBI in some respects, for example in the required expertise of the members of the ECB council. Two features are particularly relevant: the prohibition on lending money to European governments and the no bailout clause, which does not allow intergovernmental transfers within the EMU.

The Maastricht Treaty also defined the five criteria for joining the EMU. The direction (not necessarily the size, which is obviously guided by the status-quo in 1992) of two criteria reflect the literature on time inconsistency. These are that the annual budget deficit of a prospective member government must not exceed 3 per cent of its GDP and that a potential member's stock of public debt must not exceed 60 per cent of its GDP. The other three criteria deal with the interest rate and the inflation rate, which must not be higher than the average of the three lowest rates in the EMS, as well as membership in the renewed EMS, now labelled the European Exchange Rate Mechanism II (ERM II), which started after the introduction of the Euro; to become an EMU member, countries have to be a member of the ERM II for at least two years. Once an EU member country meets the criteria completely, it is obliged to join the EMU.[4]

The foundation of the EMU was highly controversial politically, particularly in Germany. But also elsewhere, some politicians and observers feared that the consensus on low inflation was endangered when the exchange rate as adjustment tool was no longer available. Carefully designed competitive devaluations between member countries would have to be replaced by more mature institutional and governance characteristics, since the instruments of a unified monetary policy, such as the short-term interest rate, could not be applied in a differentiated manner within the EMU.[5] To avoid such a scenario, the Maastricht-criteria have also been used to define the criteria of the Stability and Growth Pact (SGP), which defined sanctions in case countries did not meet these criteria.

As mentioned earlier, inflation under Bundesbank leadership was low in Europe during the 1980s and 1990s. It has been even lower between 2002 and 2021; on that measure, the track record of the ECB until early 2022 is even better than that of the Bundesbank. This changed after the latest turbulence brought about by reactions to the COVID-19 pandemic and Russian aggression in Ukraine. On balance, the Eurosystem (the monetary authority of the EUROZONE) worked smoothly: inflation was low, public budget deficits as well as the stock of public debts in the Eurosystem had been declining.[6] The critics of the Eurosystem were silenced by these developments.

However, as in the Fed's case, the ECB allowed monetary conditions to remain accommodating in the run-up to the GFC, especially

---

[4] A few EU members so far have decided not to become member of the ERM II, such as Sweden and Poland. Denmark and the United Kingdom have negotiated opt-out clauses and will not become EMU members; for the United Kingdom, after Brexit, this is self-evident.

[5] In a textbook world, this would be ideal, as competitive devaluations are welfare distorting. However, it may be politically too dangerous for governments to improve the quality of institutions; we follow that argument in Chapter 7, in particular Section 7.4.

[6] However, in the early 2000s, France and Germany, which insisted on the SGP, ran into high budget deficits for three subsequent years. The European Commission tried

with reference to asset markets and notably the property market. Spain, Ireland and Estonia are examples of countries where the property market boomed.

A second problem emerged over the years, namely the convergence of interest rates on ten-years-government bonds within the Eurosystem, despite underlying differences in creditworthiness. Some governments use this space to take up more debt than is consistent with fiscal sustainability. Market participants placed much emphasis on the currency risk at the level of the Euro, and overlooked the country risks of single members. They also might have believed that the constitutional no bail-out clause (Art. 125, European Treaty), prohibiting the bail-out of broken governments by other member countries, was not credible – this was a correct assumption. This fiscal unsustainability led to the second crisis in the Eurosystem within a few years, the so-called Eurocrisis, which strictly speaking was not a crisis of the ECB. However, it caused the ECB to react in an unprecedented manner, something that is discussed in Chapters 5 and 6.

Finally, there is a third serious difficulty for the EMU, namely the lack of fiscal co-ordination. This problem reflects an old discussion about a common currency: does it precede political union, or does it demand political union? Indeed, the term Economic and Monetary Union instead of the often falsely used term European Monetary Union, already indicates that the envisioned union was much broader than monetary policy and included fiscal policy. One may argue that it is up to the member states to overcome this problem and start fiscal co-ordination, if not unification. However, it turns out that the economic and fiscal policy models of important members, especially of France and Germany, differ significantly. Thus, the attitude of members with respect to austerity (as demanded in the SGP) also differs significantly. This is a dilemma that cannot be solved easily, as the policy models reflect general political perceptions and attitudes

to apply the SGP, but failed owing to log-rolling in the Ecofin Council in November 2003, which led to a reformulation of the SGP. See also Chapter 8.

that differ among the citizens of particular member countries. In addition, there is no right or wrong – both economic policy models, the French idea of planification and the German Ordo-liberalism (see Section 3.2), have proven relatively successful in the past (Freytag and Schnabl, 2017).

To sum up, we can observe the four trends mentioned in Section 4.2. There is an emphasis on the importance of credibility to the success of monetary policy. The ECB – as the Bundesbank – also increasingly uses explicit policy targets. It is also characterised by a high degree of ex-ante CBI. Less clear, however, is the use of feedback rules. As a consequence, the Bundesbank and to a lesser extent later the ECB use their relatively high degree of CBI to build up their reputation. In the case of the ECB, this high degree of CBI was originally safeguarded with a number of other provisions such as the no bail-out clause and the SGP. As long as the economy developed smoothly, the system worked very well – the ECB further contributed to the Great Moderation. But below the surface, the macroeconomic environment and the microeconomic structures became somewhat sclerotic. When first the GFC and afterwards the so-called Eurocrisis hit the EUROZONE, it was not equipped to meet these challenges.

4.4 THE SOUTH AFRICAN RESERVE BANK AND INFLATION TARGETING

Finally, we discuss the role of an emerging economy's central bank during the run-up to the Great Moderation. The beleaguered South African economy of the late-apartheid era suffered many afflictions, including what was called medium but stable inflation, that is, inflation in the order of 15 per cent annually. At the same time, the economy was shrinking on a per capita basis, with severe headwinds from international sanctions and isolation, together with the mounting costs imposed by the inefficiencies of the apartheid system. Nevertheless, the South African Reserve Bank (SARB), one of the oldest central banks in the developing world, implemented a policy evolution very similar to those observed in the developed world, with the same key trends: (i) an emphasis on building credibility as key to the success of monetary policy; (ii) the increasing use of explicit policy targets; (iii) rising CBI; and (iv) the use of feedback rules.

A Commission of Enquiry, later called the De Kock Commission, was constituted in 1978 to consider various aspects of the county monetary system, including the mandate and conduct of monetary policy in the post-BWS era. In the spirit of the time, the final report argued for an explicit target in the form of a goal for broad money supply growth as an anchor for monetary policy.

But the actual implementation by the SARB was more interesting than usually reported. This was not just one more experiment in broad monetary targeting during the 1980s, somewhat later than the better known experiments in the United States and the United Kingdom. Instead, the SARB implemented a nominal income target as anchor for monetary policy from 1986 until 1989. This was a deliberate choice, and as Du Plessis and Kotze (2010) show, more successful than usually reported.

The Reserve Bank Act of 1989 in South Africa also strengthened the independence of the SARB to pursue the objectives of monetary policy. But by the late 1980s, the SARB already exhibited two of the major trends reported on in this chapter – the use of nominal anchor and the role of an independent central bank in its pursuit. But the macroeconomic outcomes were not yet favourable, with inflation remaining high and output fluctuations large and centred around a low growth rate. The SARB's commitment to attaining low and stable inflation was not yet credible in the wake of major internal and external shocks in the last decade of the apartheid era.

It would fall to Dr Chris Stals, Governor of the SARB from 1989 until 1999, to establish the SARB's policy credibility and to drive down inflation expectations. He did this successfully, and finally broke the expectation of medium but stable inflation that had plagued the economy since the 1970s. The SARB under the leadership of Stals pursued credibility with an approach built around monetary growth targets augmented by an eclectic mix of indicators including the exchange rate, assets prices, the output gap, wage settlements, the current account deficit and the fiscal stance (Stals, 1997)

This period of eclectic monetary implementation, focussed on building credibility for the SARB was disrupted by the finance crises of the late 1990s. First the Asian crisis and then more significantly the Russian crisis of 1998 proved a severe test for this eclectic framework. As the Russian rouble collapsed in the third quarter of 1998, the South African rand came under increasing pressure. In the eclectic framework, the SARB's leadership responded with an ill-fated attempt to defend the currency with (much) higher interest rates. The result was both costly to the economy as it plunged into a sharp recession and to the fiscal authorities.

Following this unhappy event, and with a new governor at the SARB in the person of Tito Mboweni, the South African government decided to define the bank's policy objectives more clearly with an explicit inflation targeting framework. This framework has been in place since 2000, and has contributed to a significant stabilisation of the South African economy from a macroeconomic perspective.

This adoption of inflation targeting completed the SARB's evolution towards the system characterised by four trends seen internationally and remarked upon at the start of this chapter. An inflation targeting system is built around an explicit nominal target in the form of a target point or range for inflation, and is implemented with a forward-looking feedback rule. An inflation targeting central bank requires instrument independence to implement the feedback rule, and the successful pursuit of the stated target builds credibility for the monetary authorities, while the success of the policy depends on that same credibility. It is the credibility of the central bank's commitment to the inflation target that allows the target to function as a focal point for the public's inflation expectations. Since these expectations have a considerable influence on the process of inflation, central banks monitor inflation expectations carefully and use that information in their feedback rule.

4.5 SUMMARY

In this chapter, we have seen the connection between the progressive adoption of a modern approach to monetary policy and the benign macroeconomic outcomes called the Great Moderation. The characteristics shared by central banks in the developed and developing world include the adoption of an explicit nominal anchor; the implementation thereof with a feedback rule as well as an instrument independent central bank; and, finally, the importance of credibility for the successful implementation of monetary policy.

When credible, and conducted in this manner, monetary policy provides the background for a stable macro-economy. It does so by providing transparent and credible monetary conditions and by removing monetary policy shocks that in previous generations were highly disruptive. Milton Friedman summarised this modest, but important objective for monetary policy in his famous Presidential Address to the American Economic Association; he concluded with the following words:[7]

> By setting itself a steady course and keeping to it, the monetary authority could make a major contribution to promoting economic stability.... This is the most that we can ask from monetary policy at our present state of knowledge. But that much – and it is a great deal – is clearly within our reach. (Friedman, 1968, p. 17)

---

[7] Of course Milton Friedman had a very different kind of nominal anchor in mind when he delivered this address, and inflation targeting has proved far more practical than his favoured monetary growth targets.

5 Monetary Policy Response to the Financial Crisis

5.1 INTRODUCTION

By 2007, after a long period of monetary stability and rising house prices, risks mounted in the residential property market in the United States and elsewhere. Underlying causes included many years of accommodative monetary policy, easy regulations and even outright subsidies to encourage home ownership for households that might not otherwise be able to afford it. Mortgage-backed securities (MBS) played a critical role to lower the apparent risk in financing these homes. The subsequent GFC in 2008 signalled a call for decisive and innovative policy and regulatory action. While economists had some experience in dealing with sharp downturns in economic activity, the proximate causes of the crisis were not immediately understood. In addition, while the potential depth of the crisis was not known initially, it was clear that it would be very considerable, perhaps the deepest recession since the Great Depression for many wealthy economies. The then recent stagflation in Japan during the 1990s also encouraged strong policy action, and central banks were primed for an aggressive easing (Ahearne et al., 2002).

As the crisis unfolded and liquidity dried up in the wholesale funding market, the Federal Reserve responded to the credit crunch by cutting their policy rate incrementally on several occasions. However, simply lowering rates could not resolve the liquidity concerns raised during the crisis. Credit ratings agencies placed several securities backed by subprime mortgages on credit watch, while various financial institutions (in the United States and abroad) started reducing their exposure to MBS. These actions exacerbated the liquidity crisis as these securities were the collateral that banks had to use to fund their balance sheets in the wholesale market.

Once the Fed realised that dysfunctional financial market conditions were not improving, it further decreased the policy rate in the hope that it could avoid a recession. This was not sufficient to ease pressure in the financial markets, and liquidity shortages on the interbank funding market became commonplace, with large spikes in the primary interbank rate spreads, referred to as illiquidity waves (Sengupta and Tam, 2008). A widening of the bid-ask interest rate spread generally means that collateralised borrowing is constrained (Dicecio and Gascon, 2008).

To address the widening spread between the overnight and interbank rates, the Fed introduced a variety of liquidity facilities. This credit policy was meant to operate primarily through the liquidity channel, providing liquidity to distressed financial institutions (Sack, 2009). The first in the long line of broad-based liquidity facilities created by the Fed was the Term Auction Facility (TAF) for depository institutions, which was established in December 2007. At roughly the same time, similar actions were undertaken by other central banks, such as the Bank of Canada, BoE and ECB. The TAF was the first large-scale balance sheet policy intervention by the Fed in the wake of the crisis. Such balance sheet policies change the size and/or composition of the central bank's balance sheet.

In the following sections, we chronicle some of the proximate causes of the crisis and the resultant monetary policy response of four central banks that engaged in balance sheet measures. The monetary policy response is tracked from the fall of Lehman Brothers in 2008 to the beginning of 2016, when most of the pressure that originated from the financial crisis had subsided. In Chapter 6, we discuss more recent developments concerning balance sheet policy, primarily in response to the recent COVID-19 crisis.

5.2   THE COLLAPSE OF LEHMAN BROTHERS

In 2008, the housing bubble burst, with a decline in housing prices resulting in increased delinquencies and foreclosures (Bernanke, 2008). Mortgage markets experienced a significant downturn, and financial institutions exposed to these markets were heavily affected, suffering losses that threatened their capital adequacy and their access to liquidity (Labonte, 2015). As a result, the affected financial actors became increasingly reluctant to extend loans of any type to consumers and firms, which had a particularly severe impact on, inter alia, residential construction (Bean et al., 2010). The impact was amplified by the fact that the two publicly sponsored enterprises (since the late 1960 publicly traded companies) that facilitated the financing of home ownership in the United States since the Great Depression, Fannie Mae and Freddie Mac, also suffered severe losses and required extensive intervention (Bernanke, 2009).

In order to improve credit conditions, the Federal Reserve continued with deep cuts in the policy rate. In March 2008, with funding markets' liquidity constrained, the Federal Reserve started a securities lending programme, called the Term Securities Lending Facility (TSLF). This entailed the swap of Treasury securities for other eligible securities, a change in the composition of the balance sheet of the central bank. This facility was different from the TAF in that it included a wider range of eligible securities, including several forms of agency debt and MBS (Dicecio and Gascon, 2008).

Finally, in addition to the TAF and TSLF, the Fed introduced the Primary Dealer Credit Facility, an initiative that was initially different from the TSLF in that it accepted an even broader range of investment-grade securities as collateral. At this point in the crisis narrative, the balance sheet measures used were not considered strictly unconventional. These measures entailed an increase in the range of eligible collateral and counter-parties, but purchases were highly collateralised and considered within the normal purview of central bank operations (Bean et al., 2010).

Though the crisis was international, the United States was at the centre of the turmoil, with many crucial financial institutions becoming heavily distressed. Substantial involvement in the securitisation of MBS meant that investment bank Bear Sterns was sold to JP Morgan Chase in March 2008 at a fraction of its pre-crisis market value, a deal brokered by the New York Fed, which also provided the necessary term financing (Bernanke, 2009). In addition, several firms that were linked to mortgage markets, such as the large savings and loan association IndyMac, started to collapse. Even the support provided to Fannie Mae and Freddie Mac was not sufficient, and they had to be taken into conservatorship, with the Treasury providing enormous liquidity injections (Bernanke, 2009).

Fears of a systemic collapse were on the cards, with continued liquidity frictions in the wholesale market and increasing risk premia. Unfortunately, the position of Lehman Brothers (one of the largest players in the US shadow banking system) was unsalvageable; despite efforts on the part of monetary and fiscal authorities, it filed for bankruptcy in September 2008. This bankruptcy raised concerns for the solvency of other financial institutions with similar asset profiles, such as the insurance company AIG (which was eventually bailed out at the cost of $85 billion) and investment bank Merrill Lynch (which was acquired by the Bank of America). In a strategic move to avoid further default, large investment firms Morgan Stanley and Goldman Sachs were approved to become bank holding companies, with direct access to the term lending facilities of the Fed. At this point, market participants had lost faith in highly leveraged financial actors to meet their obligations, and co-ordination failures emerged (Falagiarda and Saia, 2013).

Shock waves from this event were felt across the globe, and policymakers started to comprehend the alarming magnitude of the crisis, perhaps best summarised by O'Rourke and Eichengreen (2010) in early 2010: 'To sum up, globally we are tracking or doing even worse than the Great Depression, whether the metric is industrial production, exports or equity valuations. Focusing on the US causes one to minimise this alarming fact. The "Great Recession" label may turn out to be too optimistic. This is a Depression-sized event.'

Central banks worldwide realised that if key financial institutions were allowed to fail, it would have a catastrophic impact on financial markets. Monetary and fiscal authorities worldwide started implementing expansionary policy measures, specifically with the goal of providing liquidity to financial institutions. As interest rates descended to the zero lower bound (ZLB) in December 2008, monetary authorities realised that they would have to provide stimulus through balance sheet policies (Labonte, 2015).

5.3 FOUR BALANCE SHEET STORIES

As described in Section 5.2, the fall of Lehman Brothers was the catalyst that escalated balance sheet operations by central banks across the globe. This section chronicles different liquidity management strategies implemented by four influential central banks, namely the Fed, the ECB, the BoE and the BoJ. It is important to gain some perspective on the balance sheet policies used by different countries, in order to determine whether there are some common trends. The goal of this section is to highlight the policies that were used most widely and that have enjoyed the greatest longevity and success. It is also meant to prepare an answer to the question of how these policy responses in the wake of the GFC have affected the independence of these central banks from political interference.

5.3.1 United States: Federal Reserve

In most developed countries, banks can deposit or withdraw liquidity in the primary market, with the central bank or in the secondary/interbank market (Catalão-Lopes, 2010). Open market operations conducted with the central bank are secure, while the liquidity traded between banks carries some risk. To alleviate concerns about an impending recession and the possible downfall of secondary markets, several facilities were established. Credit intermediation in the modern era is increasingly performed in financial markets, as only commercial banks have access to the relatively inexpensive funding provided in the wholesale funding market (Bernanke, 2009). The Fed was one of the first central banks to enact liquidity facilities to provide relief to struggling financial institutions and repair dysfunctional markets. A timeline of balance sheet operations for the US is provided in Figure 5.1.

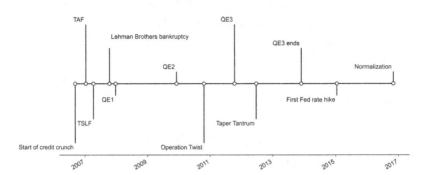

FIGURE 5.1 Timeline of US balance sheet operations

In the immediate aftermath of the Lehman collapse, the Fed created the Asset-Backed Commercial Paper and the Money Market Mutual Fund Liquidity Facility, which were guaranteed by the Treasury (Fawley and Neely, 2013). The amelioration in short-term funding markets, especially that of commercial paper, did not work out. The Reserve Primary Fund, a large money market fund, had heavy investment exposure to Lehman Brothers, with the latter's default causing its net asset value to drop below $1 per unit of invested dollars, which is referred to as 'breaking the buck', that is, investors would lose capital. As a result, there was a flight to quality, from high-yielding prime money market funds toward those that held Treasuries (safe government securities) only (Adrian and Shin, 2010). In an effort to avoid a bank run in money markets, the Fed established the Commercial Paper Funding Facility (CPFF), purchasing high-quality commercial paper (Fawley and Neely, 2013).

The failure of commercial paper funding translated into increased difficulties in meeting the credit needs of businesses and households, for institutions outside the Fed's discount window. These liquidity facilities extended the discount window to all issuers of commercial paper, to provide a backstop funding in dysfunctional markets. Increased liquidity, through the so-called liquidity channel, provides assurance to both the issuer of the commercial paper and the investor that short-term debt obligations will be met, but does not guarantee the solvency of firms (Adrian and Shin, 2010).

The establishment of these facilities entailed an increase in the size as well as a change in composition of the balance sheet of the central bank and could have potential fiscal consequences. This also meant potential concerns for CBI, as will be described.

Creating these types of facilities was the first among many steps by the Fed that moved it out of the territory of conventional monetary policy easing, as it entailed the purchase of assets that could expose the central bank to credit risk. In other words, these actions heralded the start of credit policy in the United States, with the intention of targeting specific market segments in purchasing private sector assets (Bernanke, 2009). In addition, these were also the first unsterilised purchases,[1] indicating an extraordinary expansion of the Fed's balance sheet (Fawley and Neely, 2013).

After the failure of Lehman Brothers, the Fed realised that other large investment banks were credit constrained and afforded them the opportunity to borrow at the discount window, giving them a direct credit line to the central bank (Bernanke, 2009). However, the credit extended through various liquidity facilities, and the extension of lender-of-last-resort services to a wider range of counter-parties was not enough to turn the tide (Fawley and Neely, 2013).

Even after establishing liquidity facilities to combat rapidly deteriorating conditions in short-term funding markets, the Federal Reserve could not independently reverse the fortune of financial markets, and as a recourse it solicited fiscal cooperation. In other words, the Fed was pressed to co-ordinate its efforts with the Treasury. In early October, Congress passed the Emergency Economic Stabilisation Act, which established the Troubled Asset Relief Program to the value of $700 billion, in aid of financial stabilisation (Bernanke, 2009). The objective of this stimulus was to clear toxic assets from the balance sheets of financial institutions, in order to avoid over-leveraging and potential fire sales.

---

[1] A sterilised purchase is one in which the central bank acts to counter the effect on the money supply. This is normally performed with open market operations. An unsterilised purchase is one where the effect has not been counteracted.

Having reduced the federal funds rate close to the zero lower bound (0.25 per cent), the Federal Reserve believed that to further stimulate economic activity it would have to utilise another tool in its policy arsenal, namely unsterilised purchases of government sponsored enterprises (GSE) debt,[2] and MBS to the total of $600 billion (Gagnon et al., 2011). This first round of QE or large-scale asset purchases (LSAPs), referred to as first QE (QE1), was implemented on 25 November 2008. In addition to this initial purchase, in March 2009 the Fed increased QE1 purchases, which consisted mostly of GSE debt ($100 billion), MBS ($750 billion) and long-term Treasury bonds ($300 billion). The total assets purchased in QE1 cumulated to a value of more than $1.75 trillion (Fawley and Neely, 2013).

The housing market and related institutions were the primary target of these policy actions, with more than 80 per cent of total purchases being related to the housing credit market (Fawley and Neely, 2013). In terms of the transmission channel, the Fed was looking towards the portfolio balance channel to reduce term premia on long-term assets, a channel that was explicitly mentioned by Bernanke (2009). It utilised both credit policy (GSE and MBS) and quasi-debt management (long-term securities) to achieve this goal. Importantly, even though the quantity of bank reserves increased in these operations, they did not constitute 'pure' QE, as it wasn't the explicit target of the central bank (Borio and Disyatat, 2010).

At the same time that QE1 was implemented, the central bank created the Term Asset-Backed Securities Loan Facility (TALF), which is a loan programme that entices investors to purchase AAA-rated commercial MBS. This facility was the last in the line of the Fed's special liquidity facilities (Sack, 2010). It differed from most of the other liquidity facilities in that it looked to provide support for market-based credit intermediation, rather than providing liquidity to commercial banks. It was specifically aimed at reviving securitised credit markets, opening up securitisation channels and thereby

---

[2] These were in particular Fannie Mae and Freddie Mac.

improving the 'availability and affordability of credit for households and small businesses' (Bernanke, 2009). Two features that were unique to this facility were that TALF loans were non-recourse and of longer maturities (Sack, 2010). In addition, TALF was available to a wide array of counter-parties, thereby increasing the reach of the programme.

Financial market turmoil subsided toward the end of 2010, with asset prices recovering and private sector balance sheets strengthening (Edmonds et al., 2010). However, despite the magnitude of expansionary fiscal and monetary policy, unemployment remained persistently high and disinflation continued unabated (Yellen, 2014). As emphasised by policymakers, the stagnating economic situation warranted a second round of easing in November 2010, to improve economic performance and quell some deflationary concerns (Fawley and Neely, 2013).

The second round of QE was different from the first in that the Fed decided only to purchase $600 billion in long-term Treasury debt, with purchases occurring in monthly instalments of $75 billion. In other words, the central bank was following a quasi-debt management strategy, with the goal of working through the scarcity channel to influence long-term security yields (Borio and Disyatat, 2010). In particular, the Fed wanted to push up prices and thereby drive down yields on long-term Treasury bonds, which in theory would work to increase inflation expectations (Yellen, 2014). In addition, policymakers committed to keeping the federal funds rate close to the ZLB, enacting a forward guidance strategy. It bears noting that the objective of this second round of QE was not to stabilise financial markets, but exclusively to boost economic recovery.

In September 2011, there were concerns that a double-dip recession was looming, with growth still slow and signs of distress in global financial markets. Amelioration called for another round of easing but, instead of further outright purchases of securities, the central bank experimented with maturity transformations similar to those of Operation Twist in 1961.[3] On 21 September, in what was officially called the Maturity Extension Program (MEP) and Reinvestment Policy, the Fed sold $400 billion in short-term securities with a matching purchase of long-term securities (Fawley and Neely, 2013). With this policy the central bank attempted to 'twist' the yield curve, by reducing long-term rates relative to short-term ones.

The implementation of this quasi-debt management strategy was different from before in that it took place without expansion of the monetary base, entailing only a change in composition of the assets on the balance sheet. In other words, the revived Operation Twist differed from QE2 in that liabilities (reserves) increased with the purchase of long-term assets during QE2, while there was no increase in liabilities in the MEP, but rather a change in the type of assets held by the central bank (Fawley and Neely, 2013). Operation Twist was extended in June 2012 with another $267 billion-worth of long-term government securities purchased to make broader financial conditions more accommodative.

Policy efforts to reduce persistently high unemployment rates were considered partially successful. However, the labour market remained sluggish, featuring a significant unemployment gap relative to estimates of full employment. The third round of QE was aimed directly at improving economic conditions, with a specific focus on reinvigorating the labour market (Fawley and Neely, 2013). Purchases of MBS were made on a monthly basis, to the tune of $40 billion. In addition, the central bank reinvested principal payments of MBS, which accounted for another $45 billion monthly injection into long-term treasury securities. This translated into an increase in holdings amounting to $85 billion per month (Yellen, 2013). This initiative is similar to QE1 in the variety of assets purchased, but distinctly different with regard to the communication of assets purchased (Fischer, 2015).

---

[3] Operation Twist is a monetary policy strategy used by central banks to influence the shape of the yield curve by simultaneously buying long-term government bonds and selling short-term bonds. This 'twist' in the yield curve aims to lower long-term interest rates, making borrowing more affordable and stimulating economic growth.

QE3 entailed a more open-ended structure, citing no total amount of assets that would be purchased, but rather a commitment to continue purchasing assets at regular intervals until labour market conditions improved. At first, the condition for exiting this commitment was vague, with the Federal Reserve Open Market Committee (FOMC) relaying a scenario in which there was 'significant improvement' in labour market conditions (Yellen, 2015). In early 2013, it was announced that the pace at which purchases were to be conducted would be data dependent; in particular, they were looking toward conducting purchases until the unemployment rate went below a certain threshold (in this case it was 6.5 per cent).

On 22 May 2013, Ben Bernanke revealed that the pace of asset purchases might start slowing before the end of the year if labour market conditions continued to improve. It was projected that a reduction in the unemployment rate below the suggested threshold would possibly be achieved in 2014. Shortly after Bernanke's statement, financial markets reeled at the thought of a potential taper. Further distortions in economic conditions were felt outside the borders of the United States, specifically in developing countries, with large capital outflows emanating from these countries.

Taking note of the strong adverse reaction to the announcement of potential tapering, an event called 'taper tantrum' at the time, the Fed made it clear on 18 September 2013 that it did not have any immediate plans to reduce the asset purchase programmes. This alleviated some of the pressure following the initial suggestion of winding down QE3, with emerging markets enjoying the greatest relief (Kumar and Barua, 2013). The eventual start of the taper took place on 18 December 2013, with purchases down from $85 to $75 billion a month. At this time, the FOMC also announced that QE3 would be tapered at a suggested rate of $10 billion at each successive meeting, outlining a complete winding down of the purchasing programme by October 2014.

Since the start of the financial crisis, the central bank accumulated a large portfolio of long-term securities, with the federal funds

rate being close to the ZLB for more than six years (Yellen, 2015). At
the start of 2015, with the US economy showing signs of recovery,
questions as to the normalisation of monetary policy and a potential
increase of the short-term policy rate came to the fore. As discussed
in the literature on the proximate causes of the crisis, if policy is
too accommodative for too long, it can create an environment where
excessive risk-taking takes hold again. Popular interest rate rules,
such as Taylor's rule, that take both unemployment and output gaps
into account had already necessitated increases in the policy rate.
However, the reading of these rules depends on the definitions of historical inflation and natural rates of employment (Yellen, 2015). The
experience of Japan has taught policymakers not to be too hasty in
coming out from under the ZLB.

The 'conditions for liftoff', as Stanley Fischer (2015) puts it,
are sufficient improvements in the labour market and confidence
in the fact that inflation will move to the 2 per cent objective in
the medium term. In December 2015, the Fed increased the federal
funds rate by 25 basis points, which marked the first increase in the
policy rate in a seven-year period where it was kept near the ZLB
(Yellen, 2016). One of the new-found challenges faced by the central bank is conducting monetary policy with an expanded balance
sheet. Owing to the size of the balance sheet, traditional repurchase
agreements fell by the wayside and normalised monetary policy will
entail setting of the interest on excess reserves. In addition to the
interest on excess reserves, the Fed will also be conducting overnight reverse repurchase agreements, with a wide range of eligible
counter-parties. This overnight facility will create a soft floor on
money market rates.

Our discussion of the response to the financial crisis does not
extend beyond 2016, since this is when the economy started to show
signs of recovery. We deal with the most recent developments regarding monetary policy in the United States briefly in Chapter 6, when
we focus on the further expanded size of the central bank balance
sheet in response to the 2020 pandemic.

5.3.2 European Union: European Central Bank

EMU experienced two crises within a few years. These were connected in that the GFC of 2008 triggered the sovereign debt crisis that started after Greece admitted in the autumn of 2009 that their debt statistics understated the true level of public debt – a fact that did not seem to surprise European policymakers much. It is, however, evident that even without the GFC the level of public debt in some of EMU's members was unsustainable and led to financial stress. In other countries, such as Spain and Ireland, public debt was low, and the GFC triggered a debt crisis because of the real estate bubble in these countries. Together, both crises affected other EMU members negatively.

In order to appreciate fully the policy response of the ECB, it is necessary to set the stage as to the position of EURO area banks before the crisis, as their structure differs in significant ways from the US economy. Several systemic balance sheet vulnerabilities were present in the EU before the crisis. European banks had increasingly relied on wholesale funding, but not to the extent of the United States (Pill and Reichlin, 2014). In the years leading up to the crisis, approximately 30 per cent of external funding for financial firms originated from financial markets in the EU, while in the US this figure was closer to 70 per cent (Trichet, 2009; Cour-Thimann and Winkler, 2012). Naturally, the development of other sources of external credit meant that the ratio of loans to traditional deposits started to decline (Giannone et al., 2012).

In addition to an increased dependence on external market-based funding, banks started to use newly developed financial instruments and processes. In particular, European banks started to use off-balance-sheet vehicles, securitisation and several structured financial products (Pill and Reichlin, 2014). Several European bank balance sheets were also contaminated with asset-backed securities that originated in the United States, but fortunately exposure was limited. Despite all these concerns, the structure of the European economy was still largely bank-based (Cour-Thimann and Winkler, 2012).

In fact, it was postulated by Padoa-Schioppa (2004), before the crisis, that the Eurosystem would be able to survive a run on secondary markets, as its funding originated mostly from primary markets.

Beyond the exposure to flighty assets, the EU had its own unique problems to deal with. Importantly, the cross-border exposure of banks to wholesale funding had increased significantly since the inception of the EMU. Supervision at the national level meant that retail markets remained segmented, but cross-border funding markets became more active, with increased financial integration (Pill and Reichlin, 2014). Larger economies with slow and steady growth found opportunities to finance the demand for credit in smaller developing nations (González-Páramo, 2011). Unfortunately, this meant that imbalances on the current and financial accounts of many EURO area countries were exacerbated; this was a large contributor to the sovereign debt crisis after 2009.

Successful financial integration resulted in a narrowing of spreads in the sovereign bond market, which would usually be indicative of a decrease in the market's pricing of sovereign risk (Ehrmann et al., 2010). However, it is thought that the compression of the spread could have been due to the involvement of the ECB, with their mandate providing an inherent guarantee against the failure of a sovereign entity (which further promoted risk-taking and moral hazard) (Pill and Reichlin, 2014). Taking this structure into consideration, we provide an overview of the traditional format of European monetary policy implementation and the manner in which the central bank amended its approach to address mounting concerns.

In contrast to the fixed-rate open market operations of the Fed, monetary policy at the ECB is usually conducted through refinancing operations in an auctioning process. In this set-up the ECB sets a liquidity cap, and the lowest bids are accepted, which is referred to as the variable-rate tender procedure (Cour-Thimann and Winkler, 2012). In June 2000, the ECB switched from fixed- to variable-rate tenders, in response to overbidding in the fixed-rate system (Catalão-Lopes, 2010).

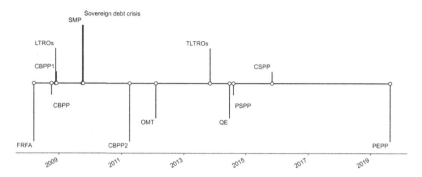

FIGURE 5.2 Timeline of ECB balance sheet operations

In general, the ECB offers two types of collateralised lending options, differentiated by maturity. Main refinancing operations (MROs) are the primary mode of policy conduct; they have a maturity of one week and are auctioned weekly. More recently, the bank introduced the longer-term refinancing operations (LTROs), which at first were presented with a maturity of three months; these are auctioned once a month (Vogel, 2016). In the months before the collapse of Lehman Brothers, the ECB tried to address building pressure by introducing reductions in the MRO interest rate. It became evident that policy rate cuts were not going to provide the necessary stimulus in constrained credit markets, which prompted the ECB to implement several liquidity management measures. These formed part of the first phase of the policy response of the ECB, namely the Enhanced Credit Support (ECS) programme.

In terms of the ECB policy response to the crisis and the surrounding fallout, four phases are identified. A timeline of these operations is provided in Figure 5.2. First, liquidity management operations started as early as 13 months before Lehman Brothers collapsed in September 2008. The demise of this institution heralded the start of the GFC and heightened the intensity of management required, which involved several alterations and additions. Second, an equally important event for the EURO area was the sovereign debt crisis that started in May 2010, specifically as a result of developments in the Greek economy, and notably Greek sovereign debt. This phase also included the resurgence of the debt crisis, with several other member states experiencing similar difficulties to that of Greece, in June 2011. This crisis reflected the asymmetric design of the EMU; it allowed for domestic fiscal policy, which needed to be very disciplined in a monetary union. The SGP enforcement mechanism turned out to be too weak. Third, the then ECB president, Mario Draghi, famously stated in 2012 that the ECB was committed to do 'whatever it takes' to salvage the EURO. Finally, the last phase is considered the one in which QE measures were adopted, in January 2015.

Financial distress in the EUROZONE following the Lehman Brothers episode was exhibited in the widening of several interest rate spreads, such as the Euribor-OIS spread (Fawley and Neely, 2013). The widening of spreads was indicative of the increased counter-party risk, emanating from the uncertainty with respect to the health of the balance sheets of financial institutions. The interbank market in the case of the ECB extends beyond several borders, and therefore segmentation becomes an important issue. Counterparties in this setting may find it difficult to participate in the interbank market, based on the 'perceived riskiness of their sovereign' (González-Páramo, 2011). Despite initial liquidity provisions, the volume of interbank lending remained lacklustre 'because of mounting insolvency and liquidity risks exacerbated by asymmetric information' (Rodríguez and Carrasco, 2014, p. 9).

In May 2009, the ECB formulated their actions with regard to liquidity management, in the form of the ECS programme. The goal was to provide liquidity to the banking sector and remedy the lack of counter-party confidence. As mentioned before, the banking sector was becoming more reliant on wholesale funding. However, the ratio of loans to traditional deposits (leveraging) had not reached the level of the United States, with the traditional banking sector still playing an important role in the extension of credit. Therefore, to address dysfunctional markets, the ECB opted to target the banking sector aggressively with the ECS programme. According to Jean-Claude Trichet (2009, p. 12), 'enhanced credit support constitutes the special and primarily bank-based measures that are being taken to enhance the flow of credit above and beyond what could be achieved through policy interest rate reductions alone'. Trichet, who was president of the ECB at the time, identified five policy cornerstones of the ECS programme (Trichet, 2009).

First, in early 2008, the ECB introduced the Fixed Rate Procedure with Full Allotment (FRFA) programme. The FRFA gave commercial banks access to unlimited amounts of liquidity against eligible collateral at the main refinancing rate, provided they were financially sound (González-Páramo, 2011). This often-overlooked policy shift is considered by several ECB central bankers to be the most significant liquidity management operation conducted to retain the health of the financial sector. Liquidity risk generated by elevated lending rates in interbank markets posed a threat to many financial institutions. Liquidity provision under this strategy aimed to facilitate interbank lending and, by extension, increase the availability of credit to households and firms (Falagiarda et al., 2015).

Lorenzo Bini Smaghi refers to the FRFA as 'endogenous credit easing', in that banks can meet all their liquidity needs. This means that they don't have to rely on external sources of funding to meet their obligations. The peak demand for liquidity before the crisis reached €95 billion (Rodríguez and Carrasco, 2014). However, during the crisis, demand for liquidity increased significantly, prompting the ECB to introduce additional measures to support the banking system and stabilise the financial markets.

In this set-up, the ECB sets the MRO refinancing rate, and interbank market rates are variable (determined by supply and demand) (Catalão-Lopes, 2010). Fluctuations in the quantity demanded reflects market sentiment, with high liquidity demand indicative of the strain in interbank lending. In addition to the mere provision of liquidity, this mechanism works by providing liquidity more cheaply than the market price; which in turn drives down money market rates (González-Páramo, 2011). Immediately following the collapse of Lehman Brothers, banks began to overbid in terms of price of the MROs, in an attempt to secure liquidity. Overbidding pressure prompted the ECB to discontinue traditional refinancing operations of all maturities (MROs and LTROs) and replace them with fixed-rate tenders (Szczerbowicz, 2015). However, this resulted in severe overbidding on the amount of liquidity, as there was no associated penalty.

Second, in addition to the FRFA, supplementary LTROs with a six-month maturity were instituted before the crisis, with the first round met with a fourfold oversubscription of bids, and €442 billion was eventually supplied (Trichet, 2009; Darracq-Paries and De Santis, 2015). In June 2009, twelve-month LTROs were created to cater for commercial bank preferences for assets of longer maturities (Fawley and Neely, 2013). This helped to address maturity mismatches where banks were looking for investments in longer-term bonds, but only finding funding in the shortest end of the market. It reduced the uncertainty involved in laying out investment strategies. Policy was designed with the expectation that banks would use long-term credit to fund long-term asset investment, rather than supply short-term liquidity.

Third, the list of assets eligible for collateral was extended by lowering the ratings threshold. Allowing a wider range of collateral affords banks the opportunity to refinance a larger portion of their balance sheet (Cour-Thimann and Winkler, 2012). Previously illiquid assets can now be transformed, potentially preventing liquidity shortages in secondary markets. In addition to the type of collateral, there is an increase in the number of counter-parties that can take part in the refinancing operations (Trichet, 2009). Fourth, international swap lines allow financial institutions to address foreign currency funding (Falagiarda et al., 2015). Cooperation among central banks is key in this respect.

Finally, the Covered Bond Purchase Program (CBPP) was created, with these purchases being the ECB's first foray into asset purchases

(Falagiarda et al., 2015). The first round of covered bond purchases, called CBPP1, amounted to €60 billion and took place between July 2009 and July 2010. A supplementary round of purchases, CBPP2, took place between November 2011 and October 2012. However, the number purchased was almost negligible during this round, amounting to less than €17 billion in total (González-Páramo, 2011). Trichet (2009) states clearly that covered bond purchases were not considered QE, as they would not result in an expansion of the ECB's balance sheet. He believed that there would be an 'automatic sterilisation', with a simultaneous reduction in purchases of LTROs. However, according to the data, the balance sheet of the bank did not remain unaltered, and expanded by 30 per cent in the most acute phase of the crisis, which indicates that sterilisation was not complete (Rodríguez and Carrasco, 2014).

In comparison with the Fed, the ECB was a latecomer to the asset purchase party, as QE1 was already well under way during this time. This was because the United States had to respond more swiftly, as financial institutions were exposed directly to mortgage markets: they had greater flexibility in the economy, and the funding structure revolved around money markets for funding, as opposed to the more traditional banking sector (Trichet, 2009). The reason for implementing CBPP hinged on two factors. First, it allowed the opportunity to address maturity mismatches between assets and liabilities (Trichet, 2009). Second, covered bonds markets are important, and these securities are different from most asset-backed securities in several ways. They are a form of recourse debt, whereby the bond holders can collect from the issuer of the bond and are entitled to the underlying collateral pool. In addition, underlying collateral is held on the consolidated balance sheet of the bond issuer, similar in spirit to originate-and-hold mortgages in the United States (Fawley and Neely, 2013).[4]

---

[4] Originate-and-hold mortgages are assets that are meant to stay on the books of the bank.

In October 2009, it was revealed that Greece had been misreporting statistics with respect to their debt. This deception meant that interbank lending to Greek banks dried up – since the quality of the collateral was suspect – and their government's fiscal sustainability became suspect (Pill and Reichlin, 2014). Uncertainty surrounding the fiscal position of the country translated into a sharp decline in the demand for Greek government bonds and, as a result, sovereign spreads widened against several countries in the Eurosystem. The possibility of sovereign debt default was on the cards as the economy struggled to find funding to meet debt payments. This was problematic for the ECB, as default would have meant an exit from the EURO area for Greece, which in turn could have spread to other countries in similar fiscal trouble, such as Ireland, Portugal, Spain and Italy (Cour-Thimann and Winkler, 2012). In addition, the portfolios of investors and financial institutions in several countries, such as Germany and France, were heavily exposed to Greek debt.

This sovereign debt crisis spurred a fire-sale on several EURO area government bonds. In order to contain the crisis and avoid financial contagion, several emergency facilities were created. The adjustment programme consisted of bilateral loans from Eurosystem countries (European Commission) and support from the IMF (Pill and Reichlin, 2014). Despite these attempts to boost sovereign solvency, confidence in Greek debt remained low. In the face of mounting pressure, the ECB was forced to act and provided ancillary support through the creation of the Securities Markets Programme (SMP), injecting liquidity into dysfunctional markets through the purchase of sovereign bonds in secondary markets (Szczerbowicz, 2015). SMP is considered a sterilised purchase programme and did not expand the balance sheet of the bank, which classifies it as credit policy (Fawley and Neely, 2013). Communication under this purchase programme was limited, with no details on the bonds purchased, counter-parties or length of the scheme made available to the public (Szczerbowicz, 2015).

The ECB justified the SMP on the grounds that it would restore the functioning of the monetary policy transmission mechanism and relieve tension in sovereign debt markets (Falagiarda et al., 2015). In practice, they were preventing a Greek default by aggressively removing debt from the market. More importantly, the ECB brokered debt restructuring for private debt holders (Pill and Reichlin, 2014). However, this was a symptomatic treatment, and public finance remained a topic for concern throughout the Eurosystem.

Contagion had spread to Ireland in 2010 and Portugal in 2011, which meant that the ECB had to step in as a lender of last resort for these sovereigns. Within the SMP, the ECB spent a total of €219.5 billion on EUROZONE government bonds, but this was not spent according to paid-in capital; rather, it focussed only on vulnerable countries, and thereby, spread the risk (Szczerbowicz, 2015). Shortly after the effective bailout of Greece, Ireland and Portugal, there was a discussion as to the fiscal health of the Italian and Spanish economies. The ECB had enough funds at its disposal to assist some of the smaller member states, but the default of large countries such as Italy and Spain would have been far beyond the reach of the monetary authority.

At the start of the financial crisis, the ECB highlighted the fact that non-standard policies were temporary, only to be used as long as they were considered necessary. However, by late 2011, fears of a sovereign debt crisis were reignited, as the solvency of Italy and Spain was considered. Sovereign bond prices plummeted and significantly altered the balance sheet positions of several banks in the EURO area (Cour-Thimann and Winkler, 2012). The widening of sovereign bond spreadss reflected the fact that market participants believed economies could potentially be leaving the monetary union. In order to preserve the union, unconventional policies became a more permanent fixture in the ECB's policy toolkit (Falagiarda et al., 2015). Mario Draghi's first response was to reinstate the SMP, which had been dormant since the bail-out of Portugal in early 2011 (Pill and Reichlin, 2014). In addition, he announced the creation of thirty-six-month LTROs, as well as the second round of covered bond purchases (Cour-Thimann and Winkler, 2012). The LTROs were specifically aimed at sovereign debt, providing liquidity over the medium term.

Talks arose about the possible exit of distressed countries from the monetary union and the ensuing reversibility of the EURO. In response, in July 2012, Mario Draghi famously stated that the central bank would do 'whatever it takes to save the EURO', as previously mentioned. The ECB followed through on the commitment with the announcement of the Outright Monetary Transactions (OMT) programme in September 2012 (Pill and Reichlin, 2014). Under this scheme, which officially replaced the SMP, the ECB agreed to intervene in secondary sovereign bond markets if this became necessary.

The OMT differed from the SMP in several ways. First, an important improvement on the SMP was that purchases of sovereign debt in the secondary market would be conditional, with the ECB buying debt only once countries had accepted and met the conditions for structural and fiscal reform set by the European Commission, ECB and IMF (often referred to as the 'Troika') (Fawley and Neely, 2013). Second, the ECB was more transparent about communicating its purchase strategies, and there would be no 'ex ante quantitative limits' on the purchases once conditions had been met (Cour-Thimann and Winkler, 2012). Third, the focus of the OMT was on shorter-term bonds, whereas the SMP focussed on longer-term securities (Szczerbowicz, 2015).

Similar to the function of the SMP, the OMT was established to improve the functioning of the monetary policy transmission mechanism. The OMT is considered to be credit policy, with purchases sterilised similarly to those of the SMP. Interestingly, the OMT was not used directly. However, it was considered successful in that it acted as an insurance mechanism against redenomination risk, signalling the commitment of the bank to prevent the exit of struggling member states (Pill and Reichlin, 2014). In fact, the mere announcement of the OMT reduced risk premia and brought sovereign interest rate spreads closer to one another (Szczerbowicz, 2015). Focussing more on communication with the general public seems to have been part of a new strategy employed by the ECB.

Deflationary pressure became of particular concern with the steady decline of inflation since the start of 2012. The ECB, under the guidance of Mario Draghi, developed a multifaceted strategy to boost economic growth in what can be considered a new framework. This framework is similar to that implemented in other central banks and combines forward guidance with credit and QE. Forward guidance, which forms an important part of this new framework, made its first appearance in July 2013, when the ECB made it clear that rates were going to remain low for an extended period of time (Falagiarda et al., 2015). Already, many observers argued that the ECB was acting beyond its mandate, and asked whether the de facto political independence of the ECB was still kept.[5]

By May 2014, the deposit rate, the lower bound on the policy rate, had dipped below the ZLB, and interbank rates followed suit. However, even negative rates failed to reignite interbank activity and spur economic growth (Valiante, 2015). In response, the ECB unveiled its credit easing package in June 2014, which was mostly an extension of measures implemented in the ECS programme. The package consisted of targeted LTROs, an Asset-Backed Security Purchase Programme and another round of covered bond purchases, CBPP3 (Falagiarda et al., 2015).

Targeted LTROs (TLTROs) are a new loan facility that is intended to encourage banks to extend credit to the private sector by reducing financing costs (Blot et al., 2015). These forty-eight-month TLTROs are supposed to provide banks access to a source of low-interest-rate funding for the following four years. The ECB hoped that these would entice banks to lend to the real economy. They are specifically aimed at small to medium-sized non-financial firms (Szczerbowicz, 2015). They differ from previous LTROs in that the amount a bank can acquire is provisioned on the amount of loans

---

[5] In addition, the sovereign debt crisis in the EUROZONE led to the breach of the so-called no bail-out-clause, which prohibits a government to bail out other members' public debt. With the introduction of the European Stability Mechanism (ESM), this rule was no longer adhered to.

extended to the non-financial private sector in the EURO area (Blot et al., 2015). However, these TLTROs did not have an immediate impact on the economy, which provided an incentive for the ECB to enact a more rapid-acting mechanism, namely a private asset purchase programme.

Asset-backed securities purchases and the third covered bond purchase programme (CBPP3) were designed to complement the targeted longer-term refinancing operations (TLTROs). They were meant as a direct intervention in secondary bond markets, purchasing the securities of European firms and residential real estate loans to affect long-term bond yields. At this point the asset purchases were still sterilised and limited to private sector debt. However, in 2015 the central bank announced an extension of the programme, called the Extended Asset Purchase Programme (EAPP) that would signal the movement to QE. The ECB claimed that it was merely expanding an existing programme of asset purchases, but under the EAPP, unsterilised purchases were added, moving from the passive management of liquidity demand to a more active intervention (Breuss, 2016). This introduced a new risk with respect to CBI.

In March 2015, the ECB announced, as part of the EAPP, the Public Sector Purchase Programme (PSPP), the first instance of QE in the EURO area. This programme diverged from previous attempts in two distinct ways. First, it would start purchasing bonds issued by 'EURO area central governments, agencies and the European institutions', which meant intervention in primary markets for sovereign debt (Falagiarda et al., 2015). Second, the scale of the programme was unprecedented, with liquidity provided by the ECB under the EAPP amounting to €50 billion a month, with a conditional commitment to keep it in place until inflation met the mandated medium-term objective (around 2 per cent) (Breuss, 2016). At the end of March 2017, the total purchased stood at €1,500 billion.

This programme was met with significant resistance, as it was felt that it contradicted the conventions of the EU Treaty, blurring the line between fiscal and monetary policy. This concern is a central theme of the book and is explored in future chapters. The next section looks at how balance sheet policies were implemented in the United Kingdom.

5.3.3 UK: Bank of England

Balance sheet policy implemented in the United Kingdom was not significantly different from that of the United States. Policy comprised the creation of several liquidity insurance facilities and successive rounds of QE. The timeline of implementation of rescue efforts by the BoE was also closer to that of the Fed's actions. Before introducing the measures used during the financial crisis, it is worth looking at how the BoE conducts monetary policy under normal circumstances, as it settled on a new monetary framework in the build-up to the crisis.

The BoE revised its operational framework for monetary policy in 2006. Management of the balance sheet was now co-ordinated under the Sterling Monetary Framework (SMF). This new system revolves around the use of reserves, standing facilities and open market operations. It has all the qualities of a reserve regime whereby banks decide on how many reserves to hold, which means liquidity issue is demand determined (Cross et al., 2010).

In contrast with the single mandate of several other central banks in developed economies, the BoE has an explicit dual mandate, with two objectives specified under its new operating framework (Joyce et al., 2012). The first of these is the pursuit and maintenance of the CPI inflation target in the medium run, which is set at 2 per cent. In normal times this is achieved through setting the policy rate. Second, the BoE is tasked with reducing the cost of disruptions to the functioning of commercial banks, which is done through the provision of liquidity insurance (Cross et al., 2010). Taking into consideration the objectives of this framework, we consider the actions taken by the BoE to abide by its mandate.

The spillover from the financial crisis significantly affected the UK economy, with real activity slowing and financial distress

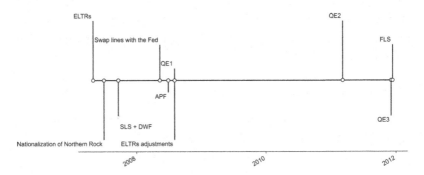

FIGURE 5.3   Timeline of BoE balance sheet operations

emerging. Prior to the collapse of Lehman Brothers, the UK financial sector was already under pressure. Northern Rock, a British bank, asked the BoE for liquidity support in September 2007. However, in February 2008, Northern Rock was nationalised in order to save it from a run on the bank. At the height of the crisis, several large UK banks, such as Halifax Bank of Scotland (HBOS) and Royal Bank of Scotland, were found to be highly leveraged in the face of mounting losses and dependent on wholesale funding. Large-scale intervention was required to save these at-risk institutions, with HBOS being acquired by Lloyds TSB with the aid of public capital. Lending conditions deteriorated, with solvency concerns about these large financial firms.

As a result of the evidence on policy implementation from the Japanese experience, the BoE reacted quickly to provide monetary policy support (Joyce and Woods, 2011). A timeline of the balance sheet operations enacted is provided in Figure 5.3. As a first line of defence, the policy interest rate was radically reduced from 5.75 per cent in July 2007 to 0.5 per cent in March 2009. In addition to interest rates cuts, several liquidity facilities were created and amended during this time. Similar to the liquidity facilities in other countries, those of the BoE were targeted at specific markets. In December 2007, the BoE announced a change to its existing three-month repo open market operations, with an extension on the range of assets viable as collateral to include AAA-rated MBS and covered bonds (Cross et al., 2010).

These newly formed longer-term open market operations were referred to as extended collateral long-term repos (ELTRs) and were initially offered at monthly auctions of £10 billion.

The BoE also formed two liquidity insurance schemes to provide liquidity to the banking sector, namely the Special Liquidity Scheme (SLS) and the Discount Window Facility (DWF). The SLS and DWF are off-balance-sheet collateral-swap initiatives that allow banks to swap high-quality illiquid securities (such as MBS) for UK treasury bills (Cross et al., 2010). Under these programmes, the banks pay a fee according to the quality of the asset offered for the swap arrangement, in order to prevent opportunistic behaviour. Finally, as a result of tension arising in US markets, the BoE engaged in temporary foreign currency swap lines with the Fed, to meet dollar-denominated obligations.

In January 2009, Her Majesty's (HM) Treasury announced the creation of the Asset Purchase Facility (APF). Operations were conducted through a limited company called the Asset Purchase Facility Fund, a legal entity that is fully under the control of the BoE (Joyce et al., 2012). HM Treasury conducted both credit and QE through this fund. Initially, the BoE was granted permission to carry out acquisitions of high-quality private sector assets amounting to £50 billion. However, the demand for private asset holdings peaked at £3 billion, suggesting that the facility was not utilised effectively. This credit easing was meant to increase the availability of corporate credit. Easing was justified on the grounds of the lender-of-last-resort function of the bank, as espoused by Bagehot. Purchases were sterilised through sales of short-term gilts, which means this was a pure credit policy (Fawley and Neely, 2013). These liquidity provisions were considered similar to those conducted by the Fed under their CPFF programme.

Despite aggressive easing, the BoE felt that it would not be able to meet its mandated medium-term goal of 2 per cent CPI inflation. The second operation under the APF was performed in March 2009 with the bank's explicit QE programme to help achieve their policy objective. More specifically, the bank adopted a combination of bank reserves policy and quasi-debt management policy, increasing the size of the balance sheet through the purchase of £200 billion of assets in the first round of easing. UK government bonds (gilts) of varying maturity (mostly from five to twenty-five years) formed the majority of the purchases (Steeley, 2015).

QE as implemented by the BoE was intended as a liquidity injection to induce spending in the economy, in order to generate an inflationary effect (Joyce and Woods, 2011). Purchases were financed by reserves, which translated into a fourfold increase in the monetary base from March to November 2009 (Cross et al., 2010). The backing by central bank money meant that this was now considered part of monetary policy. Since reserves in excess of voluntary targets were being issued, and the policy rate was near the ZLB, the SMF ceased its normal functioning. Policy was being conducted based on the size of the programme, similar to that of Japan under QE. Purchases continued until February 2010, when the Monetary Policy Committee decided not to further increase the size of the balance sheet (Steeley, 2015).

At the same time as the first round of QE, the BoE implemented several changes to their ELTRs, with an increase in the amount available for auction, as well as inclusion of securities backed by mortgage assets and corporate bonds. These credit easing operations reached a peak of £180 billion in January 2009 (Cross et al., 2010).

Two years after the first round of QE, the second round was started. In October 2011, the BoE conducted a further £75 billion worth of purchases. It was considered a necessary measure to keep inflation in line with its mandate. This increase occurred in parallel to fears of a sovereign debt crisis in the EURO area. By May 2012, the second round had come to an end, with a total of £125 billion purchased; bringing the total of QE to £325 billion (Steeley, 2015). The third round of QE quickly followed the second, owing to a contraction in GDP between the last quarter of 2011 and the first quarter of 2012. Purchases under QE totalled £375 billion by July 2012 (Fawley and Neely, 2013).

In order to improve lending conditions, the BoE and HM Treasury constructed the Funds for Lending Scheme (FLS). This scheme shares many similarities with the TLTRO programme imple-mented by the ECB, and is thought to be the inspiration for that pol-icy initiative. One of the differences between the FLS and TLTROs is that the BoE is able to co-ordinate its efforts with the Treasury in order to avoid significant losses, whereas the ECB has no single cen-tralised Treasury (Steeley, 2015).

British monetary authorities have not had reason to imple-ment large-scale changes to their balance sheet since QE3. Data from the first quarter of 2016 put inflation at 0.5 per cent, which was not close enough to the 2 per cent target. However, the price level was expected to increase over the year, as uncharacteristically low food and energy prices start to unwind. Economic growth was positive during this period and further intervention was not warranted.

5.3.4 Japan: Bank of Japan

The Japanese economy showed signs of recovery following its slump in the early part of the new millennium. In response, the BoJ started to unwind some of its unconventional measures, with QE coming to an end in 2006 (Kuttner, 2014). However, the financial crisis of 2008 resulted in a large negative shock, slowing economic growth significantly (Takahashi, 2013). Interestingly, the response of the BoJ in terms of financial markets was modest compared with other central banks, with unconventional policy not being adopted at first.

The primary reason is that Japanese banks and financial firms were not heavily invested in US mortgages or structured financial products, such as credit default swaps. In other words, they did not have toxic assets on their balance sheets. This was thanks, in part, to reform in the banking sector following the banking crisis of the 1990s (Vollmer and Bebenroth, 2012). Japanese banks were focussed on tra-ditional banking activities, instead of the dissemination of securi-tised financial products. In addition, liabilities were mostly financed though the deposit base, with only 10 per cent of financing derived from wholesale markets (Vollmer and Bebenroth, 2012).

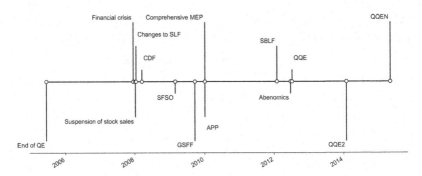

FIGURE 5.4 Timeline of BoJ balance sheet operations

Spreads on unsecured interbank markets remained relatively stable in the wake of the fall of Lehman Brothers, especially in comparison with other countries. The Tokyo interbank market rate, for example, showed little volatility. Transmission of the crisis was primarily through international capital movements, with the position on the capital, current and financial accounts deteriorating during this period (Vollmer and Bebenroth, 2012). This indicates that the crisis affected the economy through decreased exports, showing the reduced global demand and appreciation of the yen, rather than contagion in the financial markets (Takahashi, 2013).

Capital outflows translated into a sharp decrease in the Nikkei stock index, translating into a decrease in the asset values of Japanese banks, which hold a substantial portion of their high-quality capital in stocks (Vollmer and Bebenroth, 2012). Despite the limited impact on the Japanese banking system, the economy experienced a sharp decline in growth, registering one of the greatest falls in GDP among OECD countries.

The BoJ and the Financial Services Agency started to react to the movements in the financial markets in September 2008. In line with the path of other central banks, the BoJ implemented reductions to the prevailing policy rate in order to stimulate activity. In addition to the rate cuts, several measures were implemented to prevent further financial market distress. These measures are presented in Figure 5.4.

- First, the BoJ agreed to swap lines with the Fed, in order to satisfy the increasing liquidity demand for US dollars (Vollmer and Bebenroth, 2012).
- Second, in October 2008, the BoJ suspended the 'sale of stocks purchased from financial institutions on the stock exchange'. The motive for the suspension was to create space to monitor market developments.
- Third, changes were made to the securities lending facility. Usually, this facility allows repurchase agreements on Japanese government bonds (JGBs), but in October 2008 the list of eligible collateral for repurchase operations was increased. This also heralded the return to JGB purchases, which last occurred in 2002 (Fawley and Neely, 2013).
- Fourth, the BoJ showed interest in facilitating corporate financing, which was supported by the creation of a new credit facility called the 'Special Funds-Supplying Operations to Facilitate Corporate Financing' (SFSOs). Institutions are allowed unlimited three-month loans at the uncollateralised call rate using this facility, which is similar to the FRFA of the ECB (Vollmer and Bebenroth, 2012). The facility involved an expansion of the balance sheet of the bank and constituted QE (Fawley and Neely, 2013).
- In addition to the loan provision of this facility, the BoJ announced temporary purchases of commercial paper and corporate bonds, a form of credit easing. The downside of these purchases was the exposure to credit risk.

The initial response of the BoJ was a combination of the credit easing imposed by the United States and the elastic supply of loans applied by the ECB. In general, the Japanese and ECB focus appeared to be more on the banking sector, as opposed to the bond market focus of the United States (Fawley and Neely, 2013).

By the end of 2008, the BoJ had started to use its newly established 'complementary deposit facility', which provided interest on excess reserves at a fixed rate, similar to the deposit facilities found in the EUROZONE since 1999 and introduced in the United States in 2008. This facility creates a floor on the uncollateralised call rate and pays interest on reserves held at the central bank.

Toward the end of 2009 and the start of 2010, the BoJ decided to retire some of its temporary stability initiatives and replaced SFSOs with fixed rate operations (FROs) (Vollmer and Bebenroth, 2012). The newly introduced policy differed in that loans were not provided in an unlimited amount, with an initial amount of ¥10 trillion in three-month maturities being allocated (Fawley and Neely, 2013). In addition, under FROs a wider range of eligible collateral was accepted.

In April 2010, with the economy still experiencing slow economic growth, the BoJ proposed an initiative to boost growth through the provision of funds to financial institutions. By June 2010, the final details of the Growth Supporting Funding Facility were presented. Under this programme, eligible institutions were to submit proposals for one-year loans, with a possible extension to four years (Ueda, 2013). The quantity of loans under this framework was limited to ¥3 trillion. This programme was extended in June 2011, with ¥500 billion worth of credit being made available. Inflation persisted close to 0 per cent, and in September 2012, the BoJ increased the credit available from ¥3.5 to ¥5.5 trillion (Shirakawa, 2013).

The initial efforts of the BoJ were quite mild and, as a result, in October 2010, the Japanese economy was still struggling to recover from the financial crisis. In order to remain transparent regarding its policy approach, the BoJ announced a more aggressive three-pronged comprehensive monetary easing programme (Kuttner, 2014).

This programme marked the first attempt of the BoJ at large-scale usage of its balance sheet to rectify market conditions. First, it entailed lowering of the uncollateralised overnight call rate, such that it was back to the ZLB (Vollmer and Bebenroth, 2012). Second, clarification was provided for the conditions under which the bank would exit its zero interest rate policy (ZIRP) programme. Third, it involved the introduction of the Asset Purchase Program (APP).

The APP consisted of both credit and quasi-debt management policies, with private and public assets purchased (Kuttner, 2014). However, the focus was primarily on private sector securities, in order to reduce the spread between private and sovereign debt yields (Takahashi, 2013). With this programme, the bank focussed on reducing risk instead of term premia, similar in style to QE1 in the United

States. In the period from October 2011 to December 2012, additional purchases were made under the programme, this time with more of a focus on the purchases of long-term government bonds. The problem with the APP was that it was quite small compared with the equivalents in other countries. This seemed to indicate a lack of commitment on the side of the BoJ to implement an aggressive easing programme (Kuttner, 2014).

As witnessed by the data on GDP in 2012, it seemed that the measures implemented by the BoJ were somewhat successful in promoting growth. However, the third quarter of 2012 was met by a contraction in growth, which prompted further policy action. Purchases under the APP were once again attempted, with ¥11 trillion worth of public and private assets purchased.

In addition, a new framework was created to further promote lending. This new facility is called the Stimulating Bank Lending Facility. In December 2012, Shinzo Abe became prime minister and announced an economic stimulus package in response to poor growth; this approach is often referred to as 'Abenomics' (Haidar and Hoshi, 2015). Three arrows are stipulated under this policy framework. These are flexible fiscal policy, bold monetary policy and structural reform. This plan gave rise to a shift in the thinking on monetary policy implementation (Fukuda, 2015).

In March 2013, the BoJ appointed a new governor, Haruhiko Kuroda, who was sympathetic to the goals of the incumbent government and critical of the passive approach followed by the BoJ in the past (Haidar and Hoshi, 2015). Similarly to Mario Draghi, the new central bank governor indicated his resolve in ending chronic deflation and spurring economic growth (Takahashi, 2013).

A new, more radical set of easing measures was suggested to replace the CME programme. In April 2013, the BoJ introduced the Quantitative and Qualitative Monetary Easing (QQE) programme. It entails some strong commitments on the part of the BoJ, with Prime Minister Shinzo Abe referring to the shift in monetary policy as a regime change (Kuttner, 2014).

First, the bank announced an explicit inflation target of 2 per cent, with the idea of reaching this within two years. This was aimed at changing the public's deflationary mindset (Takahashi, 2013). Second, it announced QE in the form of open-ended expansion of the monetary base to aid in achieving the stated inflation target. Initially, a total of about ¥60–70 trillion per year was set; this was to replace the APP (Haidar and Hoshi, 2015). This expansionary policy commitment also generated the expectation of a higher rate of inflation.

Third, as a qualitative measure, the bank would conduct purchases of longer-term securities, in an attempt to increase the duration of bonds held on the bank's portfolio (Kuttner, 2014). This marked the first time that the BoJ used credit easing to lower long-term rates. The balance sheet of the bank has grown significantly since the adoption of QQE, with most of the purchases coming from long-term JGBs. Purchases under the QQE programme were increased to ¥80 trillion annually in October 2014, with the goal of increasing inflation more rapidly; this amendment is often referred to as QQE2. Under these expansions, the balance sheet of the bank almost doubled in size (De Michelis and Iacoviello, 2016).

In January 2016, amid declining oil prices and depressed growth of emerging market economies, the BoJ announced that in order to meet its price stability target it was going to make an amendment to the QQE programme so as to include negative nominal interest rates (De Michelis and Iacoviello, 2016). Adopting negative rates is not entirely new and has been used before by central banks in Europe, Switzerland, Denmark, and Sweden (Bech and Malkhozov, 2016). QQE with negative interest rates operates along three dimensions. Under this designation there are three tiers to the policy rate, with a positive, zero and negative rate applied to different portions on the current accounts of the financial institutions that interact with the BoJ. A positive rate is applied to existing balances with the BoJ, while the zero rate is applied to required asset holdings (De Michelis and Iacoviello, 2016). The negative interest rate is then applied to the balance of the current account in excess of the previously mentioned accounts. Thus far, the negative interest rate policy has been met with criticism and a disappointing response from financial markets, with an increase in the deflationary mindset.

5.4   SUMMARY AND CONCLUSION

In the aftermath of the GFC, central banks in the most important economies engaged in unorthodox monetary policy, which has mostly been a combination of low interest rates at the ZLB, balance sheet expansion and the purchase of government bonds. They did so reluctantly and in small steps, which were made with many new programmes to enlarge the balance sheets. Over the years, this added to a substantial balance sheet enlargement. By the end of the 2010s, the four central banks held large parts of their respective governments' debt (Reinhart, 2021).

When hope was returning that the QE could come to an end, the world was shaken by the COVID-19 crisis and thereafter by Russian aggression against Ukraine, both leading to enormous distortions on the world markets. Central banks had been stripped of their best responses to such crises and faced enormous difficulties ending in two-digit inflation rates in 2022. For example, the ECB had no chance to further reduce the interest rate at the beginning of the COVID-19 pandemic.

The string of crises since the GFC have led to some major problems for the central banks in question. In particular, their independence from daily politics was put under pressure. They were increasingly involved in general policymaking, which seemingly increased their power and importance in their societies. At the same time, they faced ever higher pressure to respond to fiscal needs, or general economic policy direction, in their countries, which can be interpreted as a loss in independence and power. Chapter 6 deals with the question of how the balance sheet enlargement relates to CBI.

6   Balance Sheet Policies
and CBI

Chapter 5 discussed the policy response of central bankers in developed economies to the financial crisis. Balance sheet policies featured prominently as a complement to interest rate policy. In this chapter, we provide a brief history of balance sheet operations and their usage in modern times, followed in Section 6.2 with a discussion on the empirical evidence about the efficacy of the broad range of balance sheet tools that were implemented in response to the financial crisis. We conclude the chapter with an overview on the potential implications for CBI from this widespread use of balance sheet policies.

By 2022, the balance sheets of central banks had expanded to a greater extent than in any other time in modern central banking history, partly in response to the COVID-19 pandemic. However, the expansion started earlier, in the wake of the GFC. Over this period, the balance sheets of central banks have become a significant part of the monetary policy narrative, and it is prudent to discuss the implications this carries for the independence of monetary authorities.

6.1   BALANCE SHEET POLICIES: EARLY HISTORY

6.1.1   Exchange Rate Policies

In the broadest sense, balance sheet policies can be viewed as any balance sheet action taken by the central bank that attempts to affect asset market conditions beyond adjusting a short-term interest rate (Borio and Disyatat, 2010). Derivatives of modern balance sheet policy were first implemented in the form of foreign exchange intervention. While the management of exchange rates is not of specific interest to the balance sheet narrative explored in this book, foreign exchange intervention is briefly discussed to demonstrate that the use of balance sheets by central banks, beyond that of interest rate management, preceded the response that became endemic following the international financial crisis.

The balance sheet operations of central banks in the post-war period were primarily performed by developing countries to exert pressure in an ever-changing exchange rate environment. These can be defined as central bank intervention in the foreign exchange market, the buying/selling of foreign currency to affect the exposure of private agents. Exchange rate policy is especially prominent in emerging Asia, with South Korea, Thailand and China identified as examples of countries that have managed to intervene in foreign exchange markets through sterilised purchases of foreign assets (Borio and Disyatat, 2010). More recently, reserve accumulation (which is an expansion of the central bank's balance sheet) has been a characteristic of developing countries in the aftermath of the 1997–1998 Asian financial crisis, in attempts to resist the appreciation of their domestic currencies (Filardo and Grenville, 2012). With that considered, the next section introduces the first part of our discussion on modern central bank balance sheet policy, which was spearheaded by Japan in a concerted effort to avoid deflation.

6.1.2   The 'Lost Decade' and the Liquidity Trap

Japan's 'lost decade' refers to the prolonged economic slump experienced since the early 1990s. A dissection of the slowdown identifies several causal factors: a protracted period of overly accommodative monetary policy; a banking crisis (on the back of non-performing loans); structural problems and slow productivity in large Japanese conglomerates; and an asset-price bubble collapse (Ito and Mishkin, 2006). During this decade, specifically in the period between 1992 and 2002, the Japanese real economy grew at a meagre rate, slightly above 1 per cent on average (Ueda, 2005). In 1995, in response to anaemic growth and disconcerting deflation, the BoJ brought interest rates close to the ZLB. Despite the expansionary efforts of the monetary authority, three large Japanese banks failed owing to sustained capital losses and, in concert with the Asian financial crisis of

1998, this heralded the return of deflation (Ito and Mishkin, 2006). The appropriate policy response was a reduction in the interest rate, but as this neared the ZLB, fears of a 'liquidity trap' emerged (Okina and Shiratsuka, 2004).

Japanese central bankers grappled with the potential loss of their primary policy lever and the possibility of chronic deflation. However, as argued by Krugman (1998) at the time, the conclusion that central banks are powerless at the ZLB is far from categorical. He proved, using an IS-LM framework, that a sustained increase in 'outside money' at the ZLB can have an inflationary impact on the economy, increasing both the general price level and output (Krugman, 1998). For this increase to be effective, the central bank is required to commit to future increases in the monetary base (Krugman, 2000). In other words, public expectation needs to be guided by the actions of the central bank as well as their commitment to future policy trajectory, for the expansionary policy to work when interest rates have hit the ZLB (Bernanke, 1999).

6.1.3 Zero Interest Rate Policy (1999–2000)

The BoJ implemented several non-standard monetary policy measures to spur economic growth and avoid deflation, in line with the policy recommendations made by Krugman (1998). In 1999, in the wake of the currency crises experienced by many South-East Asian economies, the BoJ adopted a zero interest rate policy (ZIRP), with a commitment to keeping the uncollateralised call rate at a level of zero 'until deflationary concerns are dispelled' (Okina and Shiratsuka, 2004, p. 77).

Implementing such a policy is supposed to shape public interest rate expectations, indicating the 'easy' stance of monetary policy. Achieving success with this measure requires transparency and continued communication on the side of the central bank (Woodford, 2012). In 2000, the BoJ believed the Japanese economy to be in recovery, with forecasts of the CPI indicating the possibility of at least 0 per cent inflation (Momma and Kobayakawa, 2014). Despite protestation from academics and private sector economists, the central bank reneged on their zero interest rate commitment at the first signs of growth, and increased the call rate by 25 basis points (Ito and Mishkin, 2006). However, economic conditions deteriorated rapidly in 2001 with the burst of the global information and communications technology bubble, and the BoJ reversed their rate increase with the declaration that ZIRP would continue until the 'inflation rate becomes stably above zero' (Ito and Mishkin, 2006, p. 142). However, the earlier reneging on the zero rate commitment severely damaged the credibility of the bank for several years afterwards.

6.1.4   The Quantitative Easing Programme (2001–2006)

Having blemished their reputation, the BoJ adopted a QEP in March 2001 to complement their renewed ZIRP, trying to bolster their expansionary commitment. QE as utilised by the BoJ primarily entailed providing reserves in excess of those needed to keep the interest rate at the ZLB. This approach to monetary easing was supported by several academics, such as Krugman (1998), Meltzer (1998) and McKinnon and Ohno (1997). However, there were dissidents who believed that this type of policy would have fiscal implications, with the central bank exposed to unwanted investment risk in potentially volatile asset markets (Fujiki et al., 2001). This issue has become increasingly important as central banks across the world extend their balance sheets to include a wider range of securities. It also raises the issue of CBI, which is discussed Section 6.3. In addition, there are concerns that the balance sheet expansion will be ineffective and ultimately lead to high levels of inflation. Given the levels of inflation experienced in Europe and the United States at the end of 2021 and throughout 2022, it is entirely plausible that aggressive central bank balance sheet expansion has played a role.

A simple definition of QE is an increase in the size of the central bank's balance sheet. In the case of Japan in the early 2000s, this translated into switching of the policy instrument from the short-term interest rate to the current account balance (Ito and Mishkin,

2006). The BoJ framed its approach as a three-pronged attack. First, it set a target for current account balances in a stepwise fashion, starting with ¥5 trillion in 2001 and steadily increasing this over four years to between ¥30 and ¥35 trillion (Momma and Kobayakawa, 2014). This amounts to increasing base money in the economy with the target of supplying the economy with a surplus of liquidity.

At this point, it is necessary to make a distinction between policy conducted under BoJ-governors Hayami (1998–2003) and Fukui (2003–2008). Before 1998, at the start of Hayami's term, policymakers had little practical experience in dealing with a liquidity trap (apart from the Great Depression). During that period, the first round of QE was implemented and appeared largely to be ineffective. The problem was the policymakers' failure to signal the nature of their policy commitment and in so doing to disarm deflation (Ito and Mishkin, 2006). It has been argued that this was because QE was conveyed as a temporary measure, without proper support from a tentative administration. The credibility of the bank's policies was harmed under Governor Hayami, as market participants were not always certain of the direction policy would take. Indeed, as pointed out by Ito and Mishkin (2006), Hayami constantly changed his position without providing the proposed mechanism of operation.

In 2003, when Governor Fukui was appointed, he immediately changed the message portrayed by the central bank by ratcheting up QE measures to reinforce the claims of an expansionary policy commitment (Ito and Mishkin, 2006). Communication strategies were significantly more transparent under Fukui's leadership. The necessary conditions for an exit from the ZIRP were explicitly stated. The change in rhetoric was found immediately to have an impact on the recovery of the financial sector, with a more protracted rebound of real variables (Ito and Mishkin, 2006). The forward guidance under Fukui was more successful because announcements left little room for interpretation as to the position of the bank, with the commitment of the bank being linked to actual and not forecasted values of CPI (Momma and Kobayakawa, 2014).

Discussions surrounding balance sheet measures, such as QE implemented in Japan, were not of primary importance to monetary policy discourse before the financial crisis. While there was a discussion among academics in the literature before the financial crisis, this was an almost esoteric topic in the context of developed countries. Most economists believed that the developed world operated in a context where these methods would not be implemented. The advent of the financial crisis changed this perception, and very rapidly. In the wake of nominal interest rates declining to the ZLB, many developed country central banks implemented balance sheet policies as a complement to their traditional policy measures. Chapter 5 outlines the response of central banks in retaliation to the threat espoused by the financial crisis. In the next section, we evaluate whether the empirical evidence supports the adoption of these policy tools.

6.2   EVALUATING THE IMPACT OF BALANCE SHEET RESPONSES

In his last public interview as Federal Reserve Chairman, Ben Bernanke, quipped that 'the problem with QE is that it works in practice but it doesn't work in theory' (Saft, 2014). In order to determine whether QE does indeed work in practice, this section is dedicated to a discussion of the empirical evidence as to the efficacy of balance sheet policies. Following the exploration in this section, the potential side effects from implementing such policies are fleshed out.

Generally, we have observed that central banks expand their balance sheets during periods when the policy interest rate has reached the ZLB (Woodford, 2012). As we stated in the introductory section, the earliest form of QE in the modern era was implemented by Japan, under its QEP. After the financial crisis, this unconventional measure was implemented by several advanced economies. The most prominent examples have been that of the United States and United Kingdom, which expanded their balance sheets by the largest amounts in relative terms (Gambacorta et al., 2014). It is important to note that although the corrections with relation to the financial crisis were large, in both absolute and relative terms, the recent balance sheet expansions to correct for imbalances originating from the impact of the COVID-19 pandemic dwarfed the financial crisis response.

6.2.1 Quantitative Easing Programme in Japan

We begin our analysis by looking at the results from the Japanese QEP, which was the earliest example of a 'pure' QE programme. Expanding the supply of bank reserves in this case was done to complement the use of the policy rate in conducting monetary policy, since the policy rate had reached the ZLB (Gambacorta et al., 2014). Increasing the size of bank reserves is similar in nature to a reduction in the policy rate, having the common goal of increasing expenditure, and hence stimulating economic growth. As suggested by quantity theorists, with this approach one would readily be able to see increases in nominal spending (Bernoth et al., 2015). The pressing question is whether this policy has generated the predicted effect in practice and what, if any, were the side-effects.

Econometric analysis of the Japanese policy experiment in the early part of the millennium indicates that it was rather ineffective in impacting the real economy (Ugai, 2007). Despite the monetary expansion, economic growth (and nominal expenditure) remained persistently low; the term 'zombification' of the economy was coined. More importantly, deflation appeared to be unaffected. The Japanese economy slowly started to recover by 2006, quite long after the initiation of the programme. However, although the policy might have been unsuccessful in generating real activity, it might have been effective in shaping expectations as to the future path of the policy rate, shown by longer-term interest rates decreasing throughout the early part of the 2000s.

This might be explained in part by the change in rhetoric of the central bank with regard to policy communication. Under the QEP, the credible commitment from policymakers to ZIRP stemmed from the fact that they were eliminating the possibility of increasing the policy rate in future (without first decreasing the excess reserves in the economy). This could have meant that eventually the promise of the central bank to keep rates low was transmitted through the expectations channel, from short- to longer-term rates (Woodford, 2012). After the crisis, the BoJ moved away from simply using quantitative targets for reserves with their CME programme, signalling that they did not have much confidence in QEP.

6.2.2 Large-Scale Asset Purchases in the United States

After the collapse of Lehman Brothers, the Fed was the first large central bank to undertake increases in its monetary base. LSAPs are a combination of quantitative and credit easing, with unsterilised purchases of both private and public securities. QE implemented by the Fed differed substantially from the QEP of Japan, both in terms of magnitude and rhetoric. There was a clear communication strategy, with the goal of lowering expectations with respect to the future policy rate (Gagnon et al., 2011).

The literature on the effects of QE can be divided broadly into two categories. The **first group** contains research that aims to look at the short-run policy impact, mainly through the effect on asset yields. It is mostly characterised by event studies,[1] although attempts have been made to quantify effects through time-series analysis. These studies usually utilise high-frequency data, capturing the immediate effect of announcements concerning QE programmes on financial variables (Meinusch and Tillmann, 2015).

Econometric evidence as to the existence of a reduction in long-term rates (flattening of the yield curve) through LSAPs has been easy to come by, but proper identification of the transmission channels has been more difficult (Krishnamurthy and Vissing-Jorgensen,

---

[1] An event study is a method that is utilised by economists to study the impact of a specific event or policy change. In this case, the event study considers the application of QE measures, identified by the date at which QE was imposed. Researchers then compare the performance of a set of economic variables after the event occurs to what would have been expected without the event.

2011). Modelling the complete transmission mechanism through which long-term rates operate has proven difficult, as the mechanism is poorly understood. Generally, the effect of central bank asset purchases on longer-term asset yields can be thought to affect two elements: a risk premium of some kind and the average short-term interest rate expected over the term to maturity (Gagnon et al., 2011). With the portfolio balance channel, asset purchases look to affect long-term interest rates through their impact on risk premia. Purchases of assets with long durations are swapped for bank reserves, to affect the relative supply of long-term assets and, thereby, the asset yield.

According to a statement by the Fed chairman at the time, Ben Bernanke, the Fed intended for LSAPs to work through the portfolio balance channel (Bauer and Rudebusch, 2014). In the case of the signalling channel, the mechanism works by changing expectations about the future of the short-term rate (Christensen and Krogstrup, 2015).

Several event studies, such as those by Gagnon et al. (2011), Krishnamurthy and Vissing-Jorgensen (2011), D'Amico et al. (2012), Glick and Leduc (2012), Rosa (2012), and Neely (2015), determine that the Fed was successful in reducing long-term rates through its spectrum of QE initiatives. Combining time-series and event-study methodologies, the study by Gagnon et al. (2011) is among the earliest to try and capture the portfolio balance effects of QE1. The identification strategy in the event-study methodology relies on the fact that announcements were a surprise to market participants. Immediate shifts in asset prices following these announcements show the true pass-through to bond yields, as opposed to the effect of anticipated monetary policy (Rogers et al., 2014).

Using the Kim–Wright term-structure model and event-study methods, the study of Gagnon et al. (2011) reveals that positive QE announcements cause significant reductions in the long-term interest rates of several securities. In particular, they found that the ten-year Treasury term premium dropped significantly in response to QE1 announcements, with the response of longer-term interest rates on MBS and agency debt showing an even stronger reaction. They assert that while asset purchases were effective at lowering risk premia, they failed to shape expectations as to the future of the short-term policy rate (Gagnon et al., 2011). Emphasis is placed on the portfolio balance channel while reducing the role for a signalling channel.

The results of Gagnon et al. (2011) are reinforced by the term-structure estimates of Hamilton and Wu (2012), who find a large and significant portfolio balance effect in a preferred habitat model, similar to that of Vayanos and Vila (2009). Findings provided by the event study of Krishnamurthy and Vissing-Jorgensen (2011) suggest that the portfolio balance channel is the most important driver of the reduction in long-term rates, but that the signalling and liquidity channels also contribute significantly.

Empirical evidence provided by Woodford (2012) indicates that there is a strong signalling channel component. In fact, Bauer and Rudebusch (2014) contest the claim of Gagnon et al. (2011) that the signalling channel is unimportant, citing concerns over small-sample bias in their term-structure model. Their revision of the model of Gagnon et al. (2011) aims to correct for bias and statistical uncertainty. Estimates from this revised process illustrate the extent to which the signalling channel was understated in previous attempts. The paper by Gagnon et al. (2011) only credits about 30 per cent of the movement of long-term rates to the signalling channel, while Bauer and Rudebusch (2014) identify the value to be between 30 per cent and 65 per cent.

The **second group** of research is a longer-term look at the impact of QE on the broader macroeconomy. Initial evidence on aggregate nominal expenditure shows little to support the idea that QE had an immediate impact on the real economy. In the case of the United States, the size of the balance sheet was almost quadrupled in the first four years after the crisis, with only a modest increase in the growth of nominal GDP (Woodford, 2012). However, the stated short-term objective of QE was to reduce market yields of long-term bonds, which would then eventually translate into increased availability of credit to firms and households (Woodford, 2012).

While some models focussed on the short run impact on asset yields, others tried to determine what impact QE has had in the longer-run on the real economy. During the crisis the policy rate reached the ZLB, which meant that economies had to switch to LSAPs. It is important therefore to verify whether these programmes that supplant the traditional policy tool would be able to spur economic growth and prevent deflation (Baumeister and Benati, 2013).

Unfortunately, the small sample size has made these evaluations difficult to accept. Preliminary results of a counterfactual constructed by Chung et al. (2012) reveal that without the policy intervention, the economy would have experienced decreased growth and inflation, in addition to increased unemployment. Similar results are reached with the dynamic stochastic general equilibrium (DSGE) models of Del Negro et al. (2017) and Curdia et al. (2012), who incorporate the effect of LSAPs on the broader macroeconomy.[2]

Baumeister and Benati (2013) use a time-varying parameter vector autoregression (TVP-VAR) to measure the impact of a 60 basis point increase in the ten-year term spread, which results in 0.9 per cent lower GDP, 1 percentage point lower inflation and the unemployment rate increased by 0.75 percentage points (Baumeister and Benati, 2013).[3] In order to determine whether output and price levels react to LSAPs in the United States, Weale and Wieladek (2016) use a Bayesian VAR model with several different identification specifications.[4] In this set-up they find a positive and significant effect on the

---

[2] DSGE models are a standard tool that central banks and researchers use to analyse macroeconomic phenomena. These models entail the construction of a theoretical foundation that is grounded on microeconomic principles. DSGE models are often tested against data through calibration and estimation techniques.

[3] Vector autoregressive (VAR) models are represented by a system of equations that represent a relationship between different macroeconomic variables. VAR models show how each variable is influenced by its own past values and the past values of the other variables in the system. A TVP-VAR model is one that considers potentially time varying coefficients in the system of equations, as opposed to the traditional VAR that has constant estimated coefficients across times.

[4] A Bayesian VAR model differs from the traditional VAR model in that it incorporates the idea of prior beliefs in determining what the estimated relationship between variables should be.

real economy resulting from an asset purchase shock, with a 0.36 per cent increase in real GDP and 0.38 per cent increase in CPI from the purchase of a government bond worth 1 per cent of nominal GDP (Weale and Wieladek, 2016).

Another approach is that of Meinusch and Tillmann (2015), who use a Qual VAR model, in which they find that QE was effective in stimulating real activity. With a similar result, Bork (2015) finds a significant impact on the real economy resulting from the LSAPs using a dynamic factor model. He concludes that 'industrial production, capacity utilization, inflation, and employment have significantly positive responses, and unemployment is significantly reduced' once an unconventional policy shock is applied (Bork, 2015, p. 5). In addition, in the case of a counterfactual, Bork (2015) finds that a significant downturn in the economy was avoided by the asset purchases.

6.2.3 Quantitative Easing in the United Kingdom

Once the traditional monetary policy route was exhausted in the United Kingdom, the BoE used QE to promote growth and FLS to inject liquidity and address dysfunctional financial markets; this most closely resembled the strategy followed by the United States (Churm et al., 2015). Similar studies were performed, with the results resembling those of the United States. Policies were primarily differentiated by the size of the programmes implemented, with the QE of the BoE being much smaller than that of the United States. Programmes looked at in this section, as used in the United Kingdom, are QE and FLS. Studies are grouped according to their impact on the economy.

In a similar fashion to that of the research for the United States, event studies were first used to attempt measuring the short-term effect of gilt (government bonds in the United Kingdom) purchases on the yield spreads in the UK economy. Relative to research on the unconventional measures of the Fed and ECB, studies on the policy actions of the BoE are limited. Important contributions to this literature include Meier (2009), Meaning and Zhu (2011), Joyce et al.

(2012), Breedon et al. (2012) and Churm et al. (2015), with most of the research focussing on the first phase of QE. Research performed on the UK economy is largely comparable with that of the United States in terms of methodology.

Casual empirical observation reveals that the range of credit facilities and QE mechanisms put into play in 2009 resulted in increasing asset prices as well as significant decreases in the yields of both government and corporate bonds (Joyce et al., 2012). Early studies that estimate the immediate impact on financial markets, through an event-study approach, are those of Meier (2009), Joyce et al. (2012) and Meaning and Zhu (2011). Using counterfactual analysis (constructing scenarios in which policy did not occur), Meier (2009) finds that initial QE announcements resulted in a reduction of gilt yields by between 35 and 60 basis points. In the work of Joyce et al. (2012), they find that longer-term gilt yields fell by at least 100 basis points in total for the period 2009–2010, with a similar narrowing in corporate bond yields.

In utilising the event-study methodology, there is a general disagreement in the literature about the exact approach to follow. However, most studies agree that QE contributed to the lowering of yields, as was the case for the United States, especially with regard to longer-term securities. In addition, there is a consensus that the portfolio balance channel, which is sometimes decomposed into local supply and scarcity effects, is the primary channel of operation (Joyce et al., 2012). Increased transparency with respect to QE policy changes in the United Kingdom has meant it has become increasingly difficult to identify the impact of announcements on bond yield spreads (Mclaren et al., 2014).

Event studies rely on the surprise component of policy announcements. Widely anticipated policy announcements dampen market reactions, which has led some research to show a decrease in the ability of purchases to affect asset prices (Churm et al., 2015). More recent studies, such as those of Butt et al. (2012), Mclaren et al. (2014) and Churm et al. (2015), attempt to evaluate the relative impact of the

QE2 programme, looking specifically at the financial market impact of this policy.

In terms of the effect on broad money aggregates, Butt et al. (2012) find that the effect has been largely the same over time, with transmission channels being the primary difference. Using a principal components model and counterfactual analysis, Churm et al. (2015) find that even though there was a significant reduction in gilt yields with QE2 across medium- to longer-term gilts, the registered impact across all yields was substantially lower than found during QE1.

Mclaren et al. (2014) believe that an explanation for the decreased impact of QE2 is the decrease in contribution from the signalling channel. In their study they found that the local supply effect (an element of the portfolio balance channel) is similar over time, between 40 per cent and 60 per cent of changes in asset yields, suggesting that other transmission channels are responsible for the change.

In addition to estimating the impact of QE2 on asset yields, the article by Churm et al. (2015) looks at the newly developed FLS. In particular, they are interested in the scheme's influence on marginal funding costs, similar to the study of Kapetanios et al. (2012). The conclusion reached by Churm et al. (2015) is that the introduction of FLS resulted in a drop in bank wholesale funding spreads.

There is a dearth of literature on the broader macroeconomic implications of asset purchase programmes in the United Kingdom. Kapetanios et al. (2012) use a variety of models to determine the real economy impact of the QE programmes. Empirical results suggest that the programmes that were implemented greatly improved economic conditions, and that in their absence GDP and inflation would have been much lower, perhaps even reaching negative values. Conservative estimates of the positive effect on real GDP puts it at 1.5 per cent, while inflation rose by at least 1.25 per cent as the result of QE. Similar estimates are found in the work of Baumeister and Benati (2013).

In their paper, Weale and Wieladek (2016) impose an asset purchase shock in a Bayesian vector autoregression (BVAR) framework, worth 1 per cent of nominal GDP, to determine the effect on the real economy, which delivered a 0.18 per cent increase in real GDP and 0.3 per cent increase in CPI. Also utilising a BVAR model, Churm et al. (2015) conducted an out-of-sample forecast to determine how the landscape of the UK economy would have differed if QE had not been implemented. An assumption was made, based on event-study evidence, that the stimulus reduced spreads by up to 45 basis points. In other words, the counterfactual scenario assumed that QE2 reduced the yield spread by 45 basis points. Stimulating the economy through asset purchases was found to have the equivalent impact of reducing the policy rate by between 1.5 per cent and 3 per cent, which roughly increased nominal GDP by 0.6 per cent over one year and inflation by between 0.25 and 0.6 percentage points. Churm et al. (2015) also study the impact of a lower marginal funding cost, as the result of FLS. They find that the impact of the scheme was similar to that of QE2, with a 0.8 per cent increase in GDP growth and a 0.6 percentage point increase in inflation, after a year from the start of the policy.

6.2.4 Longer-Term Refinancing Operations, Securities Markets Programmes, Outright Monetary Transactions and Public Sector Purchase Programme in Europe

The ECB also implemented liquidity injections and asset purchases throughout the crisis, but these were mostly sterilised operations and did not increase the size of the balance sheet. The first instance of expansion of the balance sheet was through the PSPP, which was implemented in 2015. There are several studies that look at the financial market impact of the ECB's policy initiatives. Usually, these studies look at one of three markets, namely, money markets, covered bond markets and sovereign bond markets (Szczerbowicz, 2015).

Early attempts by the ECB to rectify the position of failing financial markets were focussed primarily on LTROs. The impact of these exceptional liquidity provisions on interbank lending is studied through basic regression analysis in the work of Abbassi and Linzert (2012), Angelini et al.(2011) and Brunetti et al. (2011). From these studies, the general consensus is that the introduction of a range of LTROs did not contribute significantly to reducing relevant money market spreads. In other words, this policy avenue was not particularly useful in combating financial market instability.

However, of particular importance is the liquidity provided under the three-year LTROs, which Carpinelli and Crosignani (2015, p. 2) refer to as the 'largest liquidity injection ever conducted', totalling $1.37 trillion to 800 banks. They show that these liquidity injections positively affected Italian credit supply. In a similar study, Andrade et al. (2015) find that these LTROs positively impacted credit extension in France. In addition, García Posada and Marchetti (2015) argue that VLTROs increased loan supply in Spain. Szczerbowicz (2015) find that only three-year LTROs (in combination with ZIRP) contributed to removing some of the tension in stressed interbank markets, which is consistent with the result of Darracq-Paries and De Santis (2015).

Lenza et al. (2010) consider the macroeconomic effects of unconventional policies implemented during the period of enhanced credit support, before the creation of the SMP. Using a large BVAR model to construct a counterfactual, they determined that facilities created under ECS (specifically looking at FRFA) helped to reduce money market spreads, which translates into improved financial market health (Lenza et al., 2010). In addition, the ECS operated in much the same way as conventional monetary policy, by increasing industrial production by 2 per cent and decreasing the unemployment rate by 0.6 percentage points. The BVAR analyses of Giannone et al. (2011) and Baumeister and Benati (2013) corroborate the evidence that policy intervention supported market functioning by reducing money market spreads, thereby restoring the transmission mechanism of monetary policy, which helped to increase real activity across the EUROZONE.

Asset purchase strategies of the ECB during the sovereign debt crisis were subject to fierce academic and policy debate. The overwhelming majority of papers turned to the evaluation of the sovereign bond market impact of policies implemented, specifically focussing on SMP and OMT. In general, these papers looked toward the effect on asset yield spreads and the volatility associated with yields (Eser and Schwaab, 2016). Importantly, the ECB intervened in failing secondary sovereign debt markets, which had broader implications for the EURO area as a whole. We first evaluate the impact of the SMP and then the OMT (which later replaced the SMP).

The SMP was considered a temporary initiative to help stabilise the EURO economies and prevent the collapse of the monetary union. The language used by the ECB described measures that were used to restore the transmission mechanism of monetary policy (Eser and Schwaab, 2016). SMP, unlike QE in the United Kingdom and United States, was not intended to be a replacement for the short-term overnight interest rate. In other words, it was meant to normalise the movement of sovereign bond yields, not to be an accommodative monetary policy. As a result, studies rarely consider the broader macroeconomic implications of the programme, as it was not intended to boost growth or deter deflation (Szczerbowicz, 2015).

According to several studies, the initial announcement of the SMP and OMT had a powerful effect on sovereign bond yields, with the programme acting as a commitment to save the monetary union. Consequently, sovereign bond spreads for the EUROZONE periphery narrowed significantly following the announcements, as documented by Pattipeilohy et al. (2013), Krishnamurthy et al. (2014), Ghysels et al. (2014), Pooter et al. (2015), Acharya et al. (2015) and Falagiarda and Reitz (2015). However, it is argued by Eser and Schwaab (2016) that the announcement effect was not the primary driver, with actual bond purchases being more impactful in terms of lowering yield spreads and yield volatilities of sovereign bonds.

Using a panel regression, the 'impact identification' strategy performed by Eser and Schwaab (2016) on daily data reveals that bond purchases by the ECB under SMP decreased five-year bond yields across a range of countries most affected by the sovereign debt crisis. In general, the SMP appears to have had a stronger impact on the shorter end of the yield curve. Szczerbowicz (2015) uses internal ECB data and finds that purchases within the SMP and OMT significantly lowered covered bond and sovereign yield spreads.

According to Eser and Schwaab (2016), SMP operated through three primary channels:

1. reduction of liquidity risk premia through the lender-of-last resort function of the ECB;
2. local supply effect, whereby reducing supply in a specific market increases price on that asset and lowers the yield;
3. the default risk, which is reduced through country specific asset purchases to help avoid sovereign debt default.

Interestingly, since the SMP was temporary in nature and did not contain any information as to the policy stance of the ECB, we do not expect any signalling effect from these purchases (Krishnamurthy et al., 2014). In the work of Krishnamurthy et al. (2014), it is found that the dominant channels through which sovereign bond yields were affected by the SMP and the OMT were default risk and sovereign bond segmentation (local supply) effects.

The work of Altavilla et al. (2015) looks at the impact of the APP. The APP contains the PSPP as one of its policy arms, with the PSPP being the first true instance of unsterilised balance sheet expansion implemented by the ECB. They found that this APP resulted in a sizeable reduction in yields across a wide range of assets. In addition, these effects seem to intensify with an increase in the maturity and riskiness of the targeted asset. Estimates of the yield impact delivered an average reduction of 30 to 50 basis points on bonds with a ten-year maturity. Driffill (2016) finds that APP resulted in the reduction of ten-year government bond yields in troubled economies, reducing differentials between countries of the Euro area.

A comprehensive event study by Falagiarda and Reitz (2015) looks at spillovers to Central and Eastern Europe from the range of non-standard policy measures implemented by the ECB since 2007, including the newly formed APP. They find a strong announcement effect emanating from the SMP, while the OMT and PSPP had a limited impact. They identify the primary channels of transmission for non-standard policies as the portfolio balance, signalling and confidence (redenomination risk) channels (Falagiarda and Reitz, 2015).

6.2.5 CME and Quantitative and Qualitative Monetary Easing in Japan

We end the balance sheet policies narrative with the empirical evidence supplied on the Japanese economy. Since the adoption of the QEP in 2001, several other central banks have emulated the strategy, incorporating unconventional policy measures as part of their policy toolkit. Evidence as to the efficacy of non-standard policies implemented is becoming more abundant. As previously stated, most of the research has been on the LSAPs of the United States. However, the introduction of CME and especially QQE has garnered the attention of several international researchers.

As in the other sections on empirical evidence, most of the research has been conducted to determine the short-term financial market impact of asset purchases. Schenkelberg and Watzka (2013) find that QE under CME resulted in a reduction of long-term interest rates, in a similar manner to that of LSAPs in the United States. Transitory increases in output and inflation were also observed with this SVAR approach. Rogers et al. (2014) examine the effect of several non-standard policy announcements on asset prices, with policy shocks resulting in a reduction of ten-year JGBs and corporate bond yields. Although this was not necessarily the intended effect from asset purchases, with the BoJ explicitly stating that it wanted to affect the real economy, specifically inflation.

Interestingly, the study of Hiroshi (2015) points out that the signalling channel was important in the dissemination of the effect of CME, but this channel does not appear to be important under QQE. In particular, QQE caused a sharp depreciation of the yen, which is thought to operate through the portfolio balance channel. The yield of longer maturity JGBs declined with the introduction of QQE, but this reduction did not filter through to corporate bond yields (Hiroshi, 2015). The study of Hausman and Wieland (2015) also finds that the yen experienced a strong depreciation under Abenomics, as well as an increase in Japanese stock prices.

One of the stated objectives of Abenomics has been to reach an inflation target of 2 per cent in the space of two years (De Michelis and Iacoviello, 2016). This target was not reached, but inflation has turned positive for the first time in fifteen years, indicating that it has been somewhat successful. In their paper, Hausman and Wieland (2015) show that the approach of the BoJ with Abenomics was successful in providing a small increase to output, but inflation remains well below the intended target. Notwithstanding, they believe that the cost of the programme is justified. Matsuki et al. (2015) show, using an Markov-Switching VAR, that expansion of the balance sheet resulted in lowering short-term market rates and increasing inflation. De Michelis and Iacoviello (2016) use both VAR and DSGE analyses to conclude that the non-standard policies implemented by the BoJ have been effective in the battle to overcome deflation; however, owing to credibility concerns, the BoJ has not reached its intended target. Bolder measures are required if real activity is to be bolstered and deflation defeated (De Michelis and Iacoviello, 2016).

6.3 CBI AND BALANCE SHEET POLICIES

6.3.1 Balance Sheet Operations Interfere with CBI

Balance sheet policies were undoubtedly crucial policy instruments during and after the financial crisis. Nonetheless, all remedies have side effects; it is simply the severity that differs. Concerns over unintended consequences of balance sheet operations were first voiced with the initial rounds of QEP in Japan. However, owing to the unprecedented scale and pervasive usage of balance sheet policies after the financial crisis and (more recently) COVID-19 as well as the Russian aggression in Ukraine, concerns over the potential ramifications have been amplified. Some of the possible adverse consequences include international spillover effects, loss of CBI, the creation of moral hazard, permanently inflated balance sheets (no exit strategy), inflation and the depreciation of currency. These potential consequences are discussed in this section, with a focus on the effect of the crisis and their management on the relation between central banks and governments. Do balance sheet operations reduce central banks' independence from political interventions?

The British economist David Ricardo wrote in 1824 that governments should never be entrusted with the power to issue paper money, as this would ultimately lead to inappropriate servicing of public debt. His solution was to establish an independent monetary authority not subject to political influence. In fact, the central bank should 'never, on any pretence, lend money to Government, nor be in the slightest degree under its control or influence' (Ricardo, 1824, p. 11). In the rest of this section, we aim to show that political intervention in the process of money creation could severely affect the functioning of the monetary transmission mechanism, potentially causing inflation to become unmanageable.

As shown in Chapter 3, there are different concepts of CBI. Two broad classifications emerge from the literature. First, independence of objective, or goal independence, allows an organisation to determine which objectives to pursue, without input from political authorities (Ćorić and Cvrlje, 2009). Central banks do not generally have goal independence, as this would encourage opportunistic behaviour and lacks accountability, allowing the monetary authority to restructure goals so as to allow deviations from predetermined objectives. This concept remains theory, as the underlying PAP cannot be solved with a goal independent central bank.

Therefore, the second concept is in the focus of both real monetary politics and policy and this analysis. One of the defining features of the modern central bank is that it is free to achieve its mandate without regard for political agenda, using whichever instrument it chooses (Bernanke, 2010). Being able to use the tools of monetary policy to achieve stated goals without interference is at the heart of what is called instrument independence. Instrument independence is a multidimensional concept. The ability to pursue policy objectives requires the central bank to have political, technical and financial independence. Political independence means that central banks do not receive assistance or take instruction from government bodies in pursuit of their stated goals. Technical independence refers to the ability of the central bank to use monetary policy tools as they see fit. In addition, they are not allowed to use these tools for goals outside their mandate, such as the monetising of government debt. Finally, financial independence means that the central bank has to have control over its own balance sheet, with a budget separate from that of the government (Buiter, 2009).

There are several reasons government needs to be separated from the monetary authority, as we discuss extensively in Chapter 3. As a consequence, the new consensus assigned central banks the mandate of achieving price stability. As highlighted by theory, achieving this goal depends heavily on CBI, transparency and accountability (Bernanke, 2010). Inflation targeting, through adopting the inflation rate as a nominal anchor, greatly decreased inflation and output volatility. Empirical evidence supports the idea that CBI is key to achieving desired inflation outcomes. It is therefore not surprising that dissidents of unconventional policy measures identify the potential loss of CBI as too costly to ignore.

Balance sheet policies immediately raise concerns about the independence of the central bank. We identify two broad streams of argument made in the literature about the impact of unconventional monetary policy on CBI. There is some overlap between these categories, but they are largely distinct from each other. First, there are discussions about the budgetary independence of central banks with the introduction of asset purchases. Second, a large literature has formed on the portfolio management of assets purchased by central banks after the crisis. In the following section, we discuss some suggestions made to quell these fears.

We have established that instrument independence is vital in achieving price stability. However, with the start of the financial crisis, it is not the loss of freedom to use the tools of monetary policy that is mourned; instead, budgetary, or financial, independence has become the focus of discussion. In normal times, central banks have a certain structure to their balance sheet. Liabilities consist primarily of currency and reserves, while the asset side contains Treasury securities (Dudley, 2013).

In addition to the fiscal consequences of balance sheet interventions, there are also distributional consequences depending on the particular asset market within which the central bank chooses to acquire assets with the newly created central bank reserves (Goodhart, 2011).

Of course, fiscal consequences for monetary policy decisions have always occurred (e.g. Sargent and Wallace, 1981), but become more explicit when balance sheet operations are used. For the government, the central bank's actions affect the terms on which government can finance existing and new debt. Prior to extensive balance sheet operations when the central bank held few private sector assets, there was no credit risk on the portfolio. It is possible for the central bank to hold long-term government bonds, which implies some interest rate risk. However, as these long-term bonds are usually held to maturity, it eliminates much of the associated risk (Dudley, 2013). Notably, central banks typically secure some degree of profit, which they then remit to the Treasury.[5]

Not that it will be easy to use balance sheet operations in the normal course of business. Central banks are just one participant in assets markets and cannot move them with anything like the precision they have over the policy interest rate. This problem of control is compounded by an epistemological problem: we know far less where econometric estimates are concerned about the potential impact of

---

[5] It is worthwhile to note here that, for example, the Bundesbank as part of the Eurosystem did not generate profits in three years between 2020 and 2022.

balance sheet policies. It is not implausible to argue that their best work might well be done, as during the crisis, when markets are thin or liquidity risk is high. Balance sheet operations at such a time and in the right market can bring the private sector back in and return market stability (Borio and Disyatat, 2010, p. 1).

Unconventional monetary policy can have fiscal consequences. Large-scale asset purchases and maturity transformations could plausibly be unfavourable for the central bank's asset risk profile and the level of profits remitted to the Treasury (Rossi, 2013). This is of particular relevance if central banks wish to intervene in financial markets outside the traditional banking sector (Goodfriend, 2007). Purchases of private sector assets (such as MBS) and long-term government securities result in the central bank adopting the risk associated with the asset.

Broadly speaking, two types of risk are created: credit risk and interest rate risk. First, credit risk is considered the most damaging, as the central bank has little control over private asset markets. Purchases of these private sector securities expose the central bank to the volatility of the associated markets. Second, increasing long-term debt translates into greater interest rate risk. Normally, these assets would be generating income for the central bank, as has been the case in most countries. This means that the government receives seigniorage revenue from these investments. However, if long-term interest rates increase or money market investments turn sour, there could be a cessation of the stream of seigniorage revenue.

Earnings from these securities could also be negative (creating a budget deficit), which means the central bank could experience losses. Increasing interest on reserves, as in the United States, makes this situation even worse, as interest needs to be paid on this debt (Dudley, 2013). Small, temporary losses experienced by the central bank should not, however, be a cause for concern, as the burden could be shifted by increasing remittances at a later stage when the central bank becomes profitable again (Del Negro and Sims, 2015). However, in the case of the recent expansions across the last two decades, the sheer size of asset purchase programmes has amplified the potential budget risk. If losses are large, the bank might not be able to retain control over its balance sheet. Credit risk is introduced with extensive balance sheet operations, and the consequences will ultimately be borne by the taxpayer. Accordingly, it is useful to view the central bank's balance sheet as part of the consolidated public sector balance sheet (Borio and Disyatat, 2010).

One of the most hotly debated topics after the GFC is whether central banks should be allowed fiscal support when the 'system's net worth at market value is negative' (Del Negro and Sims, 2015, p. 2). In order fully to appreciate this discussion, a distinction needs to be made between fiscal support and fiscal backing. Fiscal support is defined as the 'commitment by the treasury to recapitalize the central bank if necessary' (Del Negro and Sims, 2015, p. 3). Fiscal backing, however, refers to the behaviour of the fiscal authority to 'back' the inflation target set by the central bank, making sure inflation is guided primarily through monetary policy (Reis, 2015). Fiscal backing is co-ordinated behaviour that cannot be managed by the central bank on its own (Del Negro and Sims, 2015). As illustrated frequently in the literature, for the price level to be uniquely determined, fiscal authorities need to limit their interference in monetary policy affairs.

Fiscal backing does not imply fiscal support, and vice versa. At the moment few countries have fiscal support when it comes to making losses from investments in private credit markets. Some central banks, such as the BoE, are indemnified fully by the Treasury against any loss occurring from their unconventional monetary policy spending, while other central banks have constructed charters to deal with negative dividends (Reis, 2015).

However, if the central bank receives no recapitalisation, this might influence its ability to conduct policy. If the government does not tolerate losses, then the central bank cannot guarantee price stability (Goodfriend, 2014). Without support, the central bank would try to influence inflation in order to devalue its stock of outstanding debt, which means perhaps allowing more inflation than needed (Belke and Polleit, 2010). Seigniorage revenue generated could settle their debt, but at the cost of inflation, which means that they are not pursuing their policy objective. This option can cause severe reputational damage; potentially undermining established trust in the ability of the central bank to achieve its policy objective.

During times of crisis, several lending facilities are created by central banks, often in close co-ordination with fiscal authorities. The financial institutions selected to receive credit were based on apparent need. However, because of the co-ordination with government agencies, this opened up the possibility that the selection of market intervention could have a political agenda (Bordo, 2010). One concern is that in the pursuit of this seigniorage revenue, the government could perhaps try to influence the investment decision of the central bank, potentially forcing it to contradict its mandate (Del Negro and Sims, 2015).

While the goal of most central banks, which adopted non-standard policies, has been to persuade private banks to lend, it has unearthed another interesting problem. Intervention in credit markets can create unnecessary speculation and associated volatility in asset markets (Plosser, 2009). Influencing asset prices and credit allocation also gives the central bank a lot of power. In practice this has allowed the central bank to behave like a large investor in specific market segments, managing a relatively large portfolio of assets that affects market activity. Unfortunately, this makes it the target of political pressure, opening it up to lobby groups.

The ability to intervene in specific market segments also creates moral hazard, allowing institutions to believe that they will be bailed out at the first sign of distress, inherently promoting even riskier behaviour. One of the reasons the financial agents engaged in risky behaviour before the financial crisis is that they believed banking institutions to be of such systemic importance that they would not be allowed to fail. The central bank's lender-of-last-resort function, for example, institutionalises this idea, stating that struggling financial institutions need to be provided support. In addition, if the central bank is responsible for banking supervision, then it will need to use taxpayer money to fund the strategic resolution of these institutions (Rossi, 2013).

6.3.2 How to Reconcile Balance Sheet Operations and Central Bank Independence

Several suggestions have been put forward as to how one could resolve issues on CBI. In general, central banks need to be transparent when it comes to the link between the fiscal and monetary authority, showing that a co-ordinated effort is taking place. It is essential that the objectives of policies be explained in detail, to leave no doubt about the policy direction. One solution, as mentioned before, is for governments to provide fiscal support (indemnifying losses) in the unlikely event of central bank budget deficits. This could be done through the creation of an institution that absorbs losses, such as in the case of the BoE.

Another suggestion is that of Bernanke (2010), who believes that the same independence should be extended to unconventional policies as that enjoyed by the conventional monetary policy measures. In other words, one would try to remove the influence of government when it comes to non-standard policies; for example, by assigning the central bank some financial stability objective to reach using unconventional tools, without interference from the fiscal authorities.

Finally, there is a proposal for the delineation of fiscal and monetary authorities in handling the assets of the balance sheet of the central bank. Non-Treasury securities can form part of the fiscal budget, while the central bank is left with Treasuries on its balance sheet. This resolves some of the issues over the exit strategy and its interaction with price stability (Plosser, 2009).

The expectation of a need for closer co-operation between fiscal and monetary authorities in the future, based on the more frequent use of balance sheet policies, taxes on banks and expanded financial regulation led Goodhart to one of the most surprising conclusions in monetary economics for some years: that 'the idea of a central bank as an independent *institution*' will be put aside' (Goodhart, 2011, p. 154). The italics are in the original and they are important: With reference to an older argument from the early years of central banking, Goodhart identifies the *institution* of the central bank with its balance sheet which has never been, and will not in the future be, independent from fiscal policy.

In this argument, to be a central bank requires taking responsibility for the balance sheet operations just described. By contrast, determining the level of a policy interest rate is not a necessary function of the central bank (Goodhart, 2011), though it has become conventional. 'A Central Bank is a bank', said Lord Cobbold, a former governor of the Bank of England, 'not a study group' (quoted in Goodhart, 2011, p. 146). The reference to a 'study group' need not be derogatory. It refers to a group of people engaged in a common analytical activity and captures what modern monetary policy committees do: they study the current condition and likely unfolding of the economy to determine a proper interest rate path given the goals of monetary policy.

What has been called CBI for a generation refers to the scope for the monetary authorities to set interest rate policy without fiscal dominance. It would be possible to retain such independence for interest rate policy in a central bank that is also collaborating with fiscal authorities in the management of their balance sheet.

Not that it will be easy to use balance sheet operations in the normal course of business (Du Plessis, 2012). Central banks are just one participant in assets markets and cannot move them with anything like the precision they have over the policy interest rate. This problem of control is compounded by an epistemological problem: we know far less where econometric estimates are concerned about the potential impact of balance sheet policies. It is not implausible to argue that their best work might well be done, as during the crisis, when markets are thin or liquidity risk is high. Balance sheet operations at such a time and in the right market can bring the private sector back in and return market stability (Borio and Disyatat, 2010, p. 1), but beyond the crisis they risk destabilising asset markets, incurring fiscal risk and drawing the central bank into the political fray.

PART III   The Political Economy of CBI in the Real Economy

7   Fiscal Needs and Low Interest Rates Policy in an Olsonian Setting

7.1   INTRODUCTION

The past decade (i.e. the period since the GFC) has changed the public perception of both the tasks of central banks as well as their independence from the political process. As shown in Chapters 5 and 6, central banks have taken bold measures to fight the different crises hitting the world economy since 2008. These measures seem to have worked, as economic growth recovered after 2008 (with some outliers in both directions); at the same time, inflation was low in all advanced as well as in most emerging economies.

When, in early 2020, COVID-19 started to spread in the world, most countries more or less shut down their economies. Global value chains (GVCs) were interrupted, tourism and international travel stopped, shops, universities and schools were closed. The world witnessed a combined demand and supply shock as it has not experienced since the Second World War. There are huge differences between countries, but in 2020 world GDP contracted by roughly 4 per cent in comparison with 2019, which was a bit less than predicted in June 2020 (Haas et al., 2020, p. 359).

Governments all over the world decided to react boldly and support both enterprises and employees through rescue packages. Again, these differed in scale and scope across countries, but served the same purpose, namely to allow competitive enterprises to survive without creating zombie firms and to prevent a surge in unemployment by generous short-time allowances. For this purpose, governments accepted large budget deficits, in some countries to an unprecedented extent. High budget deficits have been justified with the special character of the crisis, and have been widely accepted in politics and by the public as well as in academic circles. To finance these huge fiscal programmes, governments resorted to the capital market and additionally received support by central banks.[1]

Indeed, central banks willingly supported governments in their efforts to help their companies to survive the COVID-19 crisis. For this purpose, they could broadly utilise three policy measures (Haas et al., 2020; IMF, 2020; Mosser, 2020). The first policy option is an interest rate cut. Given that the major central banks such as the ECB, the BoE, the Fed and the BoJ had already moved close to the ZLB in late 2019, this option was mostly not available. The ECB and the BoJ did nothing, whereas the BoE and the Fed, which had started to raise interest rates again in 207 and 2016 respectively, used significant interest rate cuts in the spring of 2020. The second option included asset purchasing programmes. Haas et al. (2020) distinguish broad and narrow programmes. Whereas the first are designed to reduce long-term yields (and thus make it cheaper for governments to borrow), narrow programmes aim at specific sectors in order to expand the credit option for these sectors. The third option is to act as lender of last resort (LLR) for targeted credit through commercial or state banks such as the German Kreditanstalt für Wiederaufbau. This option enables banks to hand out credits for firms that suffer from a lockdown, but have the potential to survive the COVID-19 crisis and recover quickly after the measures end. Without the guarantee from central banks, commercial banks might be unable to take the associated risks.

The bold reaction of central banks to support the fiscal stimuli and rescue packages all over the world has been seen very positively in politics, the business community and academia. Nevertheless, this support strategy is not without risks. First, the enterprises in real economy are not automatically on the safe side with credits or bond purchases, so there is a risk of losing the investment or being forced to step in as LLR is still prevailing. The second obvious risk

---

[1] For a comprehensive list of policy responses, see the IMF Policy Tracker: www.imf .org/en/Topics/imf-and-covid19/Policy-Responses-to-COVID-19#G.

is that inflation picks up after the end of the crisis, when the spending patterns are readjusted to normal behaviour and people catch up with purchases they needed to make but were unable to, while capacities are fully utilised. Since spring 2021, there has been an increasing fear of inflation in the EUROZONE. This materialised in late 2022, with inflation rates in the range of 10 per cent in the EU and United States. The industrialised world has not experienced such rates for more than fifty years; see also Section 7.3.1. This is exactly why, as de Larosière and Marsh (2021) argued in 2021, central banks normalised their monetary policy over the course of 2022.

In addition to these risks, government debt has increased significantly after the crisis of 2008 and even more so over the course of the COVID-19 crisis of 2020 and 2021. Central banks have expanded the local currency reserves (at their discretion) and used those reserves to purchase large portfolios of domestic government bonds. Reinhart (2021) recently demonstrated the extraordinary rise in the portfolio of public debt held by the Federal Reserve Board as an example: At the end of the Second World War, the Fed held Treasuries and GSE Securities to the value of about 10 per cent of US GDP. This proportion declined and remained at about 5 per cent of GDP until the GFC. Meanwhile, other central banks had progressively increased their holding of US government debt to about 10 per cent of US GDP on the eve of the GFC. Since the GFC, other central banks have doubled their holding of US government debt relative to GDP to about 20 per cent, while the Fed's own portfolio of US debt has increased from 5 per cent of GDP to 22 per cent. And these data were compiled before the impact of the COVID-19 interventions were available, which has led to a further intensification of the same trend.

These interventions have contributed to very low (near zero, and sometimes even negative in nominal terms) bond yields, although such purchases are prohibited by most central bank statutes. For Reinhart (2021, p. 13), the impact of this rising portfolio of public debt held by central banks 'calls into question to what extent interest rates on government debt remain "market-determined"'.

Simultaneously, these large expansions of central bank reserves have affected not just bond markets, but also, owing to the integrated nature of financial markets, other asset prices, such as stock prices, exchange rates and property prices. The liquidity introduced into bond markets has led not only to low yields, but also to a rebalancing of portfolios for greater return, thus spreading the liquidity around all liquid asset markets. Stock exchanges boomed until early 2022, only briefly interrupted by temporary losses owing to the COVID-19 crisis. After the Russia–Ukraine war started, stock prices plummeted; however, as measured by the MSCI world index of stock prices, the losses suffered in the first half of 2022 had largely been recovered by the middle of 2023. The real estate market recovered in many countries, and boomed in those countries that did not experience the real estate bubble before the Great Recession, such as Germany. This has caused some distortions on the market for housing.

During the last fifteen years, many structural problems have not been tackled. In the United States, income and wealth inequality together with only modest social support mechanisms – which turned out to be disastrous during the COVID-19 crisis – have exacerbated social conflict, In Japan, structural change has been neglected if not repressed for thirty years now, and in the EU, governments have not used the time given to them by the ECB via the PSPP to reform labour market (France, Italy) or tax (Germany) policies. The demographic trends in most OECD-countries are also adverse, in particular against the background of zero interest rates. While the rescue packages helped to end the recession in the advanced economies, they did not address the structural problems – in other words, central bank activities took place in an Olsonian setting (Olson, 1982).

The policy response to repeated crises over the last decade and more suggest that policymakers have abandoned the monetarist consensus about the neutrality of money, while the desirability of responsibility assignment and the acknowledgement of the need for fiscal prudence seems to have given way to calls for new activism on both the monetary and fiscal fronts. While these ideas are presented as novel, we find many of them closer to old wine in new bottles. In addition, their short-run effectiveness has to be balanced against emerging longer-run problems. Nevertheless, they appeal to political decision-makers and gain ground in the public debate.

In the current debate, divisions run deep and *The Economist* magazine captured the controversy by quoting two very different perspectives: whereas Paul Tucker feared that the 'Bank of England has now reverted to being the operational arm of the Treasury', Olivier Blanchard argued that 'at zero interest rate it doesn't matter whether you finance by money or finance by debt' (*The Economist*, 2020, p. 15).

This unprecedented fiscal activism and the outright support by monetary authorities raises the question whether CBI as a description of policy reality and prescription for sound institutional design have lost relevance. Do central banks really need to be independent from politics, or is it indeed preferable to consolidate them again with governments, in particular with the department of finance? This is hardly a new debate: in the aftermath of the Second World War, funded by a tremendous fiscal expansion, programmes for macroeconomic stability, such as that of Friedman (1948), tied fiscal and monetary authorities closely together in their prescriptions of how to ensure sound public finance and sound money.

This chapter investigates the implications for CBI of the calls for greater macroeconomic policy action, the background of new economic theories, recent crises and the delayed structural change in many advanced economies. In Section 7.2, we briefly introduce the influential current theories that underpins the argument for greater monetary and fiscal intervention. In Section 7.3, we discuss the risk for central bankers, and show potential problems associated with current monetary policy and the additional suggestions from new theories. In Section 7.4, we take an Olsonian perspective to explain the monetary policies of the last decade in Western countries. Section 7.5 is dedicated to central banks' responses to the COVID-19 crisis and the distortions brought about by Russian aggression. Section 7.6

concludes, and discusses the consequences for the independence of central banks from a positive perspective.

7.2   ABANDONING THE MODERN MONETARIST CONSENSUS

The aftermath of the GFC overturned much that was settled in Economics. The preceding consensus was formidable. Indeed, just a few years before the crisis, the Nobel Laureate Robert Lucas argued strikingly in his Presidential Address to the American Economic Association that:

> [Macroeconomics] then referred to the body of knowledge and expertise that we hoped would prevent the recurrence of that economic disaster. My thesis in this lecture is that macroeconomics in this original sense has succeeded: Its central problem of depression prevention has been solved, for all practical purposes, and has in fact been solved for many decades.... (Lucas, 2003, p. 1)

These developments occurred against the background of disappointment with both fiscal and monetary activism since the 1970s. This demonstration effect did much to undermine the confidence in such an expansive view for macroeconomic policy, including an ambitious agenda for the central bank. In additional to the practical difficulties, confidence in the former policy regime was also undermined by theoretical developments,[2] which indicated that the disappointment was not an accident of history, but due to real shortcomings in its fundamental design.

Not only was this consensus challenged post-crisis, but also, in some instances, the consensus has been blamed for the crises.

This consensus, which had become dominant by the late twentieth century, had evolved since the mid-1970s, when economists

---

[2] See the theoretical contributions by, for example, Friedman (1968), Lucas (1976) and Kydland and Prescott (1977).

and policymakers became disillusioned with the preceding largely interventionist macroeconomic policy agenda. It is a consensus that evolved over many decades in a robust debate between Keynesian and Monetarist economists, broadly understood. The crucial monetarist insights captured by this consensus, as summarised by de Long (2000) at the turn of the century, include:

First, there was an explicit recognition of the policymaker's uncertainty both about the state of the economy and the effect of policy changes on the economy. Second, there was recognition that the criterion for good policy is not whether it is best in any specific circumstance, but whether it is best in general, therefore emphasising robustness. Third, it was argued that a stabilisation policy should be aimed at lowering volatility, not closing output gaps. And finally, it was noted that monetary policy is a very powerful tool that affects both nominal and real variables. By the late twentieth century, these points were emphasised by monetarist and Keynesian economics alike, to the extent that de Long (2000) speculated that the then ascendant 'New Keynesian' economics could equally be called 'New Monetarist' economics.

Rules-based monetary policy is a good example of this consensus in action, as it recognises the inability to fine-tune the economy, ensures the robustness of policy across many possible economic circumstances and focusses the attention of policymakers on the desired objectives. In addition, rules-based policy can improve the policymaker's credibility and ensure smoother adjustment of markets to likely policy adjustments (see also Chapter 3). In one of the most influential papers on the emergent consensus, John Taylor (1993) showed how benign the outcome was of a change in Federal Reserve behaviour towards pursuance of their stabilisation objectives in a rules-like manner from the late 1970s. What Taylor observed was also a return to the Tinbergen rule as a solution to the assignment policy in, for example, monetary policy, with a single objective formulated as the appropriate objective to pursue with a single policy instrument.

While the consensus as defined here was about monetary policy, it was part of a larger liberal agenda in economic policymaking. In this perspective, the state's role is more clearly defined and focussed on governance aspects and policy in a broadly rule-like setting. Governments have been discouraged from direct involvement in the economy, especially as the manager of businesses. Industrial policy was viewed sceptically, with limited beneficial applications such as support for research and development (R&D). Meanwhile, trade liberalisation proceeded at pace and the capital market became increasingly integrated internationally.

The practical support for this consensus was undermined by the severity of the GFC. In its wake, many supporters for the consensus proposed a much more active and interventionist role for the government. This new agenda included explicit collaboration between monetary and fiscal authorities, under the latter's leadership, and greater scepticism about lightly or self-regulated financial markets and globalisation.

This scepticism has its roots in some problematic developments of the period since 1990, when the transformation process in the former communist world began. As the then Soviet Union and communist Eastern-Bloc collapsed, the widely shared expectation was for steady progress towards capitalism and liberal democracy around the world (e.g. Fukuyama, 1992). It seemed that the combination of liberal market economics and democracy was in the ascendancy with fortunate outcomes, especially in the formerly second and third worlds. During this period, astonishing progress towards the reduction of crippling poverty globally, as measured against, for example, the United Nations' Millennium Development Goals, seems to bear that out. However, these gains were not shared equally, and while the distribution of income narrowed from a global perspective, income and wealth inequalities rose sharply within states. The tardy recovery from the Great Recession in many economies together with specific problems, such as the Euro-crisis that followed in the wake of the GFC, though this had deeper root causes, added to these difficulties. Lately, the reaction to COVID-19 has compounded the problem and further increased scepticism among the public, and also among economic researchers.

It is not just economic difficulties since the GFC that have undermined the modern monetary policy consensus, but also intellectual opposition partly developed from within the discipline of Economics and also from beyond mainstream Economics. These ideas have proven to be attractive for policymakers, and are now being discussed more seriously within the discipline too. Two of these sets of ideas, MMT and the theory of secular stagnation, deserve closer scrutiny in light of their practical relevance for the governance of central banks and their relationship with the government.

7.2.1 Modern Monetary Theory

The new paradigm of MMT emerged after the GFC, but its roots were in a venerable Keynesian tradition of the earliest vintage, such as Lerner (1943). MMT's policy implications received notable airtime during the last two US presidential elections (2016 and 2020), with support from some of the more left-wing Democratic candidates. Meanwhile, some mainstream economists have also taken an interest (Coats, 2019; Edwards, 2019; Mankiw, 2020), mostly with a critical view.

A core proposition of MMT is that governments in countries that issue their own currency face no practical budget constraints (Wray, 2015; Kelton, 2020). The government has the authority and the monopoly to print money that could be used to finance its local currency public budget. According to this line of reasoning, government spending is not constrained by public revenues; instead, public revenue rises with the tax base as the deficit-fuelled fiscal expansion has a multiplying effect on economic activity. Therefore, in a given crisis, such as the Great Recession or the COVID-19 pandemic, the state should run highly expansive fiscal policies, regardless of large deficits. Thereby, the government can increase social spending, invest in infrastructure or – as was lately discussed in

US politics – finance a New Green Deal. The multiplier effect will ensure, so the argument goes, that the government can create substantial wealth in this manner without distorting the economy. And from a financial perspective there is no risk, since the fiscal expansion will pay for itself, and to the extent that these is a residual public debt, it is of no concern as long as the debt is in the local currency. From a monetary policy perspective, one could even use MMT to justify so-called helicopter money, the direct transfer of money to every citizen.

Instead of a crowding out of private investments by government borrowing, the proponents expect a crowding in of private investment. The limit to this beneficial public intervention is only reached when the economy's productive capacity is fully utilised and the country is in a state of full employment. Such limits are of no practical concern to MMT theorists under current circumstances, and in any event they are confident that the expansionary fiscal and monetary policies could easily be turned off should a full recovery be attained.

Nor do MMT theorists share the concern about potential inflation emerging from the expansionary monetary policy, especially the expansion of central bank reserves to finance public debt. These theorists have a different theory of inflation derived from post-Keynesian cost-push arguments, and the remedy for cost push inflation might be found in wage and price controls. Curbing monetary growth to contain inflation pressure has little role in this view.

Where the institutional perspective of the central bank is concerned, MMT arrives at an ironic inversion of an old Milton Friedman argument (Friedman, 1962). As in Friedman's work, the argument is that the central bank is part of the consolidated public sector and cannot be treated as an independent institution. It is the balance sheet of the central bank with its monopoly power to create local currency reserves at its discretion that renders the central bank part of the public sector. Later in his career, Friedman argued that this required a strict rule for the annual expansion of the central bank's balance sheet, to provide inter alia an effective limit to the potentially inflationary expansion of fiscal expenditure. In this way, his programme for monetary and fiscal policy delivered macroeconomic stability, low inflation and sound public finance.

In his earlier 'A Monetary and Fiscal Framework for Economic Stability', Friedman (1948) argued in the opposite direction that an annual rule for the national budget was required and that the monetary authorities had to accommodate the associated deficit. Like the younger Friedman, theorists in the MMT paradigm assign the leading role in stabilisation policy to fiscal policy: fiscal policy has the obligation to respond vigorously with expansionary expenditure to any downswing in economic activity. Monetary policy has the obligation to accommodate the fiscal expansion with a combination of lower policy interest rates – even maintaining the ZLB in difficult circumstances – and the use of the central bank's balance sheet to purchase the resulting public debt.

Proponents of MMT admit that there are limits to the expansionary capacity of fiscal policy, limits defined by the full utilisation of resources in the economy and perhaps by the willingness of the public to hold the locally issued currency. The latter receives less attention in this literature, but is of substantial importance given the known effect that higher inflation encourages the local population to hold either alternative money (e.g. foreign currency) or alternative assets to mitigate the inflationary effect on their wealth.

When judged by academic standards, these arguments are not developed to the same degree of rigour we see elsewhere in Macroeconomics and some, for example Mankiw (2020), have portrayed this as a rhetorical device to paper over the weaknesses of the approach. One may conclude that MMT is not modern at all, and it is neither about money nor about theory. It has a mainly political thrust, which has already lost part of it appeal against the background of rising inflation, in particular in the United States from the second half of 2021.

7.2.2 Secular Stagnation and the Savings Glut

A second paradigm with implications for the role central banks play in the policy mix of modern economies derives from an empirical observation of a perceived long-run decline in aggregate demand and nominal interest rates. This approach is, appropriately, referred to as secular stagnation (Summers, 2015) and is regularly discussed in association with another phenomenon observed in the past two decades, namely the so-called savings glut (Bernanke, 2005).

As is clear from the terminology, secular stagnation refers to a trend that unfolds over a long horizon than typically associated with the business cycle. This trend emerges from several deep causes that operate over the long run, such as: demographic transitions, the technology and productivity cycle, and rising inequality especially in Western countries. The demographic transition of developed countries, with longer life expectancy, lower birth rates and an ageing population can in its advanced stages lead to a decline in aggregate demand. This slowdown could lead to slower investment growth as well, lowering the economy's long-run growth potential.

Similar factors could contribute to a savings glut. Households in an ageing Western population have to save more to provide for their extended retirement, while the state cannot provide the same on the basis of a pay-as-you go public pension scheme precisely owing to the ageing population. This trend increases the demand for safe assets and reduces their nominal yield. To these developments we can add the rising inequality in Western countries, which exacerbates the savings glut, as savings are rising with income and wealth.[3] Together, the demographic transition and the savings glut can lead to a low growth low nominal yield economy, that is, an economy at risk of falling into a liquidity trap. Paul Krugman (1998) used this lens to analyse the economic stagnation and low yield environment in Japan during the 1990s.

---

[3] Interestingly, the proponents of the secular stagnation hypotheses and the consequent policy reaction do not see the potential of low interest rate policy to increase this inequality.

The stagnation may well be caused by other factors that are related to the supply side of the economy (Gordon, 2015). He argues that US-productivity decline has its causes in a stagnating productivity development in office jobs and retailing, in a lack of education in the population and declining business dynamics. These reasons hint to an institutional problem – the regulatory environment seems to discourage productive investment.

If this is correct, the policy approach that can mitigate secular stagnation is straightforward (Summers, 2015): the first best option is structural reforms to increase the productivity of the economy, which would raise demand and solve the problem. Indeed, given the enormous shortage of capital, one wonders why aggregate demand should be so low. Summers argues, however, that structural reforms are difficult to pursue politically. A second suggestion is to boost investment, either by incentivising private investments or increasing public investment (or both). As a consequence, so the argument goes, the state should run large deficits for a long time to make up for the decreased private demand.

The secular stagnation hypothesis argues that interest rates have been falling to historically low levels since the 1980s. Recent work by Barry Eichengreen undermines this hypothesis. He shows that in the historical context (since 1800) nominal interest rates in the United States were particularly high in the 1980s and fell back to historically typical levels thereafter (Eichengreen, 2015). So the claim of a secular trend of declining interest rates is doubtful. In a current paper, Bianchi et al. (2022) argue that the declining real interest rates since the 1980s can be explained with monetary policy to about two-thirds.

7.2.3 Lessons from the New Paradigms

MMT and the secular stagnation hypothesis have in common their case in favour of large public sector deficits, with little or no inflationary cost. Whereas MMT proponents see deficits as beneficial in principle, advocates of secular stagnation see public spending as a rather unpleasant necessity. In both cases, though, the central bank's powerful balance sheet is required to help finance the resulting public sector debt.

In the case of MMT, central banks are in the centre of the policy. They expand their balance sheet and lend the money directly to the Treasury. If both Treasury and the central bank are understood to be part of the consolidated public sector, there is no net burden on the state, since the government just owes money to itself.

Central banks can use a second way to support the Treasury – even without purchasing government bonds – by reducing the policy interest rate to zero, or perhaps even into negative territory. In this case, the government is able to reduce the savings glut via deficit spending without incurring a high interest bill in the transaction. Some economists, including Willem Buiter or Kenneth Rogoff, have argued that central banks should move below the ZLB since an interest rate of –3 per cent or lower would discourage savings and increase borrowing and spending. Negative nominal interest rates create a new set of difficulties in an economy, though, one of which is the risk disintermediation from banks. To prevent the latter, the proponents of negative nominal interest rates often add the requirement to move to a cashless economy (*The Economist*, 2020).[4]

These policy recommendations are not particularly novel. They have been around for many decades and have been part of the literature that argues for broader policy objectives to be set for monetary policy, instead of a narrow focus on low and stable inflation. Although the sequence of two severe worldwide economic crises in less than fifteen years is new and unprecedented, the nature of these problems is not so new.[5] The world has experienced a number of financial crises and negative demand as well as supply shocks before.

---

[4] However, in a recent paper, Ulate (2021) argues that the effectiveness of negative interest rates the economy is lower than that of positive rates. Against the background of the rising inflation after 2021, this proposal has lost its appeal.

[5] The EUROZONE experienced at least three crises; if we include the migration crisis, we may even count four.

A bold fiscal stimulus as a response to a crisis is also not new. What is new is the emergence of a combined supply and demand shock in early 2020 as well as the severity of the crisis. In response, it was noticeable that many highly reputed mainstream economists seemed to abandon a rules-based framework for macroeconomic policies. In light of this departure, is necessary to investigate the merits of these policy recommendations more closely.

7.3 THE RISKS OF RENEWED FISCAL ACTIVISM AND MONETARY ACCOMMODATION

Both lines of argument as well as the policy conclusions have attracted much attention after the Great Recession, the interest being intensified after the beginning of the COVID-19 crisis. Whereas MMT has become very popular in political circles, its reception amongst economists has been more frosty. On the other hand, the secular stagnation hypothesis has long since enjoyed greater respectability among economists, though there are many voices critical of the consequences of increasing public debt, low interest rates and the implied diminution of CBI.

In this section, we summarise the criticism and potential drawbacks of the policy suggestions based on MMT and the secular stagnation hypothesis, and come to a conclusion with respect to our core topic: CBI. Will these theories render CBI obsolete? We use theoretical reasoning, empirical evidence and political economy arguments to understand the intended and unintended consequences of the suggested policy programmes.

7.3.1 Inflationary Risk

The risk of inflation is a basic argument against financing public debt via the central bank's balance (see also Chapter 2). As mentioned earlier, MMT advocates argue that inflation in advanced economies is not a monetary phenomenon, but is regularly driven by a cost push. If inflation is a cost-push phenomenon, so the argument goes, then monetary policy is the wrong instrument to combat the pathology.

A seemingly obvious policy response to a cost-push inflation has always been wage and price controls. Apart from the fact that price controls are not in line with a liberal market economy and will cause much resistance in the business community, the allocative distortions may be enormous. Price controls dampen investments and thus may lead to shortages in downstream industries. This may lead to even higher job-losses (or fewer new jobs), initiating a vicious cycle.

It is not disputed that price shocks on the supply side of the economy can feed the process of inflation expectations. However, those shocks are by definition relative price shocks, and can only enter the process of inflation when they raise expected future inflation. This cost-push model of inflation is not consistent with the modern literature on the process of inflation. Apart from its inadequacy as a theory of inflation, the cost-push model creates the impression that fiscal stimulus financed by monetary expansion holds no inflationary risk. This is incorrect for, at least, two reasons.

First, the theory is based on the existence of chronically under-utilised capacity in the economy. As long as capacity is under-utilised and labour is unemployed to a large extent, an additional monetary injection leading to higher purchasing power of the government may indeed not end in inflation. This at least holds if the government exactly demands those goods that can be produced with additional labour and idle capacity. In this case, inflation is not very probable.

However, these assumptions are unlikely to describe the relevant circumstances in an economy. Increasing aggregate demand may well fail to employ the idle capacity owing to structural mismatches.[6] In this case, additional public spending will lead to a boom in a few sectors where prices increase, which leads to strained capacity and inflationary pressure in downstream industries. This is not implausible as public demand programmes often address construction services. If the industry is already operating at stretched or even

---

[6] It may also have other problems: see Sections 7.3.2 and 7.3.3.

full capacity, prices will increase. In addition, the price increases crowd out private businesses and may rather cost jobs – crowding in is unrealistic in this scenario. Thus, we see a negative side effect: other than expected additional jobs will not be created in the short run by this demand-side policy.

Second, the Cambridge-equation still holds. The question then is whether the purchase of public bonds by the central bank will result in an increase in broad money (including credit) beyond the central bank's balance sheet, which is sufficient to trigger inflation. This logic is known to MMT proponents, but mostly ignored. The process of money creation and the contribution of public debt to it in practice is quite complicated and should not be overlooked when proposing monetary budget financing (Coats, 2019). MMT in advanced economies may avoid hyperinflation, but already inflation rates between 5 and 10 per cent may cause significant welfare losses and reduce economic growth (Barro, 1995).

Sebastian Edwards argues in exactly that direction. He shows that in Latin America throughout the 1960s, 1970s and 1980s, populist government pursued monetary policy as suggested by MMT. The state ran large budget deficits and financed these with the printing press. As a consequence, Latin America became known as the world's most inflation-ridden continent, with disastrous consequences for economic and social development (Freytag, 2002; Edwards, 2019). The legacy of high inflation in Latin. America cast a long shadow over the economic development of that continent.

An additional threat stems from the political consequences of the secular stagnation hypothesis. If the central bank – as demanded by the proponents of this concept – reduces interest rates and keeps them artificially low, the real interest becomes and stays negative. This is called financial repression. Krueger states that the United States in the period directly after the Second World War reduced its debt burden relative to GDP with the help of substantial financial repression (Krueger, 2020). She argues that the level of public debt in the United States in mid-2020 poses the threat of a new period of financial repression. Its consequences are distributional – the debtor is favoured over the creditor – but also allocational, since financial depression reduces economic growth. The risk of higher inflation through a permissive monetary policy to finance huge public spending as conducted by the Fed and the ECB after the COVID-19 crisis has become obvious in the course of 2021, when inflation rates in the United States and the EMU hit 7 and 5 per cent respectively.

7.3.2   The Risk of a Zombie Economy and Repressed Structural Change

Very low, even negative policy interest rates, have been widely encouraged since the GFC and widely implemented. These decisions imply a number of the following risks.

First, both zero interest rates and an extensive role for government in totally economic activity increase the risk of distorting economic development and repressing structural change. The macroeconomic perspective on both issues may well lead to a misconception, namely that cheaper credit or higher public spending will benefit the economy neutrally. This is highly unrealistic. Low interest rates may prolong the life of unfit enterprises and harm fit ones (Banerjee and Hofmann, 2018). By the same token, public demand may support certain sectors at the expense of others. If we additionally consider the structure of subsidies and protection in advanced economies, we can observe that mostly old and relatively unproductive industries are supported, whereas new and promising as well as successful industries are neglected (e.g. Baldwin and Robert-Nicoud, 2007). They may even suffer from the support of the laggards because they have to pay taxes, at least if governments do not completely rely on seigniorage.

Second, the lower the interest rate, the less chance investors have to distinguish between good and bad risks, between promising and risky investment opportunities. A relatively high interest rate with a functioning yield curve (i.e. with higher long-run than short run interest) also allows an adequate interest rate spread between good and bad risks. With zero interest or even with negative interest, every investment project appears similarly attractive.

Third, with low or zero interest, banks cannot generate profits with the traditional business case of borrowing from savers with positive but lower interest rates and lend to investors or house owners with a significant higher interest rate. This argument particularly applies to traditional banks, not to investment banks. It may take some time until this problem becomes obvious (Schnabl, 2017). Since banks in the Western world operate in an oligopoly, their profits can shrink without their going bankrupt. Nevertheless, the reduction of profits through interest rate differences for borrowers and savers may have strong negative consequences for structural change in an economy. It may prove to be too risky for banks to finance young enterprises without a track record. Instead, the banks tend to prolong credit to old enterprises that otherwise would leave the market – structural change in the economy is repressed, and productivity growth slows down. The economy becomes a zombie economy. This argument may even lead to a reversed causality: zero or negative interest policy reduces the productivity further.

Japan is a case in point. The downturn of the economy began in the 1980s, when observers in the West were still afraid of Japanese superiority. Regulation, protection of old and powerful industries and an unfavourable mix of monetary and fiscal policies producing too little inflation and maintaining unproductive economic structures (Hoshi and Kashyap, 2011; Shimizu, 2019) led to a long-term decline in interest rates. As a result, public debt reached record-levels and the zombification of the economy proceeded (Caballero et al., 2008). This could be shown at plant level (Kwon et al., 2015) as well as for small and medium-sized enterprises (Imai, 2016). Since the early 1990s, Japan has struggled with this phenomenon. It needs urgent structural reform that stops protection and regulation that favours unproductive industries (Hoshi and Kashyap, 2011).

However, not only in Japan, but also in other advanced economies, low interest rates are allowing governments to borrow enough funds to substitute for economic reform that enables the economy to raise productivity growth. Such reforms normally need time to develop their positive effect. Directly after the reform starts, the economy will be worse off, since unproductive enterprises are no longer subsidised and firms dismiss unproductive workers formerly protected by labour market regulations. Unemployment increases in the short run. Only in the medium to long run do the intended effects – new firms, new jobs, higher productivity – unfold; economists speak of a J-curve over time (Cooper and Williamson, 1994). The time until the positive effects unfold may be so long that governments cannot claim success before the next election. Thus, economic reforms are politically unattractive. Instead, governments can use the debt to pay for social programmes or other subsidies, keeping uncompetitive firms in the market, and thereby rescuing unproductive jobs. This substitution process leads to economic sclerosis (Olson, 1982), but raises the chance of a government staying in office after the next election.

Another practical example of the risks of low interest rates is the run up to the GFC. From the dotcom bubble to the advent of the GFC, the Federal Reserve Board kept the Fedfunds rate lower than would have been suggested by the policy rule that describes the Fed's own behaviours since the late 1970s. This argument was articulated most clearly by John Taylor (2009), whose analysis showed the connection between this overly accommodating monetary policy and the rise in US house prices that played a major role in creating the circumstances for the GFC. Low interest rates also contributed to risks within the international banking sector itself, including encouraging banks to pursue high yielding and higher risk investments (notably equity investment) while, at the same time, inflating the value of assets held by banks that presented their balance sheets as safe, despite the implied interest rate risk (Gambacorta, 2009; Adrian and Shin, 2010).

Central banks are aware of this problem, as the example of the ECB shows. Mario Draghi, in his capacity as CEO of the ECB, constantly reminded the governments in the EUROZONE of the necessity to reform the economies structurally; he used almost all his press conferences for a reminder. He argued that a flexible economy can much more easily react to an economic crisis (Draghi, 2017). Consequently, the ECB understood its rescue packages including the PSPP after the Eurocrisis as buying the governments time for reform. Indeed, there are examples of EUROZONE members reforming their economic policies (Rieth and Wittich, 2020), in particular Ireland, Spain and Portugal, and to a lesser extent Greece. Other countries such as France and Italy, partly also Germany, have missed this opportunity to initiate structural reforms of their labour market, bureaucratic burdens and tax reforms so far.

However, it may be doubted that a too accommodative monetary policy, that is a monetary policy that allows governments to buy political support via generous lending to governments, puts enough pressure on governments to reform. The cases of reform mentioned here all were cases in dire need. A the political economy also shows, the probability of reforms increases with a dire economic situation – this has been labelled pathological learning (Freytag and Renaud, 2007). Cheap credit moves countries away from the political need to apply unpleasant reform measures and reduces the likelihood of much-needed structural reform.

7.3.3 The Risk of the State as Entrepreneur

The sort of zombie economy described here has another problematic aspect. If the average productivity of the economy declines in the course of the low interest rate policy in combination with expanding public demand, this also means that technological and economic transformation of the kind needed in the early twenty-first century will be hampered.

To overcome the negative consequences of the COVID-19 crisis and to master the challenges of climate change and the need for further digitalisation, many innovative processes are needed. New climate-friendly technologies as well as digital business solutions, and also solutions in medicine, education and other sectors are best developed in a competitive environment with creative entrepreneurs. If the mix of monetary and fiscal policy disincentivises private entrepreneurs, more state activity is needed – either to subsidise private enterprises or to run state-owned enterprises (SOEs).

Both avenues are much less promising than a competitive and thriving private new-tech/high-tech industry undistorted by state interventions (other than pro-competition measures). Subsidies are very rarely granted to the most promising enterprises (see earlier comments). The rent-seeking process invited by subsidy schemes normally leads to a sort of adverse selection in that the least productive enterprises are most successful in winning subsidies. Moreover, subsidies are regularly in conflict with international rules, and the mix of monetary and fiscal policies advocated by MMT and secular stagnation proponents risks further distortion of an already shaky global trade order.

In addition, the state's capacity to be an innovative and unconventional entrepreneur can be doubted, as too many bureaucratic processes may hinder a state-owned would-be start-up. The problem is not simply the typically bureaucratic nature of the public sector but the lack of feedback via the system of profit and loss that is especially crucial in early stage start-up firms. Empirical evidence suggests that SOEs are less successful than their private competitors, at least on average (Mueller, 2003, pp. 373–380). Return on investment is larger in private business; resources are used more efficiently. There is also the logic that governments as owners of large-scale enterprises such as utilities may even invest more in R&D than comparable private enterprises; the question of whether the efficiency of these investments is higher remains.

In sum, the policy mix suggested by MMT and the secular stagnation hypothesis bear the risk that SOEs replace private enterprises in dynamic markets. This does not reflect an optimal division of labour between the state and the private sector. As a consequence, productivity growth may decline further – even in comparison with the problems of the zombie economy.

7.3.4   The Risk to Old-Age Protection
and Distributional Problems

Zero interest rates render savings less attractive and boost consumption – this is the explicit theoretical plan of their proponents. This holds particularly in ageing societies, such as Japan, where secular stagnation is a real problem. However, this mix may present some serious problems for savers who want to protect against income losses towards the end of their working life through private savings.

Low interest rates are adverse for savers, in particular those savers that are interested in safe investment. One may argue, as often done by central bankers, that there is no right of positive interest rates and that real interests have been negative regularly in history. Nevertheless, psychologically a positive and varying (with risk) interest rate might give savers a better feeling. In addition, there is a harder argument. Savers with small incomes are not able to diversify their savings – and thereby increase their potential return on investment by choosing riskier assets. They may also not be able to invest in those assets that will be potentially in demand, such as real estate. They might also save in cash, which increases the personal risk for those keeping the cash at home and leads to policy recommendations such as the suggestion to abolish highly denominated banknotes (*The Economist*, 2020).

A policy of sustained low interest rates risks exacerbating the skewed distribution of wealth (Hoffmann and Schnabl, 2016). Apart from different investment opportunities for small income receivers as compared with high income earners, asset prices add to this picture. Those with a substantial portfolio of financial (or non-financial) assets may not be hurt by low interest rates, but even benefit. As a vignette, one may point to the boom in the market for superyachts in the wake of the COVID-19 pandemic (Dempsey, 2021). It is not clear yet to what extent low interest rate policies are stimulating demand for existing assets such as shares or real estate. It is clear that stock prices quickly recovered after all the crises considered here; it is also obvious that house and other real estate prices also recovered quickly or have starting rising sharply in other countries, an example being Germany. Consequently, rents for flats and houses also have risen, at least in Germany. It would be naïve to dismiss the role of monetary policy in these price increases completely.

7.3.5 Interim Conclusion: MMT and Secular Stagnation Pose Risks to Central Bank Independence

We have already indicated the reasons to be sceptical about the case made for renewed fiscal and monetary activism by MMT and the secular stagnation paradigm. Even if the objectives of inflation-free sustainable growth are met to a certain extent, which is rarely the case, the side effects may be substantial: inflation, zombification, increasing state intervention in the economy, gaps in old age protection and unfavourable redistribution. In some quarters, the word 'stagflation' has been whispered (*The Economist*, 2020).

Another side effect affects central banks themselves. It has become clear that the potential risks of the new economic thinking are high. These risks are mostly of a political or rather political economy nature. Central banks lose degrees of freedom to pursue monetary policy according to their own judgement. Both MMT and the secular stagnation hypothesis interpret central banks as a crucial part of, but not independent from the government. MMT does so explicitly by asking for the printing press as source of taxes, whereas the proponents of the secular stagnation hypothesis argue implicitly by demanding low costs of borrowing for governments.

This interpretation does not deny an important role of central banks in economic policy, but does not see CBI as important because its proponents do not see the trade-off between price stability and other objectives, as laid out in Chapter 3. This interpretation has been questioned earlier in this chapter. The following section discusses the emerging threat to CBI in many countries from a broad political economy perspective. We also have to acknowledge that this threat is not based on academic exercises, but on serious political thinking backed by academic exercises: it is much more real than an academic discussion.

7.4 CBI RECONSIDERED IN AN OLSONIAN SETTING: AN ALTERNATIVE INTERPRETATION

7.4.1 *The Basic Hypothesis*

This chapter so far has shed light on the major current economic problems in most advanced economies as well as on prominent theoretical approaches to solve the current problems. Until the recent resurgence of inflation in the developed world – in late 2022 at its highest level since the early 1970s in the United States and since the Second World War in Europe – policymakers were not overly concerned with inflation, but rather focussed on financial stability, employment, growth and fiscal stability. That said, it is also evident that in a traditional policy assignment with clearly defined responsibilities in a rule-bound policy framework, the central bank would only play a minor role in supporting other government agencies in their efforts to solve a crisis.

However, central banks have moved to the centre of political action after the Great Recession and have remained there since. As seen in Chapter 6, central banks have taken bold measures to expand their balance sheets to fight the different crises. The hypothesis presented here claims that we are in a 'new era of economics' (*The Economist*, 2020, p. 13), which renders traditional mainstream or orthodox economic policy models obsolete and calls for a new policy model, which gives more weight to the state and uses monetary policy more aggressively. CBI becomes obsolete in this policy model. The renowned Monetary Economist Charles Goodhart observed the same trend more than a decade ago, in the immediate aftermath of the GFC, in his words: 'But the range and scale of interaction [by the central bank] with government, on the bank tax, on regulation and sanctions, on debt management and on bank resolution, is likely to increase. The idea of the central bank as an independent institution will be put aside' (Goodhart, 2011, p. 154).

This section offers an alternative interpretation and hypothesis, based on political economy reasoning and arguing in an Olsonian setting of societies displaying signs of economic sclerosis (Olson, 1982). From this perspective, the intensive involvement of central banks in economic policies – the proliferation of tasks – is due to structural changes and challenges in the world economy that overburden democratically elected and responsible governments. Instead of taking the necessary and potentially bold structural measures, which will definitely cause some temporary frictions and endanger economic rents and social positions, governments prefer an easier option, which in turn is less likely to cost votes on election day. This easy option is to take recourse in the balance of the central bank and public debt. Consequently, central banks have become central to a larger discussion about economic reform.

This strategy may save governments from being punished by voters in the short term, but will probably not address underlying structural challenges in the long term. Easy policy options do not solve the underlying problems, but rather increase them and postpone a solution. As a side effect, populist politicians with even simpler policy options may emerge (Hoffmann and Schnabl, 2016). That said, our hypothesis also claims that there is no 'New era of economics'; rather it seems as if the current situation calls for a return to rule-based policies and to a definite policy assignment.

7.4.2   The Underlying Structural Challenges

The existence of structural change is not a new phenomenon; it is also not restricted to international relations. It is a permanent feature of modern economies. Their ability to cushion the consequences is often impressive. Old firms go bankrupt; new companies emerge and hire the abundant labour and capital. Social policies are used to help those who (temporarily) lose their jobs and have difficulties in finding a new position shortly. Lifelong learning enables people to adjust to new challenges. In such a situation, monetary policy indeed focusses on price stability and can act independently from daily politics. However, it seems that since the end of the Cold War, the speed and intensity of structural change has increased. Several aspects are relevant.[7]

- First, we witness the ascent of so-called emerging economies (EMEs), above all China. Former developing countries integrate themselves into the global economy, industrialise, catch up and offer fierce competition for established enterprises in the OECD. The governments of EMEs also develop a sense of their own relevance, and challenge the world order and their main actors. Their emergence is also associated with major geopolitical changes.
- Second, the decline of transportation and communication costs as the result of a combination of technological advancements and political liberalisation measures has also contributed to fierce global competition, resulting in the emergence of GVCs.
- Third, the social impacts of this globalisation were underestimated in many advanced countries until the GFC hit them. In the United States, for instance, the industrial base has been shrinking since the 1970s, leaving more and more members of the middle-class behind. In a nutshell, globalisation has reinforced structural changes leading to social problems in the longer run, which have been hidden under the undeniable benefits of a deeper integration.
- Fourth, digitalisation requires new business models and new policy concepts in both the economic and political sphere. Many observers fear that the fourth industrial revolution will disrupt the labour markets in advanced economies enormously, leaving millions of people jobless (Baldwin, 2019). However, at the same time, many new job opportunities emerge from this trend; history suggests that the net effect is positive.
- Fifth, the challenge of climate change is becoming increasingly visible. Many governments have too long ignored the problem and pursued policies that would rather speed up climate change, for example, fossil fuel subsidies for the rural population. A serious climate policy will necessarily lead to increasing costs for mobility and energy, at least in the short run. Governments have recently been starting to acknowledge the need for transformation, and plan huge spending programmes (European Commission, 2019).

[7] The order of these challenges does not imply a ranking in terms of urgency.

- Sixth, the recent sequence of crises has disturbed the world order both politically and economically. The Great Recession has led to huge spending programmes and a proliferation of protectionist measures. In Europe, the Eurocrisis followed suit, obviously fostered by the Great Recession, but still an independent crisis, caused by a lack of fiscal austerity that would have been necessary for a smooth interaction of national economic policies with a common monetary policy. The COVID-19 crisis added another serious demand and supply shock, leading again to a nationalisation of economic policies and the demand for high public spending to rescue large parts of the business communities in advanced and developing countries. Similarly, Russian aggression in Ukraine has led indirectly to significantly higher energy prices as well as food and fertiliser shortages, which has fuelled inflation and reduced growth further.[8]

All these factors contribute to faster and deeper structural changes. Jobs have been lost and will continue to be under threat. Knowledge will be written off ever faster, so it seems. People will have to learn and adjust their whole lives. This poses a threat to those who may overlook the complexity and interplay of various factors. They expect governments to deal with the situation and are probably not patient when it comes to accepting the adjustment processes needed. They may also ask for simple solutions.

In sum, these challenges demand efforts in different policy spheres. They also have in common that the necessary policy measures will not be easily digested by society, since they may lead to the erosion of rents for established sectors and firms, and cause further job losses in the short term (the J-curve). However, they are not exclusively responsible for the awkward political situation many governments find themselves confronted with, which is responsible for the grip on monetary policy in many countries. There is also the investment gap in many countries, which seemingly demands more public debt and monetary expansion.

---

[8] At the time of writing (late 2022), the consequences of the COVID-19 crisis and the Russian aggression could not be seen in their totality. See also Section 7.5.

7.4.3   Low Investment as a Supply-Side Problem

The secular stagnation hypothesis claims that investment is low because of a mix of demand side factors, intensified by a global savings glut (Summers, 2015). As a consequence, low interest rates are suggested to encourage investment. The alternative explanation is that supply-side factors rather than a demand gap are responsible for the moderate investment activity in advanced economies (Gordon, 2015). In addition, without supply-side restrictions one would expect high demand for capital and thus returns on investment in developing countries with low capital abundance. We will take a closer look at this hypothesis.

When analysing the capital stock across different countries in the world, it is obvious that many parts of the world are in dire need of capital – be it public or private. Public capital includes infrastructure such as roads, harbours, airports, electricity and water networks, hospitals, schools and universities. These gaps are not limited to developing countries, although they come to mind first. But also in developed countries, physical infrastructure is either in bad shape or lacking. This is a fundamental gap, as it is an obstacle to private business success. Thus, one gets the impression that there should be high demand for public investment all over the world. In addition, private investments are also not sufficient to employ the youth cohort. This is the case in Southern Europe as well as in many developing and emerging countries with high population growth, which need private investment to employ the younger cohorts.

In 2020, the COVID-19 crisis had a negative impact on investment. Transnational private investments (FDI) went down by 42 per cent when compared with 2019.[9] It seems highly implausible that these investments are repressed because of too high interest rates. If there is a savings glut, a statement not every observer subscribes to

---

[9] See UNCTAD (2021), Global Foreign Direct Investment Fell by 42 per cent in 2020 – Outlook Remains Weak, https://unctad.org/news/global-foreign-direct-investment-fell-42-2020-outlook-remains-weak, 24 January 2021, retrieved 16 March 2021.

(see earlier comments and Eichengreen, 2015), these savings should almost by themselves find investors, as the interest rate would be low anyway. In addition, the last decade witnessed central banks moving towards ZLB or even below. Nevertheless, the investment gap does not close. The explanation for the investment gap seems to be different from the savings glut hypothesis, at least regarding the gap before COVID-19.[10] It is not a lack of demand, which needs fresh money in public accounts to be compensated for. Rather it seems that investment conditions are unfavourable. Partly, such unfavourable conditions may be explained with low productivity. However, there is undeniable need for people in developing countries to have access to electricity or water, to mobility and schooling. There is also an unquestionable extra cost factor for industrial countries if the highways are in a poor state, so that traffic jams prevent the fast transport of goods, or if the digital network is too slow.

This raises two questions: first, who is responsible for poor roads, a lack of electricity grids or outdated digital networks? Second, what can central banks do to close the gap? The first question can be answered easily. It is the government of the country or state that is responsible. It is a political decision to invest in electricity grids, digital networks or roads. To put it differently, the same factors that slow down political responses to the structural challenges discussed in Section 7.4.2 prevent satisfactory investment conditions. The second question can be answered similarly quickly. Central banks can provide credit to governments or care for financial and price stability; they cannot make the investment. The answer to this question is even clearer when private investments are considered. Central banks can provide banks with base money; the banks then grant credit to investors. If investors do not seize chances, a central bank cannot be blamed. That said, we must look at supply-side conditions in the economy and analyse political obstacles. This requires an

---

[10] Investment prevented by COVID-19 will have to be tackled with one-time rescue measures rather than long-term supply-side policies.

institutional economic analysis and a political economy perspective, as bureaucratic hurdles often prevent investments.[11]

7.4.4 Climate Change and the Central Bank

In 2019, another discussion about the role of central banks emerged in the context of climate change. This discussion takes place in parallel with the discussion of green and social taxonomy. Governments can use this taxonomy to force banks and other financial institutions to invest in green technologies. Since the ECB has decided to purchase both government bonds and corporate bonds, it has been argued in Europe that the purchases of corporate bonds should concentrate on green bonds, that is, on companies that are active in the environmental sectors. While 'greening the economy' seems adequate against the background of the need to protect the climate and decarbonise the economy, it is highly questionable whether central banks should engage in this policy.

Central banks are not meant to pursue industrial policies. If they do, they move away from their mandate. With respect to their independence from daily politics, it is ambiguous. On the one hand, their power seems to increase with another policy objective, On the other hand, they give in to the wishes of governments with respect to certain political action. Probably even more problematic, the intervention by central banks into the bond market is not an effective climate policy measure.

According to the Tinbergen principle, this task should be assigned to a special organisation at the global level, since the climate is a global common. If the members of the Intergovernmental Panel on Climate Change agree on credible commitments, national policies must be implemented to secure that these commitments are

---

[11] It is beyond the scope of this section to give an overview of investment conditions of all countries, but a few hints may be sufficient to understand the responsibilities. In different publications by the World Bank, UNCTAD and the World Economic Forum, the causes for low investments are highlighted (World Economic Forum 2018, UNCTAD 2020, World Bank 2020). They place the responsibilities with governments and do not mention central banks.

met. If this works well, there will be structural change towards a rising number of 'green companies'. This again implies that the mixture of corporate bonds available for the ECB or the Fed becomes 'greener' over time without affirmative action from the ECB.

7.4.5 What Role for Central Banks? The ECB as an Example for Practical Implications

As already mentioned, it is often politically difficult to reform policies or reduce administrative burdens. Many countries, among them some in Europe, face an Olsonian type of sclerosis (Olson, 1982). Some European countries, for example France, Spain, Greece and Italy, face high youth unemployment; at the same time, labour market regulation is still rigid and protects insiders, which makes it difficult for youngsters to enter the labour market. Obviously, governments feel politically unable to perform the necessary reforms. In such circumstances, it seems much easier to call for higher budgets and pay for political support, for example through social spending and subsidies for green technologies. At this point, the central bank is required to step in.

However, there has to be a trigger for this mechanism to work; otherwise the political equilibrium, that is having an independent central bank with high reputation, is difficult to overthrow – think of Operation Goldfinger (Chapter 3). The sequence of crises offered a good opportunity. Urged by politicians, central banks all over the world responded to each crisis. In the instance of the GFC, they reduced interest rates, expanded the monetary base (QE), purchased government bonds (despite the prohibition of budget financing) and announced further measures (forward guiding). They may also have taken more responsibility for financial stability.

As a consequence, central banks are going through an interesting and ambiguous process. On the one hand, they seem more powerful, as they are in charge of addressing multiple policy problems. Instead of only being responsible for price stability, they are now supposed to consider employment, investments, public finances

and even the green transformation process when making policy decisions. Furthermore, the appearance of central bankers in the public
is very different than in the old days. Whereas the Bundesbank was
associated with its greyish buildings in Frankfurt until the 1990s,
and most Germans did not know the names of the members of the
Bundesbank council, this is very different today. The ECB resides in
a modern tower and its president is a public figure, as are the ECB's
counterparts at the Fed. Their speeches and press conferences are followed closely.

On the other hand, the decisions made by central bankers after
the Great Recession (and again after COVID-19) are driven by political pressure. As long as the official objective is not compromised
by their policies to address multiple objectives, they can convince
themselves and the public that their political independence is still
substantial and that they follow their mandate by supporting the government in their general economic policy. However, the litmus test
is a situation in which there is increasing inflation; this is the situation that emerged in the second half of 2021 and continued the following year. The response of central banks to these inflation rates in
more than a generation will test their independence severely.

The ECB is both a typical and a special case. It is typical
because many of the issues raised here can be seen in the practice
and discourse of European monetary policy. But the ECB is also special, as the relationship between the ECB and Treasury is different
from the situation in nation states; the ECB is confronted with many
Treasuries and is subject to those various interest groups. The ECB is
involved in distribution conflicts within the EU, which makes things
even more complicated than it is for other central banks. In some
twenty years of its existence, the ECB has experienced a substantial change of perspective on its working methods and has been challenged substantially by European Treasuries.

Before the ECB was founded, the issue of CBI was being heavily
debated in Europe, with at least two different positions towards
independence of central banks. Since its founding in 1957, the

Bundesbank had been perceived as the driving force of monetary policy in Europe, and was why the EMS worked. Elsewhere in Europe,
notably in France, this was sometimes perceived as imposing German
preferences on the other states. The French government, for example,
was unhappy with the stability oriented monetary policy, labelled as
'franc fort', adopted by the Bank of France as part of its commitment
to the EMS (Steuer, 1997). French top politicians consequently disap-
proved of an independent ECB. In addition, the French government
from the start of the EMU insisted that the first ECB president, Wim
Duisenberg, should step down 'voluntarily' after four (of officially
eight) years in office to give way for a French candidate; this eventually happened.

In Germany, the sentiment was exactly the opposite, with a
public convinced of the concept of CBI. The Bundesbank enjoyed a
very high reputation; the EMU was never understood as an economic
necessity, but rather as a political bargain. German observers were
afraid of a general European lack of stability culture (Steuer, 1997).
The founding of the EUROZONE was seen in some quarters as surrender, which raised the risk of accommodating monetary policy.

With the Maastricht Treaty, German monetary policy institutions were made standard in the EUROZONE. The ECB is among the
most independent central banks in the world. First, the entry standards were clearly defined with the Maastricht criteria. In the course
of the preparation for the EMU and in light of the discussion about
the weighing-in effect, that is, countries meeting the Maastricht standards prior to joining the EMU and thereafter neglecting them, the
SGP was introduced. This used the same criteria as the Maastricht
Treaty (preventive arm) and foresaw sanctions if governments repeatedly failed to meet these criteria (corrective arm).[12] In addition, price
stability was laid down as the main objective, and the ECB was not
allowed to lend money to governments. Governments themselves

---

[12] However, it was already then suspected that the need to use the corrective arms with
qualified majority in the Ecofin Council (consisting of the Ministers of Finance of the
EUROZONE) would politicise the process, which proved true in 2003.

were prohibited from lending money to each other (no bail-out clause, Art. 125, European Treaty). According to all measures of CBI (Section 3.5), the ECB is an independent central bank.

This institutional setting ameliorated public concerns in Germany, at least for a few years. However, scepticism did not disappear. Indeed, the launch of the EMU allowed the ECB to work unencumbered for only about five years. In November 2003, after being threatened with sanctions by the European Commission, France and Germany, with the support of other members, managed to avoid these sanctions in the Ecofin Council. As a consequence, the SGP was reformed, with a higher focus on the process of debt or deficit reduction than on numbers and on unforeseen shocks (Morris et al., 2006). This reform has weakened the SGP substantially.[13]

Nevertheless, in subsequent years and up to the Great Recession, the ECB worked smoothly with low inflation. Monetary policy in the EUROZONE was not a public issue; see Chapter 4. At the same time, budget deficits were moderate and the average debt stock in the EUROZONE fell, with Spain and Ireland being particularly successful with debt reduction. The Great Recession changed the situation dramatically. Owing to the subprime crisis, real estate prices in Spain, Ireland and other EMU members fell dramatically. Many banks were under pressure and had to be supported by the governments, with massive fiscal consequences. Still, the ECB played a minor role, and doubts about its independence did not emerge.

This changed with the so-called Eurocrisis, when the ECB engaged more actively in the support of financially fragile EMU member states. This crisis was not caused but triggered by the Great Recession. It was rooted in fiscal problems of the member countries, which emerged independently from the Great Recession. In 2009, Greece had to admit that its official numbers had been understating

---

[13] In October 2002, Romani Prodi, then President of the European Commission, called the SGP 'stupid and rigid' (Interview with *Le Monde*, 17 October 2002).

the debt level for many years. It subsequently became obvious that other members also lacked fiscal sustainability.

As a consequence, in May 2010, the European Council decided to bail out Greece; this was done with the support of the IMF and the ECB. This was only the beginning of a series of rescue packages for Greece. In order to structure these measures and take care of the threat of contagion, the EMU first introduced a temporary facility, the European Financial Stability Facility, which in 2012 was replaced by the permanent ESM, commanding roughly 700 billion Euros. Ireland, Portugal and Spain used this facility in the years after 2010.

The ECB has supported the rescue packages, first with a series of reductions in the interest rate on the MROs, starting in November 2011.[14] In September 2019, the MRO rate reached 0 per cent, the deposit facility went down to –0.5 per cent. During the last decade, the ECB consequently argued that it has acted within its mandate to ensure an inflation rate under but close to 2 per cent. It did not refer to the secular stagnation hypothesis of the MMT.

In July 2012, ECB President Mario Draghi announced that the ECB would do 'whatever it takes' to save the Euro. This was interpreted as a signal the ECB would buy public bonds almost infinitely. In December, the OMT programme was announced, but it was never activated. Since March 2015, the ECB has engaged in its PSPP and bought public bonds of the Eurozone members up to an amount of 60 billion Euros per month. The programme ended in January 2019, but was restarted in December 2019 when a recession was feared. To fight the COVID-19 crisis, the ECB installed its Pandemic Emergency Purchase Programme (PEPP) with total funds of 1,850 billion Euros.[15]

---

[14] Since late 2008, the ECB had reduced the MRO rate, but increased it shortly to 1.50 per cent in July 2011 (www.ecb.europa.eu/stats/policy_and_exchange_rates/key_ecb_interest_rates/html/index.en.html).

[15] See also Section 8.5. On the ECB's website, the programmes are shown: www.ecb.europa.eu/mopo/implement/pepp/html/index.en.html.

Third, the ECB has become an active part of the European System of Financial Supervision (ESFS);[16] it is responsible for 'significant credit institutions'. There are both arguments against and in favour of commissioning the central banks with the supervision and regulation of the domestic financial system. There are two arguments against such an arrangement. First, the central bank can face a conflict of interests if banks have liquidity problems. Adding liquidity to the system may rescue these banks. Second, if a financial institution fails, the central bank may receive bad publicity and lose reputation. The primary argument for an active role of the central bank is that co-ordination of monetary policy and prudential regulation will enhance efficiency. Second, central banks act as lender of last resort. Therefore, it makes sense that they regulate the financial system to recognise as well as to prevent a financial crisis as early as possible. In sum, it is not unusual and does not interfere with their policy independence if central banks take a leading role in the regulatory regime.

How does this affect our subject, CBI? Since the beginning of the Eurocrisis, there has been a controversial discussion in politics and the academic world about the legitimacy of the whole rescue programme including fiscal and monetary policies, which many observers interpreted as a breach of the European Treaty (Art. 125). The whole discussion is often misguided as it appears to be a discussion in favour of or against the EURO, or even the EU. This simplification does not do justice to the discussants and it also understates the complexity of the issue. It would be way too easy to dismiss criticism of the rescue packages as anti-European propaganda.

It is beyond the scope of this section to discuss this in detail. However, it can be argued that the traditional political positions of member countries and individuals are more or less reflected. On the one hand, voices from those countries that were sceptical about CBI from the beginning do not express concern and do not see the ECB

---

[16] Details about the ESFS can be found on the website of the European Parliament: www.europarl.europa.eu/factsheets/en/sheet/84/europaisches-system-der-finanzaufsicht-esfs.

as compromised through the policy measures taken since the beginning of the Eurocrisis. The ECB itself has repeatedly acknowledged that the Bundesbank and its president have opposed the PSPP, but otherwise they have mostly not participated in the discussions. An exception is a recent interview with a new member of the directorate, Isabel Schnabel, who has tried to delegitimise critics of the ECB by complaining about their 'narratives' (Horn, 2020).

On the other hand, voices mostly in Germany – including former members of the ECBs directorate – are very critical. Jürgen Stark, former chief economist of the ECB, has expressed his view that the ECB is financing government budgets and is therefore overstepping its mandate (Stark, 2020). Repeatedly, critics of the ECB have sued it at the German Constitutional Court of Justice (BVG). In May 2020, the BVG judged that the ECB is not financing government budgets, and is therefore not overstretching its mandate, but needs to be more transparent and accountable to national parliaments and governments, as its policies definitely affect other – domestic – economic policies, for instance old-age protection. This has been interpreted both as attacking the independence of the ECB (Bofinger et al., 2020) and strengthening it (Freytag, 2020). The public discussion about central banks often touches the topic of CBI.

7.5   MONETARY POLICY SINCE THE BEGINNING OF COVID-19: THE ECB AS EXAMPLE

The ECB faced a completely new challenge after the outbreak of COVID-19. This has been interpreted a s a combination of supply and demand shock for the world economy. States were in demand to quickly support citizens and businesses with huge sums. Central banks helped with freshly created base money and lent huge sums to governments, which according to a broad consensus among economists, including the authors of this book, was a necessity. The ECB initiated its PEPP in March 2020 to temporarily purchase private and public assets up to 1,850 billion EUROS. By February 2021, the ECB had purchased the sum of roughly 870 billion EUROS. By the end of

January 2023, it had become some 1,680 billion EUROS; in January 2023, the holdings were reduced by 3.5 billion EUROS.[17]

However, given the already large balance sheet of the ECB and other central banks, this policy made them vulnerable to huge increases in broad supply. Inflationary pressure rose. After the Russian invasion of Ukraine and the subsequent economic sanctions against Russia, energy prices went up sharply. Because of the war, the world's supply of cash crops plummeted as both Russia and Ukraine, traditionally large wheat exporters, were respectively unwilling and unable to export their wheat until late 2022. As a consequence, inflation rose in 2022: it hit 10 per cent in the EUROZONE and the United States by late 2022. In other countries, it was even higher: Argentina, with about 100 per cent inflation in early 2023, stood out again.

In Europe, central bankers were hesitant. By the end of 2021, inflation in the EURO area was below the ECB's 2 per cent target. That is why the policy was not ended even when the signs were already pointing to an increase in inflation rates. Well into the second half of 2021, leading ECB representatives were still claiming that deflation rather than inflation was looming. At the time, the directors could not have made this statement out of ignorance of the theoretical context, but because of political pressure.

In the course of the period of increasing inflation, the members of the ECB Board obviously changed their mind. The ECB changed its strategy well after the Fed, and began to raise key interest rates. In July 2022, all three interest rates used by the ECB were raised for the first time since 13 April 2011. These are the interest rates for the main refinancing operations, marginal lending facility and deposit facility. After that, there were only cuts until the last rate decision on 18 September 2019. Most recently, all three interest rates were increased by 50 basis points on 8 February; the interest rate for the main refinancing operations stood at 2.5 per cent.[18]

---

[17] See again www.ecb.europa.eu/mopo/implement/pepp/html/index.en.html, retrieved on 16 March 2021.

[18] On 8 February, the ECB announced another increase of 50 basis points in March.

This means that the so-called *Zeitenwende* (English: turn of the times) also arrived at the ECB. These interest rate steps since July 2022 can certainly be described as very drastic. Since its foundation, the ECB has increased the interest rate for its main refinancing operations only once by 0.75 per cent (on 1 January 1999) and three times by 50 basis points. Since September 2022, it has now done so twice by 0.75 per cent and three times by 0.5 per cent, namely from −0.5 to 2.5 per cent; the increases were identical for all three rates in each case but started at different levels.

The Interest rate steps have naturally triggered concerns in the real economy. In particular, they have made construction very expensive. In addition to building materials becoming more expensive owing to supply chain problems following the lockdowns related to the COVID-19 response, the cost of debt financing has also roughly quadrupled in a very short time. This is a hard blow to the industry and to builders, including governments. The latter are now paying considerably higher interest rates for borrowing on the capital market or from its principal banks.

And that is precisely why the ECB's interest rate policy for the first six months of 2022 is so astonishing and such good news at the same time. After all, the policy of the last few years has been very much geared to making life easier for finance ministers (mentioned earlier). To cope with the COVID-19 crisis, a permissive monetary policy was still understandable. In previous years, when the ECB tried to buy governments time for urgently needed supply-side policy reforms, which they let pass unused, the impression was that the ECB had given up some of its independence and had now become a recipient of instructions from finance ministers. In return, the ECB seemed to have been granted an increase in political importance, the sustainability of which would be doubtful (Section 9.2).

Therefore, it had to be feared that the ECB would give in to pressure from the finance ministries and lower the interest rate cuts. Of course, it is very difficult to precisely determine the optimal level of interest rate steps. In this respect, the statement is not correct in this absolute form; perhaps the ECB did indeed give in to the pressure and did not make even larger interest rate hikes.

However, the sequence of steps described here can truly be described as historic. Of course, the inflation of up to 10 per cent that had to be fought can also be described as historic. In Germany in particular, people have become accustomed to very low inflation rates since the second oil crisis in 1979/1980 at the latest. This is one of the reasons why criticism of the ECB has been particularly loud in that country. But what Otmar Issing, the former chief economist of the ECB, said in January 2023 in an interview is also worth considering.[19] Most of today's central bankers were too young to sense the real dangers of inflation, he said. They believed that the dangers of deflation were much greater.

A positive interpretation of the ECB's responses to the last two crises would argue that with the strong interest rate hikes in 2022, the ECB tried to regain the lost confidence of the markets and break inflation expectations. When this chapter was being written in the middle of 2022, it was still too early to pass final judgement on whether and to what extent the ECB succeeded in doing so. It was also not yet clear to what extent it will be able to regain its damaged independence, which politicians have by no means enthusiastically conceded to. But it can be said that it is on the right track.

7.6 INTERIM CONCLUSION: CBI AT RISK

Since the Great Recession, Treasuries in advanced economies have spent trillions of dollars or EUROS to combat the cascade of crises that hit them (and partly the rest of the world). In the course of this fight, central banks have had to use monetary policy in support. After governments successfully overcame the first crisis, monetary

---

[19] Otmar Issing in the *FAZ*, 8 January 2023: *'Ich bin von der EZB enttäuscht'*, www.faz
.net/aktuell/wirtschaft/ich-bin-von-der-ezb-enttaeuscht-18583123.html?premium.

policy did not return to its traditional path. It has remained expansionary, which is partly supported by new academic paradigms, such as MMT and the secular stagnation hypothesis, and partly forced by national governments eager to finance their new debts as cheaply as possible.

It was not just the role of central banks that changed; they also became much more prominent in the public eye than they were before. Up to the 1990s, except for politicians, bankers and academics, not many individuals knew the names of central bankers. But central bankers have become political superstars, culprits or even public enemies, depending on the perspective of the observer.

In any case, in the public perception, central banks seem to have gained power and importance. They have assumed responsibility for a number of policy objectives, which traditionally are in the realm of the Treasury, investment agencies, social partners and capital market participants. The public has paid increasing attention to statements of, for example, ECB Board members; they have become prominent public figures.

However, more power does not imply a higher CBI. The activities are driven by political actors who are unable or unwilling to take care of their main tasks. President Draghi's statement to do 'whatever it takes' was indeed an obvious appeal to policymakers to reform the supply side of the economy so that monetary policy could soon be 'normalised'. It remained unheard in the European political system. Moreover, central banks seem unable to concentrate on the main objective of central banking, as laid down in most central bank laws and statutes: price stability.

Therefore, we conclude that the independence of central banks in some advanced countries, for instance the United States, the United Kingdom, Japan and the EUROZONE, has come under threat in recent years. It appears, however, as if these central banks have risen to the challenge of high inflation in 2022. As we have tried to show in this chapter, this decline in independence and gain in public importance may have severe economic costs in the long run.

These risks suggest that the underlying political PAP is still relevant. Governments as agents of a population with limited information may exploit this asymmetric information to increase welfare in the short run, thereby increasing the chances of re-election, at the expense of long-run costs, which at the end of the day render short-term gains worthless. This danger is real and should encourage academics and policymakers to reconsider CBI and the conditions under which it can sustain and help governments to achieve welfare objectives, also in the short run.

8 Are Central Banks Too Independent?

CBI and Democracy after the Crises

8.1 INTRODUCTION: CENTRAL BANKERS UNDER POLITICAL PRESSURE

In Chapter 7, we discuss the economic and fiscal threats to CBI. These are based on two trends: first, the inability of governments to solve different crises without turning to central banks to support their expansive fiscal policies implied a proliferation of Central banks' objectives. Second, the intellectual foundation for this expanded mandate rests on two economic theories, one new and the other resurrected from an earlier era.

However, there is more criticism, which can be labelled the political dimension of threats to CBI. These political threats originate in both academic analysis and political action. The discussion about the increase in political power and medial visibility of central bankers has revived a discussion that was current in Political Science and to some extent also within the Economics literature during the late 1990s. In this debate, critics are concerned with the appropriateness of CBI at a fundamental level within a democracy, and refer to the so-called democratic deficit of an independent central bank (e.g. Briault et al., 1996). The tension between CBI and democratic governance is discussed in this chapter.

In addition to this discussion, and probably much more disconcerting for central banks and price stability than this academic dissent, is the real threat to the independence of central banks internationally. Both democratic and autocratic governments have put central bankers under pressure, and this has become more frequent and intensive since the Great Recession. For example, countries with large public debt and/or deficits have repeatedly pressured central banks to support these fiscal positions despite the central banks' official independence. More recently, democratic governments have aggressively attacked their central bankers, and these have often been populist attacks, whether from the right or the left. In 2019, President Trump asked rhetorically on Twitter: 'who is our bigger enemy, [Fed Chairperson] Jay Powell or [Chinese President] Chairman Xi'.

The first case to mention is Argentina, a country stricken with inflation since the early Peronist days after the Second World War. The country has not managed to avoid fiscal problems since then, and has regularly used the central bank to help out the government (Freytag, 2002). Despite this history, the presidential action during the debt crisis in early 2010 was unusual. The president urged the central bank to sell foreign reserves, which were held on an account at the Bank for International Settlement (BIS) in Basel, and thus by BIS statute protected from the government. When the president of the Argentine central bank, Martin Redrado, refused to do so, he was fired. Later, President Kirchner got her way (Freytag and Voll, 2010). Even for the country's standards, this was a particular strong neglect of the central bank's autonomy in a democracy. In similar style, President Erdoğan of Turkey appointed a compliant governor, Şahap Kavcıoğlu, to lead Turkey's central bank in the 2010s after inflation started to rise and the Turkish lira depreciated sharply. President Erdoğan nevertheless insisted on accommodating monetary policy with low interest ceilings. Several central bank CEOs were fired as they did not want to respond to these needs. The Turkish economy heavily suffered from these governmental interventions.

The Great Recession has encouraged governmental aggression towards central banks in other democracies too. President Trump hired Jerome Powell as the Fed's governor in 2018 as replacement for Janet Yellen, who had served one term quite successfully. The president obviously expected his candidate to be more accommodating, which the Fed mostly refused; it proceeded to raise interest rates four times until late 2018 under Governor Powell. President Trump frequently publicly complained about the governor in harsh words, even once calling him an enemy of America, and discussed the potential for firing him. The president's attempts to undermine the Fed's independence resulted in the nomination of a candidate for the Fed's Board of Governors who was heavily criticised as being ill suited for the position, but expressed views supporting the president (Tappe, 2020). This sort of criticism was almost unheard; it displayed a lack in confidence in the Fed and lack of respect for the institution of CBI.

Further examples can be found in the United Kingdom, this time not from government officials, and in Hungary (Jones and Matthijs, 2019). Criticism of the ECB in the EU must be interpreted differently. There have been frequent attacks on the ECB from domestic politicians, many of whom have the domestic audience as addressee and are searching for a scapegoat (Vaubel, 1986; Jones and Matthijs, 2019). For instance, in 2016, Wolfgang Schäuble, German finance minister from 2009 to 2017, blamed the ECB for the success of the right-wing party Alternative für Deutschland (Jones and Matthijs, 2019), which is definitely not correct.[1] The ECB was rather overburdened with financing the member states, while their governments did not see the urgency to solve the underlying problems of the Eurocrisis (Chapter 7).

The remainder of this chapter elaborates upon the relationship between CBI and democracy in two steps. After the Great Recession and with a more visible and seemingly powerful central bank, the old discussion about the alleged democratic deficits of rule bound policies has re-emerged. Political scientists argue that rules diminish the rights of elected politicians. We discuss this claim in some detail in the next section. In Section 8.3, we briefly recall the discussion about accountability and transparency. Section 8.4 discusses how economic problems and political threats reinforce each other.

---

[1] Alternative für Deutschland was founded – by a group of economics professors – in response to the European rescue packages of 2011. If someone is so easily to be blamed for its successes, it is the German government for allowing the very far-reaching interpretation of the European Treaties. See Section 7.4.

8.2 IS CBI COMPATIBLE WITH DEMOCRACY?

For Public Choice disciples as well as new political economics scholars it is obvious that rule bound policies are economically sensible. They first allow to avoid trade-offs between different policy objectives, when applied according to the Tinbergen rule, and second prevent short-term orientation of policymakers constrained by the election cycle, when long-term strategies should rather be applied, for example in monetary policy. The economic argument is theoretically straightforward and has been destroyed neither by MMT nor the secular stagnation hypothesis.

These scholars also would not question that rule-bound policies are in line with democracy, if not building blocks for a democratic society. This, however, has frequently been contested by political scientists who argue that rule-binding is moving policies away from democratic control (Berman and McNamara 1999; Best, 2017). Best (2017) claims first that rule-bound policies as suggested by the Public Choice school is anti-democratic, as it is an indication that elected policymakers cannot be trusted. In fact, she claims that Public Choice is anti-democratic or New Right. This is an utter misunderstanding of the political economy of modern societies in which organised interests have become very powerful. Public Choice simply argues that rules protect policymakers from being prone to these vested interests, in other words: from the 'slavery of the rent-seeking society'. Public Choice arguments also have to be seen against the background of election cycles, which encourage short-termism. Rules (including the Rule of Law) in this understanding protect democracy against vested interest and short-sighted politicians (Brennan and Buchanan, 1981; McDonough, 1994; Blinder, 1996; Drazen 2002).

However, Best (2017) also argues that CBI is a form of exceptionalism or emergency power, which allows almost unlimited power. As a consequence, right-wing populists can attack the central bank (see also Section 8.1). This argument has a grain of truth given that central banks have taken over many tasks in the aftermath of the Great

200 RECONSIDERING CENTRAL BANK INDEPENDENCE

Recession (Chapters 5 and 7).[2] However, as shown in Chapter 7, this proliferation of tasks is not in line with CBI. It rather reflects the inability of governments to fulfil their tasks within the policy assignment and to perform necessary structural reforms. Instead, they have found a convenient scapegoat (Jones and Matthijs, 2019).

Berman and McNamara (1999) additionally argue that CBI is part of a neoliberal catechism that unnecessarily narrows the objectives of monetary policies to price stability. This argument neglects the trade-off between policy objectives and the subsequent difficulties to meet several objectives with one policy instrument. The Tinbergen rule is ignored, which tries to give every agency some policy space – again, it is clear that policy actors from different policy areas do not work in isolation. It becomes obvious that this criticism is not so much addressing a lack of democracy, but the policy assignment as such.

There is another argument against CBI, which is based on the regular claim that central bankers are not elected politicians but technocrats. Since they are not accountable to the public, they act in isolation and are able to impose their preferences on the public. They hold unelected power (Tucker, 2018). This argument points to two different aspects. First, participation of elected politicians in monetary policy is denied; they do not participate, which some central bankers find in order because of the complexity of the matter at hand (Blinder 1996). Parliamentarians or cabinet members cannot override decisions by the central bank directorate. Second, central banks act in secret and do not share their insights with parliament or government. Thus, democratic legitimacy of monetary policy is said to be too low. This is not shared by central bankers who are aware of the rising influence of vested interest should monetary policy be controlled in parliament (Hetzel, 1997).

To answer the question of whether or not CBI is in line with democratic principles, it is sensible to develop criteria

---

[2] This has led to many accusations of similar kind; see the debate on the ECB in Section 7.4.

(Bini Smaghi, 1998). Bini Smaghi defines three criteria: ex-ante control, answerability and popular mandate. Ex-ante control refers to the legal foundation of the rule in question (here, CBI) for the objectives and principles. It is unquestioned by economists and central bankers that independence does not include the ability to define the objectives; CBI means instrument independence and not goal independence (Blinder, 1996; Debelle and Fischer, 1994). It obviously depends on the democratic nature of the process leading to the definition of rules, objectives and principles, including the appointment procedures for central bankers,[3] for the extent to which CBI is compatible with democratic principles can be judged. The second criterion is answerability: this refers to the necessity for any public policymaker to report about her work. This is an undisputed element of the policy of an independent central bank, which is discussed in its own section (see Section 8.3).

The third criterion is popular mandate. This can be seen in two ways. With independent central banks, political parties cannot put monetary policy on policy platforms; at least the instruments are decided outside their competencies. However, they may present election platforms with other than current objectives of monetary policy – if such a platform is successful, it is possible to reduce CBI again. Interestingly, this has not been observed so far; in most democracies, it may be highly risky to deviate from the goal of stability in an election platform. In the case of the ECB, this mechanism does not work; the ECB lacks this sort of democratic legitimacy (Van't Klooster, 2018). Second, central banks can get a popular mandate through a credible monetary policy. The more credible the policy, the higher the reputation of the central bank. Many sceptics argue that, for instance, the Bundesbank would have been as successful even without the strong independence it has enjoyed since its foundation (Stiglitz, 1998). This can be doubted, as the Bundesbank's high

---

[3] Critics of the Fed, for instance, argue that not all members of the regional boards are appointed by elected policymakers; this has been identified as a flaw (Stiglitz, 1998).

reputation may have to do with its politically undistorted and highly successful policy from the start. This sort of public mandate is also dependent on stability culture in a country (Hayo, 1998), which again is certainly endogenous.

Against this background, it is interesting to assess the empirical picture. In two empirical studies, the relation of CBI and democracy has been analysed from different angles. One paper shows that independent central banks are more likely to discipline governments and assure low inflation in democracies than in autocracies (Bodea and Hicks, 2015). This outcome confirms that – unless the objective of low inflation is not accepted (Stiglitz, 1998) – in democracies it pays off to make the central bank independent. A second paper shows that CBI can safeguard the transparency of distribution mechanisms and thus also safeguard the democratic order (Destefanis and Rizza, 2007). This is even stronger empirical support for the hypothesis that CBI is compatible with democracy.

Finally, it may be relevant to clarify the way in which the monetary policy framework is legally introduced, because this also indicates the mechanism with which CBI can be repealed again. One can think of a government decree, a central bank law or even a constitutional decision. Some authors argue that – given the importance of price stability – objectives of monetary policy should be decided at a constitutional level (Blinder, 1996; Hetzel, 1997). In any case, the higher the level of political decision-making, the more independent the central bank and the less likely this CBI can be reversed. This may be seen as critical in a case where the central bank is given more tasks and develops its own agenda (Best, 2017). To avoid such a concentration of power, it is ideal to make price stability as the first and primary objective to be followed by an independent central bank.

The upshot of this discussion leads to the conclusion that rule-bound policies including CBI are well in line with democracy as long as democratic procedures have led to the decision to apply the rules, and as long as they can be changed or repealed in democratic procedures if they have proven ineffective, inefficient or outdated. As long as they are valid, they allow for non-discriminatory policy, as they block vested interests.

However, central banks may lose legitimacy if members of the public fail to understand their policies. That said, any independent agency is of course accountable and should be as transparent as possible. This aspect has been understated in the economic and political discussions about CBI for years. In the 1990s, the topic became more important, in particular when the EUROZONE was founded. The next section discusses this in some detail.[4]

8.3 THE IMPORTANT ROLE OF ACCOUNTABILITY AND TRANSPARENCY

The discussion presented so far has revealed the high potential for misunderstanding. Politically independent actors such as central banks are not free from being controlled and supervised.[5] They do not set their objectives and plan their resources; they are only independent from political influence in their efforts to achieve the given objectives. In addition, they are accountable to the public as represented by elected politicians. In all central bank legislations, there are reporting provisions for central banks. Governments have to be informed; and central banks also have to get in touch with the public. Against this background, the claim that CBI offends democracy is inadequate, in particular when considering the historical reasons for CBI, namely the negative economic and social consequences of inflation.

For many years, however, economists and central bankers did not quite understand the concerns of citizens, politicians and political scientists who were not so easily convinced of the time inconsistency logic and the benefits of the Tinbergen rule, and who regard

---

[4] Since this book is on CBI, the extensive literature on accountability and transparency will only be touched upon here. Dincer and Eichengreen (2013), give a good overview of the state of research in the field.

[5] The same arguments hold for other independent, technocratic policy actors such as competition agencies or regulatory offices.

monetary policy as one of several policy fields for which governments are responsible. They often consolidate all official policymaking agencies in the government. In practice, monetary policy was conducted by unknown central bankers who would exchange views with academics and argue that the public should not bother with understanding them – as monetary policy is very complex (Blinder, 1996). In addition, the result of monetary policy has been low inflation in most countries over many years, which has also discouraged central banks from bothering the public and politicians with the details. It seemed that the audience was satisfied and did not show much interest in specifics. Politicians and scientists who demanded more governmental or parliamentarian influence and transparency were often denied their demands because their arguments were mistaken as the wish to conduct different monetary policy was based, for example, on the Phillips curve.[6]

This has changed over the last three decades. A discussion of central bank accountability started in the 1990s, beginning before the founding of the ECB (De Haan et al., 1998) and took off with the start of the EUROZONE. This is justified by the quite unusual nature of the two-stage PAP in the EUROZONE. Whereas national central banks act as agent for the respective exclusive principal government (who is the agent of the domestic public), the ECB was the agent of multiple principals. Therefore, the issue of accountability was discussed from the beginning in the EUROZONE (Bini Smaghi, 1998; Buiter, 1999; Issing, 1999).

What does accountability mean? According to the Bank for International Settlements (2009, Chapter 7), it has three characteristic dimensions: scrutiny by third parties, regular disclosure of actions and negative consequences when underperforming. Central banks can be held accountable for the inflation rate, for other monetary as well as financial regulatory objectives and for the use of resources including the profitability of reserves invested. The process

---

[6] See Chapter 3.

of accountability can be formalised to different degrees, from formal reporting to the legislature/parliament or formal reporting to the government, that is the minister of finance or head of state, to public reports only. The consequences can range from nothing to the governor being fired if the central bank misses the inflation objective (BIS, 2009).

The link between CBI and accountability is transparency (IMF, 2019). Transparency describes the flow of information from the central bank to political actors and the public; it is meant to reduce the degree of informational asymmetries between the central bank and its principals. It can be generated actively by the central bank (signalling) through hearings in parliament, reports to governments, annual, quarterly or monthly public reports, press conferences, publication of targets, predictions, policy models or even of the central bank council meeting minutes. The more detailed and regular the information has to be, the higher the transparency. Transparency can also be raised by observers such as journalists, bank economists and academics. This can be interpreted as screening.

A particularly disputed tool is the publication of the central bank councils' or board of governors meeting minutes, as this information gives valid information about the individual members' positions (Chappel, McGregor et al., 2004). Such information can be misused to put pressure on individual members of the council or board. It may also lead to meetings becoming short technical events, with all relevant discussions taking place before them in informal settings.[7]

Transparency can be measured in a methodically similar way to CBI, for instance through an analysis of central banks' websites (Dincer and Eichengreen, 2013). Dincer and Eichengreen distinguish five categories of transparency: political, economic, procedural, policy and operational. Three questions are asked in each category: if a

---

[7] The topic has been the subject of a vivid and highly readable controversy between Willem Buiter (1999) and Otmar Issing (1999) about the ECB's transparency.

question can be answered with yes, transparency is high. The constructed index ranges from 0 to 15, with a score of 15 indicating the highest possible degree of transparency.[8]

The degree of transparency of central banks has increased in the last twenty years. In a sample of 110 countries, only 10 did not increase transparency between 1998 and 2008 (Dincer and Eichengreen, 2013). The IMF and the BIS both expect central bank transparency to increase against the background of the extension of central banks' mandates owing to the series of economic crises experienced since 2008 (BIS, 2009; IMF, 2019); it is also necessary as a tool to stabilise the expectations from the financial sector and the public. In addition to this necessity, there has been substantial pressure in the public on governments to increase their transparency in general (Dincer and Eichengreen, 2013).

8.4   CONCLUSION: ECONOMIC AND POLITICAL THREATS REINFORCE EACH OTHER

To summarise this chapter, it has become obvious that politically independent agencies such as central banks must place high emphasis on their accountability and transparency. Apart from the necessity for every public actor to be accountable, the particular circumstances for central banks after the Great Recession and subsequent, but not necessarily related, crises call for high transparency.

Central banks have experienced quite different responses to their policies in the past decade. With much political pressure on them in advanced economies to become engaged in other policy fields than monetary policy, on the one hand they have increased their power, at least temporarily. Governments have made themselves dependent on central banks as a leading financier of their increasing debts; they need low interest rates to have fiscal policy space in the future. Such support finds strong academic support (see Chapter 7).

---

[8] Dincer and Eichengreen (2013) also present an overview of the literature in the field, where similar indices are developed.

On the other hand, in the long run this situation threatens to reduce their political independence, because it will be increasingly difficult for them to retreat from expansionary monetary policy. In addition, the perception of their influence and power leads to political resistance in both academic and political quarters. Whereas the first may not be considered as a serious threat, the political pressure by often populist politicians, regardless of their position as members of government or opposition, may reduce their reputation. This may not only reduce their current power again, but lead to a long-run reduction in CBI. In this vein, the two types of threat – economic and political – must be seen together, as they may reinforce each other.

9   The Future of CBI

9.1   THE CHANGING ROLE OF CENTRAL BANKS SINCE THE SECOND WORLD WAR

The concept of CBI is relatively new. It became prominent in the 1980s, although some central banks – such as the Bundesbank and the Swiss National Bank – had previously operated with significant independence; a history that was not just an example but an argument for wider application. The increasing prominence of CBI and the improvement of both monetary policy conduct and outcomes internationally over the last forty years occurred jointly; indeed, it is the argument of this book that CBI contributed significantly to the improved monetary policy outcomes.

The case for CBI is based on several economic and political considerations, discussed in this book.

First, as Tinbergen (1952) has shown, policymakers should use one policy instrument for each policy objective. This introduces the assignment problem in monetary policy – the selection of an appropriate objective to assign to the instrument of monetary policy.

From society's perspective, the pathology of inflation is undoubtedly costly – economically, socially and politically. Many empirical studies confirm these costs. The evolving theory of monetary policy, together with the practical outcomes of forty years, demonstrates that using the policy interest to combat inflation is a practical tool to control inflation over the medium-term. Therefore, the appropriate objective for monetary policy is low and stable inflation, or price stability, pursued by the judicious adjustment of the policy interest rate within a modern monetary policy framework. Because of Tinbergen's logic – which we call the Tinbergen rule – monetary policy should focus on price stability and should not also target additional objectives, such as employment or the public budget. When central banks follow this logic in real life, the policy mix in the respective country works relatively well. The first argument for an independent central bank is, therefore, that it allows the monetary authority to use its instrument independence to pursue the appropriate objective of monetary stability without the imposition of other objectives.

Hyperinflation only occurred historically when governments had no alternative to finance their budgets or existing debt. Additionally, inflation is often the result of other unresolved economic problems, based either on the attempt to boost short-term growth and employment or on fiscal problems. Inflation is not the objective in these cases, but can be a side-effect of attempts to meet other policy objectives. If governments use one instrument to meet more than one objective, they face trade-offs, which often cause inflation. This is known to politicians; beginning in the 1980s, the institutions (or rules) for central banks began to evolve to embody these lessons. This is the second reason for CBI: to assign effective instrument independence to central banks in order to prevent governments from being tempted to misuse monetary policy for purposes other than inflation control.

The third argument for CBI extends the Tinbergen argument with so-called time-inconsistency models (though other economic schools of thought such as the Virginia School of Public Choice or the Freiburg School of Law and Economics (Ordoliberalism) come to similar conclusions). These models emphasise the credibility of policy announcements that have a time-lagged effect, and thus the degree to which the public can form reliable expectations about the future policy conduct and outcomes such as the inflation rate. It is the striking demonstration of these models that rules-based monetary policy achieves lower inflation than well-intentioned discretionary policy, at no output cost. An independent central bank with an appropriate policy rule can achieve the benign outcomes foreseen by these models.

This evolution of the institutional framework with the central banks being independent from daily politics in their exercise of the policy instrument, proved very successful. During the 1990s, many European governments granted their central banks such independence, including those such as France and the Netherlands that were forced by the Maastricht Treaty of 1992. In the United Kingdom too the BoE was first granted independence to set the policy interest rate in the late 1990s, and many developing countries followed suit.

As the empirical literature shows, the scope provided by being independent from daily politics has allowed central banks to perform well and guarantee a stable financial and monetary environment for the economy. Since the two oil crises in the 1970s, central banks in the OECD countries contained inflation successfully. Even in Latin America, inflation fell in the 1990s to an unprecedently low level. In the first decade of the twenty-first century, in a period known as the Great Moderation, inflation was low and the economic growth path was relatively stable. Strong monetary growth in the United States during the Greenspan years was not perceived as a problem. Inflation remained low throughout these years, until 2021.

Thus, CBI added to the credibility of the policy conducted by central banks over this period. The explicit focus on low and stable inflation by an independent central bank also allowed better co-ordination with other macro-policies, given the credibility of the monetary framework that also rendered it highly predictable for fiscal authorities.

By the turn of the century, commentators went so far as to announce the advent of a New Economy, a world without inflation and business cycles (Blinder, 2000b). CBI was seen as a crucial part of a sustainable institutional framework for monetary policy. This happy result was part of a wider complacency that emerged in the new century regarding the challenges of macroeconomic policy. The Nobel prize winner Robert Lucas exemplified this complacency in the opening of his Presidential Address to the American Economic Association in 2003. As mentioned in Chapter 7, he argued that macro-economists had learnt the lessons the Great Depression had to offer and were able to advise politicians in order to prevent further depressions; the challenges of stabilisation policy had been solved, or so he argued.

Little did he know, or anticipate, that the Great Moderation was about to end in the second half of the first decade of this century, when the housing market in the United States collapsed, precipitating the GFC. As discussed earlier, it seems that governments had grown complacent. The US government subsidised housing to a large extent, and thereby encouraged banks to lend excessively to clients who eventually could not repay their debts. Since the banks were able to securitise their loans, they shifted the risk to institutional investors such as pension funds and insurance companies. That way the financial crisis, which started in the United States, became a global financial and subsequent economic crisis.

The EUROZONE was disrupted by two economic crises in this period, since directly after the GFC had reached its peak with the demise of Lehman Brothers, some member states ran into fiscal difficulties, partly as a consequence of the GFC, and within a few years owing to the fiscal woes of the Greek government and others. This crisis led to several new objectives for the ECB, as discussed in Chapter 7. The fundamental question is how these new tasks have affected the role of central bank and their independence from daily politics.

An Olsonian perspective on this era suggests that OECD governments did not do enough to implement structural change and keep the dynamic forces of the Western economies strong. The good years and decreasing interest rates after the founding of the EMU were not used to modernise economies in the EUROZONE – instead, some countries such as Greece used the low interest rates to increase public consumption, financed by debt. This perspective leads to the fundamental argument that the supply-side deficiencies caused the structural problems that were revealed by the two crises. This was the case in the EUROZONE but partly also in other OECD countries, such as Japan.

Even during and after the global financial and economic crises, it became obvious that these governments were not able to solve their economic problems. Despite the support by the ECB ('Whatever it takes'), governments in the EUROZONE were politically unable to implement reforms necessary to unleash productive forces in their economies. Instead, they had to rely on central banks that were assigned the task to stimulate the economies. In the EUROZONE, the ECB was forced to buy more government bonds than probably initially planned. This new direction for monetary policy implied an enormous balance sheet expansion for central banks, which was used to purchase government bonds and keep unproductive businesses, often labelled as zombies, alive. Instead of supply-side reforms, governments increased public debt, financed cheaply with central bank balance sheet policies.

In addition to public debt increase, monetary expansion since 2012 and even more since 2015 contributed to an asset price inflation. This shows the supply-side problems, as the additional money was not used to invest in new activities and enterprises, but rather to purchase existing assets, that is, real estate, shares and even collectors' items such as classic cars. Monetary policy turned a blind eye to this development. Nevertheless, central banks in OECD were perceived as an important actor to solve the GFC. The same expectations were laid upon the ECB in the second crisis of the early twenty-first century, the Eurocrisis, and in its third and fourth major disruptions, the COVID-19 crisis and the energy crisis after the Russian aggression against Ukraine. In all these cases, central banks were actively supporting governments with new loans.

The permissive balance sheet operations potentially disarmed the central banks in the OECD; they were no longer able to reduce the interest rate further in the event of another crisis. These operations also contributed to asset price bubbles, and had the potential to increase monetary aggregates, posing inflationary risk in the medium term.

Whereas the central banks faced no inflation until 2021, this changed in the course of 2022 when inflation in the United States, the United Kingdom and the EMU hit double-digit levels, at least for a short period until late 2022. This posed a new challenge for central banks. In order to contain inflation, they had to start raising interest rates; which they did. This was a painful decision owing to the well-known short-term trade-off between inflation and growth, as higher interest rates might discourage economic activity such as investment. However, we have seen that unduly low interest rates disallow a discrimination of investment projects and create zombies, thereby not spurring investment. On the same token, we can expect that a moderate increase in interest rates will not automatically lead to another recession, as banks use the interest rate tool to discriminate between the risk of potential projects once the time-value of money has returned.

Increasing interest rates are, however, a problem for governments that have been used to declining and minimal interest rates for more than ten years. For them, a rising interest rate means a higher share of debt service in their budget, which – in particular in a recession or in the aftermath of the COVID-19 pandemic – may lead to a vicious circle. Higher interest payments reduce scope for other spending, which in turn demands more public debt. Because of higher public debt, interest payments increase further (see also Section 9.2).

This new situation has consequences for central banks. With the current need to combat inflation, central banks can disconnect a bit from Treasuries and move back to a more traditional monetary policy. They can resist the pressure more easily than in times of low interest rates and low inflation, when it seems almost costless for central banks to expand the balance sheet further and allow states to indebt themselves further.

9.2 GAIN IN POWER OR LOSS OF INDEPENDENCE?

After the string of economic, political and health crises experienced between 2008 and mid-2023 (the time when the text of this book was finalised) in many countries, central banks are in a different position than they were fifteen years ago. Their mandate seems to have been expanded, with a concomitant gain in power. The perception of central bankers has also changed. They are no longer grey technocrats, whose names nobody in the public knows, but rather omnipotent superstars with a significant public and media presence. The public as well as professional observers wait, almost with excitement, for the bi-weekly press conferences of the ECB, for instance. They pronounce not only on monetary policy, but also on climate change. Central bankers are inevitably present at G7 summits or World Bank/IMF spring meetings and annual meetings, as well as Davos and other gatherings of the economically and politically powerful.

However, this expansion in the roles and responsibilities of central banks and their governors is not applauded by everyone. Many observers, especially economists, have criticised the persistently accommodating monetary policy of the last decade; this book also argues along these lines. However, in the context of this book, the question is not whether central banks are operating beyond their mandates – which at least for the ECB seems clear from an economic perspective (though less so through a legal lens); rather, we are interested in the question of whether central banks really have gained power in these fifteen years of crises.

At first glance, it is obvious that central banks have a broader mandate today than fifteen years ago. They still care for price stability, but have also become responsible for other macroeconomic and structural policy objectives. They finance public budgets, are looking at employment and investment, and have also become relevant actors in climate policy because they are supposed to 'green' their portfolio, and use regulation to encourage others to follow suit. In this way they conduct structural or industrial policy. This is significantly more responsibility than central banks had in 2007. In addition, central bankers are increasingly listened to when they give statements about general economic policy. They demand fiscal stability and even suggest structural reforms, which is also not within their traditional mandate. Together with their public appearances, this adds to the impression that central banks have gained power in the past one and a half decades.

From a different perspective, we observe that this new policy setting has also imposed constraints on central banks, as their responsibility as well as public awareness has risen. We are concerned whether central banks are really in every instance able to decide on the timing and scope of their monetary measures under the circumstances of a weak supply side and poor economic policy conditions, very low interest rates and high public debt. Let us first discuss the example of an increase in interest rates as observed between late 2022 and mid-2023 in the United States, in the United Kingdom and in the EUROZONE.

Each time a central bank increases the interest rate or ends a purchasing programme, the government faces a problem with respect to the national budget. As long as the average interest rate of government bonds – along the different settlement dates – is declining, implying that bonds with higher interest will be replaced with bonds bearing lower interest, there is scope for small interest rate increases without the governmental payments for interest increasing. However, a rising interest rate environment increases the burden of existing government debt tremendously; for example, an interest rate increase of 3 per cent within a decade and 1 trillion EUROS debt leads to an increase of interest payments to the amount of 30 billion EUROS. Governments will certainly try to prevent that kind of fiscal pressure, which sets fiscal and monetary authorities on a collision course.

The good news is that central banks increased interest rates during 2022 and 2023, despite this logic, and the opposition from governments – except in the EUROZONE for the Italian government – was limited. Governments seem to have accepted the need to combat inflation for now.

Central bank laws all over the world assign a high degree of CBI to many central banks. As mentioned earlier, this was the result of an intellectual and political consent about the necessity to secure price stability. These laws have not changed, but possibly their interpretation has. As the pressure to react to the increasing challenges of the past fifteen years has increased, Western governments have acted in a pattern typical of democracies. They have opted for a range of short-term solutions, the advantages of which can be seen immediately. Thereby, governments showed their ability to master crises. In the cases we have discussed, governments put pressure on central banks to accommodate fiscal programmes that covered structural weaknesses of the Western economies. This has led to short-term political gains and long-term economic costs – in the form of higher inflation and repressed structural change.

We have discussed this development carefully, presenting all arguments. Our conclusion is that CBI was at risk until 2022, and still may be so. The latest stepwise interest rates increase may, however, indicate that the 'old normal', the division of labour in economic policy before the GFC, is slowly reappearing under the pressure of double-digit inflation. Nevertheless, central bankers should not believe that their newly gained influence protects them from ever more interventions or even maintains their independence.

9.3 THE NEED FOR A REVISED MANDATE AND HIGH ACCOUNTABILITY

In principle, the normative conclusions of policy developments in the last fifteen years are the same that led to the increasing independence of central banks from daily politics forty years ago. The case for CBI is as strong as ever. However, this insight comes at a time when governments remain under the pressure they have experienced since the beginning of the GFC. Their willingness to refrain from the printing press as a silver bullet in the future cannot be taken for granted.

Therefore, a repeated appeal to governments to honour central bank legislation and to stop the pressure on central banks to accommodate fiscal needs is probably not helpful. Instead, it will have to be a mixture of incentives for governments and actions by central banks that will let the pendulum swing back to less glamorous, but more independent and mandate-adhering, central banks.

The high inflation in Western economies since mid-2022 into the first quarter of 2023 has brought the main mandate of most central banks, namely to ensure price stability, back onto the agenda. High inflation has discredited the economic theories that enthusiastically supported the enlargement of the central banks' balance sheets, such as MMT and the theory of secular stagnation, which theoretically are rather poor and are now also weakened empirically.

In several steps, central banks have increased official interest rates to combat inflation. At the time of writing this chapter (end of 2023), this has already led to a significant reduction in inflation in the major economies. The general perception of inflation as negative is helpful and supportive for central banks; the increase of interest rates does not come without economic costs, at least in the short term.

Indeed, the downside of central banks raising interest rates is obvious: long-term interest rate rise and bond prices fall. In March 2023, this combination led to the collapse of Silicon Valley Bank, as their depositors withdrew parts of their capital and their assets lost part of their value.[1] In general, increasing interest rates are seen as a problem for short-term economic activity, which holds all the more in times of multiple crises. The economic consequences of the COVID-19 crisis had not been fully overcome by March 2023, while at the same time Russian aggression and the subsequent economic sanctions against Russia and to a limited scale against China added to the negative business cycle.

Notwithstanding these negative effects, central banks are attempting to regain reputation and act credibly as they move to a more 'normal' monetary policy. Thus, their policies have been

---

[1] For a discussion of the causes of that collapse, see Ball (2023). A similar case in Switzerland a few days later sent another round of shockwaves through the system. One is tempted to ask why the financial industry and governments refuse to learn from past mistakes.

acknowledged by the public, as well as by academic and professional observers, as appropriate. Governments – until the time of writing – did not object despite the fiscal consequences of higher interest rates. This suggests that the old consensus has not been fully surrendered: inflation is still perceived as a major problem that is better avoided.

Central banks can adjust their policies and public appearances so as to reduce the potential for governmental interventions and attempts to utilise monetary policy for other objectives than price stability (and in line with the mandate of central banks gain the general support of economic policymakers).

- A first step in this direction is to ensure the clear accountability and transparency of central banks. As Chapters 4–6 of this book show, central banks, particularly the ECB, have created many special programmes since the beginning of the GFC in 2008. The latest of these, the Transmission Protection Instrument, is intended to keep borrowing costs low for countries with high public debt and, thus, maintain a low spread over the German bond rate. This instrument does not raise the transparency of the ECB and the credibility of its policies. Instead, it appears to be designed to keep Italian borrowing costs below market assessment. Rather than creating more special instruments, central banks should keep their toolkit lean. Any attempt to discriminate between market participants may provoke a backlash to efforts to regain trust.
- A second step is to focus on the objectives laid down in central bank legislation, which in most countries (and regions) is a mix of price stability and general support of national economic policies. This can only be a slow and cautious process in order not to distort expectations. With respect to the economic situation in the Western world in March 2023, we would argue that a focus on inflation control is the correct policy. Other objectives, such as government finances, jobs or investment, are never ignored, but do not become specific targets. Instead, they are constraints on the pace with which disinflation is pursued.
- With respect to the green economy, central banks should be more explicit and deny their responsibility to finance green investment. As we have shown, central banks cannot conduct industrial policy, not even in an ideal world. Doing so leads to a conflict with their mandate, as governments might at times find it difficult to finance climate

protection initiatives without abandoning other expensive projects. If central banks are seen as lenders of last resort for the so-called green industries, their balance sheets might explode again. Apart from this, it does not seem easy to clearly and faultlessly distinguish green investment from other types. The Tinbergen rule suggests that the task of climate protection should be left to specialised organisations at domestic and global levels. Currently, central banks appear to be eager to assume this task. While this enthusiasm is understandable, the expected outcome is poor. Green monetary policy might end up as being neither green nor good monetary policy.

Edward Gibbon (1787, pp. 17–18) opened his *Decline and Fall of the Roman Empire* with the first Roman emperor's discovery 'that Rome, in her present exalted situation, had much less to hope than to fear from the chance of arms; and that, in the prosecution of remote wars, the undertaking became every day more difficult, the event more doubtful, and the possessions more precarious, and less beneficial'. This book delivers a similar, if less colourful, message: that there are limits to how we can profitably pursue monetary policy, and that an independent central bank using its instruments to implement a modern, rules-based monetary policy may circumscribe the beneficent monetary policy regime as sensibly as the 'Atlantic ocean; the Rhine and Danube on the north; the Euphrates on the East; and towards the south, the sandy deserts of Arabia and Africa' demarcated the Empire in the will of Augustus. And if we overstep this boundary by 'assigning to monetary policy a larger role than it can achieve', as Milton Friedman (1968, p. 5) cautioned, we risk 'preventing it from making the contribution it is capable of making'.

We are concerned that these boundaries have been overstepped since 2008 in the scope of policy objectives assigned to monetary policy, with an eroding effect on the independence so necessary to deliver benign monetary outcomes. This trend has to be reversed, to restore the independence of central banks and to reaffirm their appropriate and narrow objective as low and stable inflation over the medium term.

References

Abbassi, P., & Linzert, T. (2012). The Effectiveness of Monetary Policy in Steering Money Market Rates during the Financial Crisis. *Journal of Macroeconomics, 34* (4), 945–954.

Acharya, V. V., Imbierowicz, B., Steffen, S., & Teichmann, D. (2015). Does Lack of Financial Stability Impair the Transmission of Monetary Policy? *HIT-REFINED Working Paper Series.*

Adrian, T., & Shin, H. S. (2010). Financial Intermediaries and Monetary Economics, Ch. 12. In B. M. Friedman & M. Woodford (Eds.), *Handbook of Monetary Economics* (vol. 3, pp. 601–650). Amsterdam: Elsevier.

Agénor, P. R. (2000). *The Economics of Adjustment and Growth.* New York: Academic Press.

Ahearne, A., Gagnon, J., Haltmaier, J., Kamin, S., Erceg, C., Faust, J., Guerrieri, L., Hemphill, C., Kole, L., Roush, J., Rogers, J., Sheets, N., & Wright, J. (2002). Preventing Deflation: Lessons from Japan's Experience in the 1990s. *Board of Governors of the Federal Reserve System International Finance Discussion Papers* (729).

Alesina, A., & Tabellini, G. (1988). Credibility and Politics. *European Economic Review, 32* (2–3), 542–550.

Altavilla, C., Carboni, G., & Motto, R. (2015). Asset Purchase Programmes and Financial Markets: Lessons from the Euro Area. *ECB Working Paper Series* (1864).

Andrade, P., Cahn, C., Fraisse, H., & Mesonnier, J. S. (2015). Can the Provision of Long-Term Liquidity Help to Avoid a Credit Crunch? Evidence from the Eurosystem's LTRO. *Banque de France Working Paper.*

Angelini, P., Nobili, A., & Picillo, C. (2011). The Interbank Market after August 2007: What Has Changed, and Why? *Journal of Money, Credit and Banking, 43* (5), 923–958.

Arnone, M., Bernard, L., & Segalotto, J.-F. (2006a). The Measurement of Central Bank Autonomy: Survey of Models, Indicators, and Empirical Evidence. *IMF Working Papers, 06* (227), 1.

Arnone, M., Bernard, L., & Segalotto, J.-F. (2006b). Measures of Central Bank Autonomy: Empirical Evidence for OECD, Developing, and Emerging Market Economies. *IMF Working Papers, 06* (228), 4.

Arnone, M., & Romelli, D. (2013). Dynamic Central Bank Independence Indices and Inflation Rate: A New Empirical Exploration. *Journal of Financial Stability*, 9 (3), 385–398.

Backus, D., & Driffill, J. (1985). Rational Expectations and Policy Credibility Following a Change in Regime. *The Review of Economic Studies*, 52 (2), 211–221.

Bagehot, W. (1873). *Lombard Street: A Description of the Money Market*. New York: Charles Scribner's Sons.

Bailey, M. J. (1956). The Welfare Cost of Inflationary Finance. *Journal of Political Economy*, 64 (2), 93–110.

Baldwin, R. E. (2019). *The Globotics Upheaval: Globalisation, Robotics and the Future of Work*. Oxford: Oxford University Press.

Baldwin, R. E., & Robert-Nicoud, F. (2007). Entry and Asymmetric Lobbying: Why Governments Pick Losers. *Journal of the European Economic Association*, 5 (5), 1064–1093.

Ball, C. (2023). The How, Why and What Next of the Silicon Valley Bank Failure. *Global Economics Blog*. https://globalecon.substack.com/p/the-how-why-and-what-next-of-the?utm_source=substack&utm_medium=email

Banerjee, R., & Hofmann, B. (2018). The Rise of Zombie Firms: Causes and Consequences. *BIS Quarterly Review* (September), 67–78.

Bank for International Settlement. (2009). *Issues in the Governance of Central Banks.*, cited as BIS.

Barro, R. J. (1995). Inflation and Economic Growth. *Bank of England Quarterly Bulletin*, 35, 166–176.

Barro, R. J., & Gordon, D. B. (1983a). A Positive Theory of Monetary Policy in a Natural Rate Model. *Journal of Political Economy*, 91 (4), 589–610.

Barro, R. J., & Gordon, D. B. (1983b). Rules, Discretion and Reputation in a Model of Monetary Policy. *Journal of Monetary Economics*, 12 (1), 101–121.

Bauer, M. D., & Rudebusch, G. D. (2014). The Signaling Channel for Federal Reserve Bond Purchases. *International Journal of Central Banking*, 10 (3), 233–289.

Baumeister, C., & Benati, L. (2013). Unconventional Monetary Policy and the Great Recession: Estimating the Macroeconomic Effects of a Spread Compression at the Zero Lower Bound. *International Journal of Central Banking*, 9 (2), 165–212.

Bean, C., Paustian, M., Penalver, A., & Taylor, T. (2010). Monetary Policy after the Fall. *Proceedings – Economic Policy Symposium – Jackson Hole*, 267–328. http://ideas.repec.org/a/fip/fedkpr/y2010p267-328.html

Bech, M., & Malkhozov, A. (2016). *How have Central Banks Implemented Negative Policy Rates?* BIS Quarterly Review March, 31–44.

Belke, A., Freytag, A., Keil, J., & Schneider, F. (2014). The Credibility of Monetary Policy Announcements: Empirical Evidence for OECD Countries since the 1960s *International Review of Economics and Finance*, 217–227.

Belke, A., & Polleit, T. (2010). How Much Fiscal Banking Must the ECB Have? The Euro Area Is Not (yet) the Philippines. *International Economics, 124*, 5–30.

Benati, L. (2009). Long Run Evidence on Money Growth and Inflation. *Working Paper Series 1027, European Central Bank.*

Berger, H., de Haan, J., & Eijffinger, S. C. W. (2001). Central Bank Independence: An Update of Theory and Evidence. *Journal of Economic Surveys, 15* (1), 3–40.

Berman, S., & McNamara, K. R. (1999). Bank on Democracy: Why Central Banks Need Public Oversight. *Foreign Affairs, 78* (2), 2–8.

Bernanke, B. S. (2004). The Great Moderation. *The Federal Reserve Board, Remarks at the Eastern Economic Association, Washington D.C., February 20, 2004.*

Bernanke, B. S. (2005). *The Global Saving Glut and the U.S. Current Account Deficit.* St Louis, Homer Jones Lecture, St. Louis, Missouri, USA, 14 April, 2005.

Bernanke, B. S. (2008). Housing, Mortgage Markets, and Foreclosures. *Speech 437, Board of Governors of the Federal Reserve System (U.S.).*

Bernanke, B. S. (2009). Financial Reform to Address Systemic Risk. *Speech 448, Board of Governors of the Federal Reserve System (U.S.).*

Bernanke, B. S. (2010). Central Bank Independence, Transparency, and Accountability. *Speech at the Institute for Monetary and Economic Studies International Conference, Bank of Japan, Tokyo, 25 May 2010.*

Bernanke, B., Laubach, T., Mishkin, F. S., & Posen, A. S. (1999). *Inflation Targeting. Lessons from the International Experience.* Princeton: Princeton University Press.

Bernholz, P. (1995). Necessary and Sufficient Conditions to End Hyperinflations. In P. L. Siklos (Ed.), *Great Inflations of the 20th Century* (pp. 257–287). Cheltenham: Edward Elagar.

Bernoth, K., Köning, P., & Raab, C. (2015). Large-Scale Asset Purchases by Central Banks II: Empirical Evidence. *Politik im Fokus, 61*, 1–8.

Best, J. (2017). *Bring Politics Back to Monetary Policy – How Technocratic Exceptionalism Fuels Populism. Foreign Affairs, December 2017,* www .foreignaffairs.com/articles/world/2017-12-06/bring-politics-backmonetary-policy.(6).

Bianchi, F., Lettau, M., & Ludvigson, S. C. (2022). Monetary Policy and Asset Valuation. *The Journal of Finance, 77* (2), 967–1017.

Bini Smaghi, L. (1998). The Democratic Accountability of the European Central Bank. *BNL Quarterly Review, 51* (205), 119–143.

Blinder, A. S. (1996). Central Banking in a Democracy. *Federal Reserve Bank of Richmond, Economic Quarterly, 82* (4), 1–14.

Blinder, A. S. (2000a). Central Bank Credibility: Why Do We Ware? How Do We Build It? *American Economic Review, 90* (5), 1421–1431.

Blinder, A. S. (2000b). The Internet and the New Economy. *Brookings Institute Policy Brief.* No 60. June 2000. Washington, DC.

Blot, C., Creel, J., Hubert, P., & Labondance, F. (2015). The QE Experience: Worth a Try? *OFCE Briefing Paper* (10), 1–21.

Bodea, C., & Hicks, R. (2015). Price Stability and Central Bank Independence: Discipline, Credibility, and Democratic Institutions. *International Organization, 69* (1), 35–61.

Bofinger, P., Hellwig, M. F., Hüther, M., Schnitzer, M., Schularick, M., & Wolff, G. (2020). Gefahr für die Unabhängigkeit der Notenbank. *Frankfurter Allgemeine Zeitung (FAZ)* (29 May 2020), 18.

Böhm-Bawerk, E. (1914). Unsere Passive Handelsbilanz. In F. X. Weiss (Ed.), *Gesammelte schriften von Eugen von Böhm-Bawerk.* Salzwasser-Verlag.

Bordo, M. D. (2010). The Federal Reserve: Independence Gained, Independence Lost ... *Shadow Open Market Committee, March 26, 2010.*

Bordo, M. D., & Schwartz, A. J. (1999). Monetary Policy Regimes and Economic Performance: The Historical Record. In J. B. Taylor & M. Woodford (Eds.), *Handbook of Macroeconomics, Volume 1* (pp. 149–234). Amsterdam: Elsevier.

Borio, C., & Disyatat, P. (2010). Unconventional Monetary Policies: An Appraisal. *Manchester School, 78* (SUPPL. 1), 53–89.

Bork, L. (2015). A Large-Dimensional Factor Analysis of the Federal Reserve's Large-Scale Asset Purchases. *Available at SSRN:* https://ssrn.com/abstract=2618378 or http://dx.doi.org/10.2139/ssrn.2618378

Brash, D. T. (1996, July 1996). Reducing Inflation in New Zealand: Some Practical Issues. Annual Symposium of the Kansas City Fed, Jackson Hole, Wyoming.

Breedon, F., Chadha, J. S., & Waters, A. (2012). The Financial Market Impact of UK Quantitative Easing. *Oxford Review of Economic Policy, 28* (4), 702–728.

Brennan, G. H., & Buchanan, J. M. (1981). *Monopoly in Money and Inflation: The Case for a Constitution to Discipline Government.* London: Institute for Economic Affairs. Hobart Paper (Vol. 88).

Breuss, F. (2016). The Crisis Management of the ECB. *WIFO Working Papers* (507), 1–45.

Briault, C. B., Haldane, A., & King, M. A. (1996). *Independence and accountability.* Bank of England working papers, Bank of England.

Broaddus, J. A. J. (1995). Reflections on Monetary Policy. *Federal Reserve Bank of Richmond, Economic Quarterly, 81* (2), 1–11.

Brunetti, C., Di Filippo, M., & Harris, J. H. (2011). Effects of Central Bank Intervention on the Interbank Market during the Subprime Crisis. *Review of Financial Studies, 24* (6), 2053–2083.

Buiter, W. H. (1999). Alice in Euroland. *JCMS: Journal of Common Market Studies, 37* (2), 181–209.

Buiter, W. H. (2009). What's Left of Central Bank Independence? *Financial Times.* http://blogs.ft.com/maverecon/2009/05/whats-left-ofcentralbankindependenc e/#axzz3RhiPobiY

Burns, A. F. (1979). *The Anguish of Central Banking* (The 1979 Per Jacobsson Lecture). In M. Cirovic & J. J. Polak. Belgrade: The Per Jacobsson Foundation.

Butt, N., Domit, S., McLeay, M., & Thomas, R. (2012). What Can the Money Data Tell us about the Impact of QE? *Bank of England* (1), 321–331.

Caballero, R. J., Hoshi, T., & Kashyap, A. K. (2008). Zombie Lending and Depressed Restructuring in Japan. *American Economic Review, 98* (5), 1943–1977.

Cagan, P. (1956). The Monetary Dynamics of Hyperinflation. In M. Friedman (Ed.), *Studies in the Quantity Theory of Money* (pp. 25–117). Chicago: The University of Chicago Press.

Capie, F., Fischer, S., Goodhart, C., & Schnadt, N. (1994). *The Future of Central Banking: The Tercentenary Symposium of the Bank of England.* Cambridge: Cambridge University Press.

Capie, F., & Wood, G. (2013). Central Bank Independence: Can It Survive a Crisis? In Owen F. Humpage (Ed.), *Current Federal Reserve Policy Under the Lens of Economic History* (pp. 126–150). Cambridge University Press.

Carpinelli, L., & Crosignani, M. (2015). The Effect of Central Bank Liquidity Injections on Bank Credit Supply. *Working Paper.*

Catalão-Lopes, M. (2010). Fixed- and Variable-Rate Tenders in the Management of Liquidity by the Eurosystem: Implications of the Recent Credit Crisis. *International Journal of Central Banking, 6* (2), 199–230.

Cecchetti, S. G. (1998). Policy Rules and Targets: Framing the Central Banker's Problem. *Federal Reserve Bank of New York Economic Policy Review, 18* (37), 1–14.

Cecchetti, S. G., & Wynne, M. A. (2003). Inflation Measurement and the ECB's Pursuit of Price Stability: A first Assessment. *Economic Policy* (October), 395–434.

Chappel, H. W. J., McGregor, R. R., & Vermilyea, T. (2004). Majority Rule, Consensus Building, and the Power of the Chairman: Arthur Burns and the FOMC. *Journal of Money, Credit and Banking, 36* (3), 407–422.

Christensen, J. H. E., & Krogstrup, S. (2015). Transmission of Asset Purchases: The Role of Reserves.

Chung, H., Laforte, J. P., Reifschneider, D., & Williams, J. C. (2012). Have We Underestimated the Likelihood and Severity of Zero Lower Bound Events? *Journal of Money, Credit and Banking, 44* (SUPPL. 1), 47–82.

Churm, R., Joyce, M., Kapetanios, G., & Theodoridis, K. (2015). Unconventional Monetary Policies and the Macroeconomy: The Impact of the United Kingdom's QE2 and Funding for Lending Scheme. *Bank of England Staff Working Paper* (No. 542).

Clarida, R., Gali, J., & Gertler, M. (2000). Monetary Policy Rules and Macroeconomic Stability: Evidence and some Theory. *Quarterly Journal of Economics, 115* (1), 147–180.

Coats, W. (2019). Modern Monetary Theory: A Critique. *Cato Journal, 39,* 563–576.

Cooper, R., & Williamson, J. (1994). The Political Economy of Policy Reform. *Foreign Affairs, 73* (3), 154.

Ćorić, T., & Cvrlje, D. (2009). Central Bank Independence: The Case of Croatia. *University of Zagreb Working Paper Series* (14), 1–14.

Cour-Thimann, P., & Winkler, B. (2012). The ECB's Non-Standard Monetary Policy Measures: The Role of Institutional Factors and Financial Structure. *Oxford Review of Economic Policy, 28* (4), 765–803.

Cross, M., Fisher, P., & Weeken, O. (2010). The Bank's Balance Sheet during the Crisis. *Bank of England Quarterly Report* (February), 34–42.

Crowe, C. (2006). Goal-Independent Central Banks: Why Politicians Decide to Delegate? *IMF Working Papers, 256.*

Crowe, C., & Meade, E. E. (2007). The Evolution of Central Bank Governance around the World. *Journal of Economic Perspectives, 21* (4), 69–90.

Crowe, C., & Meade, E. E. (2008). Central Bank Independence and Transparency: Evolution and Effectiveness. *European Journal of Political Economy, 24* (4), 763–777.

Cukierman, A. (1992). *Central Bank Strategy, Credibility, and Independence: Theory and Evidence.* Cambridge, MA and London: The MIT Press.

Cukierman, A. (2000). Establishing a Reputation for Dependability by Means of Inflation Targets. *Economics of Governance, 1,* 53–76.

Cukierman, A., Miller, G. P., & Neyapti, B. (2002). Central Bank Reform, Liberalization and Inflation in Transition Economies: An International Perspective. *Journal of Monetary Economics, 49* (2), 237–264.

Cukierman, A., & Webb, S. B. (1995). Political Influence on the Central Bank: International Evidence. *The World Bank Economic Review, 9* (3), 397–423.

Cukierman, A. S. (1995). Rapid Inflation: Deliberate Policy or Miscalculation? In P. L. Siklos (Ed.), *Great Inflations of the 20th Century* (pp. 125–182). Cheltenham: Edward Elgar.

Curdia, V., Ferrero, A., & Chen, H. (2012). The Macroeconomic Effects of Large-Scale Asset Purchase Programs. *Economic Journal, Royal Economic Society, 122* (564), 289–315, November.

d'Amico, S., English, W., López-Salido, D., & Nelson, E. (2012). The Federal Reserve's Large-Scale Asset Purchase Programmes: Rationale and Effects. *The Economic Journal, 122* (564), F415–F446.

Darracq-Paries, M., & De Santis, R. A. (2015). A Non-Standard Monetary Policy Shock: The ECB's 3-year LTROs and the Shift in Credit Supply. *Journal of International Money and Finance, 54*, 1–34.

Davis, S. J. K., & James, A. (2008). Interpreting the Great Moderation: Changes in the Volatility of Economic Activity at the Macro and Micro Levels. *Journal of Economic Perspectives, 22* (4), 155–180.

De Gregorio, J. (1992). The Effects of Inflation on Economic Growth. *European Economic Review, 36* (2–3), 417–425.

De Haan, J., Amtenbrink, F., & Eijffinger, S. C. W. (1998). Accountability of Central Banks: Aspects and Quantifications. *Banca Nazionale del Lavoro Quarterly Review, 52* (209), 169–193.

De Jong, E. (2002). Why Are Price Stability and Statutory Independence of Central Banks Negatively Correlated? The Role of Culture. *European Journal of Political Economy, 18* (4), 675–694.

De Larosière, J., & Marsh, D. (2021). Central Banks Need to Change Gear. *Official Monetary and Financial Institutions Forum.* www.omfif.org/2021/02/central-banks-need-to-change-gear/

De Long, J. B. (2000). The Triumph of Monetarism? *Journal of Economic Perspectives, 14* (1), 83–94.

De Michelis, A., & Iacoviello, M. (2016). Raising an Inflation Target: The Japanese Experience with Abenomics. *European Economic Review, 16*, 1–33.

Debelle, G., & Fischer, S. (1994). How Independent Should a Central Bank Be? In J. C. Fuhrer (Ed.), *Goals, Guidelines, and Constraints Facing Monetary Policymakers* (pp. 195–225). Federal Reserve Bank of Boston.

Del Negro, M., Eggertsson, G., Ferrero, A., & Kiyotaki, N. (2017). The Great Escape? A Quantitative Evaluation of the Fed's Liquidity Facilities. *The American Economic Review, 107* (3) (March 2017), 824–857 (34 pages).

Del Negro, M., & Sims, C. A. (2015). When Does a Central Bank's Balance Sheet Require Fiscal Support? *Journal of Monetary Economics, 73*, 1–19.

Dempsey, H. (2021). Superyacht Market Surges as Wealthy Seek Luxury and Seclusion. *Financial Times*, 29 May 2021.

Destefanis, S., & Rizza, M. O. (2007). Central Bank Independence and Democracy: Does Corporatism Matter? *Rivista Internazionale di Scienze Sociali, 115* (4), 477–502.

Dicecio, R., & Gascon, C. S. (2008). New Monetary Policy Tools? *Monetary Trends* (May).

Dincer, N. N., & Eichengreen, B. (2013). Central Bank Transparency and Independence: Updates and New Measures. *Bank of Korea Working Paper No. 2013-21.*

Dluhosch, B., Freytag, A., & Krüger, M. (1996). *International Competitiveness and the Balance of Payments: Do Current Account Deficits and Surpluses Matter?* Cheltenham: Edward Elgarl.

Draghi, M. (2017). Structural Reforms in the Euro Area. *Introductory remarks by Mario Draghi, President of the ECB, at the ECB conference 'Structural reforms in the euro area', Frankfurt am Main, 18 October 2017.*

Drazen, A. (2002). Central Bank Independence, Democracy, and Dolarization. *Journal of Applied Economics, 5* (1), 1–17.

Driffill, J. (2016). Unconventional Monetary Policy in the Euro Zone. *Open Economies Review, 27,* 387–404.

Du Plessis, S. A. 2012. *Assets Matter: A New and Old View of Monetary Policy.* Presidential Address prepared for the Annual General Meeting of the Economic Society of South Africa. 25 September 2012. Presented at the University of Johannesburg.

Du Plessis, S. A., & Kotze, K. (2010). The Great Moderation of the South African Economy. *Economic History of Developing Regions, 25,* 105–125.

Dudley, W. C. (2013). Unconventional Monetary Policies and Central Bank Independence. *No 119, Speech, Federal Reserve Bank of New York.*

Dvorsky, S. (2000). Measuring Central Bank Independence in Selected Transition Countries and the Disinflation Process. *SSRN Electronic Journal.* https://ssrn.com/abstract=1016043

Easterly, W., & Fischer, S. (2001). Inflation and the Poor. *Journal of Money, Credit and Banking, 33* (2), 160–178.

Edmonds, T., Jarrett, T., & Woodhouse, J. (2010). *The Credit Crisis: A Timeline. House of Commons Standard Note, SN/BT/4991.* researchbriefings.files.parliament.uk/documents/SN04991/SN04991.pdf

Edwards, S. (2019). Modern Monetary Theory: Cautionary Tales from Latin America. *Cato Journal, 39,* 529–561.

Ehrmann, M., Fratzscher, M., Gürkaynak, R. S., & Swanson, E. T. (2010). Convergence and Anchoring of Yield Curves in the Euro Area. *Review of Economics and Statistics, 93* (1), 350–364.

Eichengreen, B. (2015). Secular Stagnation: The Long View. *American Economic Review: Papers and Proceedings, 105* (5), 66–70.

Eser, F., & Schwaab, B. (2016). Evaluating the Impact of Unconventional Monetary Policy Measures: Empirical Evidence from the ECB's Securities Markets Programme. *Journal of Financial Economics, 119* (1), 147–167.

Eucken, W. (1923). *Kritische Betrachtungen zum deutschen Geldproblem.* Jena: Gustav Fischer.

Eucken, W. (1955). *Grundsatze der Wirtschaftspolitik.* Freiburg: Mohr Siebeck.

European Commission. (2019). *A European Green Deal – Striving to be the First Climate-Neutral Continent.* https://ec.europa.eu/info/strategy/priorities-2019-2024/european-green-deal_en.

Falagiarda, M., & Reitz, S. (2015). Announcements of ECB Unconventional Programs: Implications for the Sovereign Spreads of Stressed Euro Area Countries. *Journal of International Money and Finance, 53,* 276–295.

Falagiarda, M., & Saia, A. (2013). Credit, Endogenous Collateral and Risky Assets: A DSGE Model. *Working Papers wp916, Dipartimento Scienze Economiche, Universita' di Bologna.*

Fawley, B. W., & Neely, C. J. (2013). Four Stories of Quantitative Easing. *Federal Reserve Bank of St. Louis, 95,* 51–88. https://doi.org/10.20955/r.95.51-88

Fetter, F. W. (1977). Lenin, Keynes and Inflation. *Ecomica, 44* (173), 77–80.

Filardo, A., & Grenville, S. (2012). Central Bank Balance Sheets and Foreign Exchange Rate Regimes: Understanding the Nexus in Asia. *BIS Papers 66,* 76–110. www.bis.org/events/cbbsap/filardogrenville.pdf

Fischer, S. (1995). *Modern Approaches to Central Banking.* Boston. *NBER Working Paper No. 5064.*

Fischer, S. (2015). Conducting Monetary Policy with a Large Balance Sheet. *Speech 837, Board of Governors of the Federal Reserve System (U.S.).*

Fischer, S., Sahay, R., & Végh, C. A. (2002). Modern Hyper- and High Inflations. *Journal of Economic Literature, 40* (3), 837–880.

Forder, J. (1996). On the Assessment and Implementation of 'Institutional' Remedies. *Oxford Economic Papers, 48,* 39–51.

Forder, J. (1998). Central bank Independence-Conceptual Clarifications and Interim Assessment. *Oxford Economic Papers, 50* (3), 307–334.

Forder, J. (2005). Why Is Central Bank Independence So Widely Approved? *Journal of Economic Issues, 39* (4), 843–865.

Franzese, R. T. J. (1999). Partially Independent Central Banks, Politically Responsive Governments, and Inflation. *American Journal of Political Science, 43* (3), 681–706.

Freedman, C. (1993). Designing Institutions for Monetary Stability. A Comment. *Carnegie-Rochester Conference Series on Public Policy, 39* (2), 85–94.

Freytag, A. (2001). Does Central Bank Independence Reflect Monetary Commitment Properly? – Methodical Considerations. *BNL Quarterly Review, 54,* 181–208.

Freytag, A. (2002). *Success and Failure of Monetary Reform.* Cheltenham: Edward Elgar.

Freytag, A. (2005). The Credibility of Monetary Reform – New Evidence. *Public Choice, 124* (3–4), 391–409.

Freytag, A. (2020). Sprengt das Bundesverfassungsgericht die Europäische Union? *Wirtschaftswoche online,* www.wiwo.de/politik/europa/freytags-frage-sprengt-das-bundesverfassungsgericht-die-europaeische-union/25829884 .html.

Freytag, A., & Renaud, S. (2007). From Short-Term to Long-Term Orientation? Political Economy of the Policy Reform Process. *Journal of Evolutionary Economics, 17* (4), 433–449.

Freytag, A., & Schnabl, G. (2017). Monetary Policy Crisis Management as a Threat to Economic Order. *Credit and Capital Markets, 50* (2), 151–169.

Freytag, A., & Voll, S. (2010). Staatsbankrott einmal anders: Argentinien 2010. *WirtschaftsWoche* (11/2010 of March 13, 2010), 43.

Friedman, B. M. (2000). *Monetary Policy.* Boston. *NBER Working Paper No. 8057.*

Friedman, B. M. (2002). *The Use and Meaning of Words in Central Banking: Inflation Targeting, Credibility, and Transparency.* Boston. *NBER Working Paper No. 8972.*

Friedman, M. (1948). A Monetary and Fiscal Framework for Economic Stability. *American Economic Review, 38,* 245–264.

Friedman, M. (1962). Should There Be an Independent Monetary Authority? In L. B. Yeager (Ed.), *In Search of a Monetary Constitution* (pp. 429–445). Harvard University Press.

Friedman, M. (1968). The Role of Monetary Policy. *American Economic Review, 58,* 1–17.

Friedman, M. (1970). *The Counter-Revolution in Monetary Theory.* Institute of Economic Affairs, London, IEA Occasional Paper, No. 33.

Friedman, M. (1977). Nobel Lecture: Inflation and Unemployment. *Journal of Political Economy, 85*(3), 451–472.

Friedman, M., & Schwartz, A. J. (1963). Money and Business Cycles. *The Review of Economics and Statistics*, 45 (2), 32–64.

Fry, M., Goodhart, C., & Almeida, A. (1996). *Central Banking in Developing Countries*. Routledge.

Fujiki, H., Okina, K., & Shiratsuka, S. (2001). Monetary Policy under Zero Interest Rate: Viewpoints of Central Bank Economists. *Monetary and Economic Studies*, 19 (1), 89–130.

Fukuda, S.-I. (2015). Abenomics: Why Was It So Successful in Changing Market Expectations? *Journal of the Japanese and International Economies*, 37, 1–20.

Fukuyama, F. (1992). *The End of History and the Last Man*. New York: The Free Press.

Gaettens, R. (1955). *Inflationen: das Drama der Geldentwertungen vom Altertum bis zur Gegenwart*. R. Pflaum.

Gagnon, J., Raskin, M., Remache, J., & Sack, B. (2011). The Financial Market Effects of the Federal Reserve's Large-Scale Asset Purchases. *International Journal of Central Banking*, 7 (1), 3–43.

Gambacorta, L. (2009). Monetary Policy and the Risk-Taking Channel. *BIS Quarterly Review*, 2009 (December), 43–53.

Gambacorta, L., Hofmann, B., & Peersman, G. (2014). The Effectiveness of Unconventional Monetary Policy at the Zero Lower Bound: A Cross-Country Analysis. *Journal of Money, Credit and Banking*, 46 (4), 615–642.

García Posada, M., & Marchetti, M. (2015). *The Bank Lending Channel of Unconventional Monetary Policy: The Impact of the VLTROs on Credit Supply in Spain*.

Ghosh, A., & Phillips, S. (1998). Warning: Inflation May Be Harmful to Your Growth. *Staff Papers – International Monetary Fund*, 45 (4), 672.

Ghysels, E., Idier, J., Manganelli, S., & Vergote, O. (2014). *A High Frequency Assessment of the ECB Securities Markets Programme. ECB Working Paper Series, 1642 (February)*.

Giannone, D., Lenza, M., Pill, H., & Reichlin, L. (2011). *Non-Standard Monetary Policy Measures and Monetary Developments (9781139044233)*. http://papers.ssrn.com/sol3/papers.cfm?abstract_id=1739051

Giannone, D., Lenza, M., Pill, H., & Reichlin, L. (2012). The ECB and the Interbank Market. *Economic Journal*, 122 (564), F467–F486.

Gibbon, E. (1787). *The Decline and Fall of the Roman Empire (Volume I)*. London: Frederick Warne & Co.

Gischer, H., Herz, B., & Menkhoff, L. (2005). *Geld, Kredit und Banken – Eine Einführung* (2nd ed.). Springer.

Glick, R., & Leduc, S. (2012). Central Bank Announcements of Asset Purchases and the Impact on Global Financial and Commodity Markets. *Journal of International Money and Finance, 31* (8), 2078–2101.

Goodfriend, M. (2007). *Elements of Effective Central Banking: Theory, Practice, and History.* http://ideas.repec.org/p/ess/wpaper/id1245.html

Goodfriend, M. (2014). Monetary Policy as a Carry Trade. *Monetary and Economic Studies, 32,* 29–44.

Goodhart, C. A. E. (2011). The Changing Role of Central Banks. *Financial History Review, 18* (2), 135–154.

Gordon, R. J. (2015). Secular Stagnation: A Supply Side View. *American Economic Review: Papers and Proceedings, 105,* 54–59.

Greenspan, A. (1997). Remarks at the 15th Annual Anniversary Conference of the Center for Economic Policy Research. In Stanford University, 5 September 1997.

Grilli, V., Masciandaro, D., Tabellini, G., Malinvaud, E., & Pagano, M. (1991). Political and Monetary Institutions and Public Financial Policies in the Industrial Countries. *Economic Policy, 6* (13), 342–392.

Grimes, A. (1991). The Effects of Inflation on Growth: Some International Evidence. *Weltwirtschaftliches Archiv, 127* (4), 631–644.

Griswold, D., & Freytag, A. (2023). Balance of Trade, Balance of Power How the Trade Deficit Reflects U.S. Influence in the World, Cato Policy Analysis, April.

Haas, J., Neely, C. J., & Emmons, W. R. (2020). Responses of International Central Banks to the COVID-19 Crisis. *Federal Reserve Bank of St. Louis Review. Fourth Quarter 2020, 102* (4) 339–384.

Haidar, J. I., & Hoshi, T. (2015). Implementing Structural Reforms in Abenomics: How to Reduce the Cost of Doing Business in Japan. Boston. *NBER Working Paper Series.*

Hall, R. E., & Mankiw, N. G. (1994). Nominal Income Targeting. In N. G. Mankiw (Ed.), *NBER Studies in Business Cycles* (pp. 71–94). Chicago: The University of Chicago Press.

Hamilton, J. D., & Wu, J. C. (2012). The Effectiveness of Alternative Monetary Policy Tools in a Zero Lower Bound Environment. *Journal of Money, Credit and Banking, 44* (SUPPL. 1), 3–46.

Hansen, A. H. (1941). *Fiscal Policy and Business Cycles.* New York: W. W. Norton & Company.

Hausman, J. K., & Wieland, J. F. (2015). Overcoming the Lost Decades? Abenomics after Three Years. Brookings Papers on Economic Activity, 510.

Hayek, F. A. (1990). *Denationalisation of Money – The Argument Refined.* London: Institute of Economic Affairs. Hobart Paper Special (Vol. 70).

Hayo, B. (1998). Inflation Culture, Central Bank Independence and Price Stability. *European Journal of Political Economy, 14* (2), 241–263.

Hayo, B., & Hefeker, C. (2002). Reconsidering Central Bank Independence. *European Journal of Political Economy, 18* (4), 653–674.

Hazlitt, H. (1964). *What You Should Know About Inflation.* New York: D. Van Nostrand Company, Inc.

He, L. (2017). *Hyperinflation: A World History.* Routledge.

Hetzel, R. L. (1997). The Case for a Monetary Rule in a Constitutional Democracy. *Federal Reserve Bank of Richmond, Economic Quarterly, 83* (2), 45–65.

Hibbs, D. A. (1977). Political Parties and Macroeconomic Policy. *American Political Science Review, 100* (4), 1467–1487.

Hielscher, K., & Markwardt, G. (2012). The Role of Political Institutions for the Effectiveness of Central Bank Independence. *European Journal of Political Economy, 28* (3), 286–301.

Hiroshi, U. (2015). Transmission Channels and Welfare Implications of Unconventional Monetary Easing Policy in Japan. *Working Papers e102, Tokyo Center for Economic Research.*

Hoffmann, A., & Schnabl, G. (2016). Adverse Effects of Unconventional Monetary Policy. *Cato Journal, 36* (3), 449–484.

Horn, K. (2020). In einer außergewöhnlichen Situation sind außergewöhnliche Maßnahmen erforderlich – Interview mit Isabel Schnabel. *Perspektiven der Wirtschaftspolitik, 21* (2), 137–148.

Hoshi, T., & Kashyap, A. K. (2011). Why Did Japan Stop Growing? *Report for the National Institute for Research Advancement (NIRA).*

Hume, D. (1777). Of Money, and Other Economic Essays. Reprint. Independently published 2022.

Imai, K. (2016). A Panel Study of Zombie SMEs in Japan: Identification, Borrowing and Investment Behavior. *Journal of the Japanese and International Economies, 39,* 91–107.

IMF. (2019). *Staff Proposal to Update the Monetary and Financial Policies Transparency Code* IMF Policy Paper (May 2019). Washington, DC: IMF.

IMF. (2020). *Central Bank Support to Financial Markets in the Coronavirus Pandemic.* Monetary and Capital markets. Special Series on COVID-19. Washington, DC: IMF.

Issing, O. (1999). The Eurosystem: Transparent and Accountable or 'Willem in Euroland'. *JCMS: Journal of Common Market Studies, 37* (3), 503–519.

Ito, T., & Mishkin, F. S. (2006). Two Decades of Japanese Monetary Policy and the Deflation Problem. In Takatoshi Ito & Andrew K. Rose (Eds.), *Monetary Policy with Very Low Inflation in the Pacific Rim* (pp. 131–202). Chicago: University lof Chicago Press.

James, M. H. (1996). *International Monetary Cooperation since Bretton Woods.* Washington, DC: International Monetary Fund.

Jevons, W. S. (1863). *A Serious Fall in the Value of Gold Ascertained, and Its Social Effects Set Forth.* London: E. Stanford Ltd.

Jevons, W. S. (1865). On the Variation of Prices and the Value for the Currency since 1782. *Journal of the Royal Statistical Society, 28,* 294–325.

Johnson, H. G. (1977). A Note on the Dishonest Government and the Inflation Tax. *Journal of Monetary Economics, 3* (3), 375–377.

Jones, E., & Matthijs, M. (2019). Rethinking Central Bank Independence. *Journal of Democracy, 30,* 127–141.

Joyce, M., Miles, D., Scott, A., & Vayanos, D. (2012). Quantitative Easing and Unconventional Monetary Policy: An Introduction. *The Economic Journal, 122* (564), F271–F288.

Joyce, M. A. S., & Woods, R. (2011). The United Kingdom's Quantitative Easing Policy: Design, Operation and Impact. *Bank of England Quarterly Bulletin, 51* (Quarter 3), 200–212.

Kapetanios, G., Mumtaz, H., Stevens, I., & Theodoridis, K. (2012). Assessing the Economy-Wide Effects of Quantitative Easing. *Economic Journal, 122* (564), F316–F347.

Kasper, W., & Streit, M. E. (1998). *Institutional economics: Social Order and Public Policy.* Cheltenham: Edward Elgar.

Kelton, S. (2020). *The Deficit Myth.* New York: Public Affairs.

Keynes, J. M. (1923). *A Tract on Monetary Reform.* Macmillan.

Keynes, J. M. (1924). *The Economic Consequences of the Peace.* Macmillan and Co.

Kiehling, H. (2004). Die Ansteckung der Realwirtschaft durch den Aktien-Crash – der Beginn einer neuen Ära? In L. Schuster et al. (Eds.), *Wege aus der Banken- und Börsenkrise* (pp. 239–255). Springer.

Kirchgässner, G. (1996). Geldpolitik und Zentralbankverhalten aus der Sicht der Neuen Politischen Ökonomie` In P. Bofinger & K. H. Ketterer (Eds.), *Neuere Entwicklungen in der Geldtheorie und Geldpolitik* (pp. 21–41). Tübingen: Mohr (Siebeck).

Klein, B. (1974). The Competitive Supply of Money. *Journal of Money, Credit and Banking, 6* (4), 423–453.

Klomp, J., & de Haan, J. (2010). Central Bank Independence and Inflation Revisited. *Public Choice, 144* (3–4), 445–457.

Krishnamurthy, A., Nagel, S., & Vissing-Jorgensen, A. (2014). ECB Policies Involving Government Bonds Purchases: Impact and Channels. *NBER Working Paper Series*, 1–57. http://faculty.haas.berkeley.edu/vissing/efa_krishnamurthy_nagel_vissingjorgensen.pdf%5Cnpapers2://publication/uuid/8953AEE7-7111-42E2-B109-13008F56ACFA

Krishnamurthy, A., & Vissing-Jorgensen, A. (2011). The Effects of Quantitative Easing on Interest Rates: Channels and Implications for Policy. *Brookings Papers on Economic Activity, 2011* (2), 215–287.

Krueger, A. (2020). Financial Repression Revisited. *Project Syndicate*. www.project-syndicate.org/commentary/financial-repression-for-us-debt-after-covid19-by-anne-krueger-2020-08?utm_source=Project+Syndicate+Newsletter&utm_campaign=057940dd79-sunday_newsletter_23_08_2020&utm_medium=email&utm_term=0_73bad5b7d8-057940dd79-107185814&mc_cid=057940dd79&mc_eid=1d5c86659f(August 20, 2020).

Krugman, P. (1998). It Baaack: Japan's Slump and the Return of the Liquidity Trap. *Brookings Papers on Economic Activity, 1998* (2), 137–205.

Krugman, P. (2000). Thinking About the Liquidity Trap. *Journal of the Japanese and International Economies, 14* (4), 221–237.

Kumar, N., & Barua, A. (2013). The Impact of Fed Tapering in Emerging Economies: Struggling with the Ebb. *Global Economic Outlook 7*.

Kuttner, K. (2014). Monetary Policy during Japan's Great Recession: From Self-Induced Paralysis to Rooseveltian Resolve. *Peterson Institute for International Economics Policy Brief 14-4, 2014*.

Kwon, H. U. N., Narita, F., & Narita, M. (2015). Resource Allocation and Zombie Lending in Japan in the 1990s. *Review of Economic Dynamics, 18*, 709–732.

Kydland, F. E., & Prescott, E. C. (1977). Rules Rather than Discretion: The Inconsistency of Optimal Plans. *Journal of Political Economy, 85*(3), 473–491.

Kydland, F. E., & Wynne, M. A. (2002). Alternative Monetary Constitutions and the Quest for Price Stability. *Economic & Financial Policy Review, 1* (1), 1–19.

Labonte, M. (2015). Monetary Policy and the Federal Reserve: Current Policy and Conditions. *Congressional Research Service Report for Congress, 1*, 1–20.

Laidler, D., & Parkin, M. (1975). Inflation: A Survey. *The Economic Journal, 85* (340), 741.

Lenza, M., Pill, H., Reichlin, L., & Ravn, M. (2010). Monetary Policy in Exceptional Times. *CEPR Press Discussion Paper No. 7669*.

Lerner, A. (1943). Functional Finance and the Federal Debt. *Social Research, 10*, 38–51.

Lucas, R. E. (1996). Nobel Lecture: Monetary Neutrality. *Journal of Political Economy, 104* (4), 661–682.

Lucas, R. E. (2003). Macroeconomic Priorities. *American Economic Review, 93* (1), 1–14.

Mankiw, N. G. (2020). A Skeptic's Guide to Modern Monetary Theory. *American Economic Review Papers and Proceedings, 110*, 141–144.

Marsh, D. (1992). *The Bank That Rules Europe.* London: William Heinemann.

Matsuki, T., Sugimoto, K., & Satoma, K. (2015). Effects of the Bank of Japan's Current Quantitative and Qualitative Easing. *Economics Letters, 133*, 112–116.

McCallum, B. (1995). Two Fallacies Concerning Central Bank Independence. *American Economic Review (Papers and Proceedings), 85*, 207–211.

McDonough, W. J. (1994). An Independent Central Bank in a Democratic Country: The Federal Reserve Experience. *Federal Reserve Bank of New York, Economic Quarterly, 19* (1), 1–6.

McKinnon, R. I., & Ohno, K. (1997). *Resolving Economic Conflict between the United States and Japan.* The MIT Press.

McLaren, N., Banerjee, R. N., & Latto, D. (2014). Using Changes in Auction Maturity Sectors to Help Identify the Impact of QE on Gilt Yields. *Economic Journal, 124* (576), 453–479.

Meaning, J., & Zhu, F. (2011). The Impact of Recent Central Bank Asset Purchase Programmes. *BIS Quarterly Review, 2011*, 73–83.

Meier, A. (2009). Panacea, Curse, or Nonevent? Unconventional Monetary Policy in the United Kingdom. *IMF Working Paper* (09/163).

Meinusch, A., & Tillmann, P. (2015). The Macroeconomic Impact of Unconventional Monetary Policy Shocks. *Journal of Macroeconomics, 47* (PA), 58–67.

Meltzer, A. H. (1998). Time to Print Money. *Financial Times.*

Mishkin, F. S. (2000). What Should Central Banks Do? *Federal Reserve Bank of St Louis Economic Review* (November/December), 1–13.

Mishkin, F. S., & Savastano, M. A. (2002). Monetary Policy Strategies for Emerging Market Countries: Lessons from Latin America. *Comparative Economic Studies, 44* (2–3), 45–82.

Momma, K., & Kobayakawa, S. (2014). Monetary Policy after the Great Recession: Japan's Experience. In J. Vallés (Ed.), *Monetary Policy after the Great Recession.* Madrid, Spain: FUNCAS Social and Economic Studies.

Morris, R., Ongena, H., & Schuknecht, L. (2006). The Reform and Implementation of the Stability and Growth Pact. *ECB Occasional Paper Series, 47.*

Mosser, P. C. (2020). Central Bank Responses to COVID-19. *Business Economics, 55*, 191–205.

Mueller, D. C. (2003). *Public Choice III*. Cambridge: Cambridge University Press.

Mundell, R. A. (2000). A Reconsideration of the Twentieth Century. *American Economic Review, 90* (3), 327–340.

Murphy, K., Shleifer, A., & Vishny, R. (1991). The Allocation of Talent: Implications for Growth. *The Quarterly Journal of Economics, 106* (2) (May): 503.

Neely, C. J. (2015). Unconventional Monetary Policy Had Large International Effects. *Journal of Banking and Finance, 52*, 101–111.

Nordhaus, W. D. (1975). The Political Business Cycle. *Review of Economic Studies, 42* (April), 169–190.

North, D. C. (1984). Transaction Costs, Institutions, and Economic History. *Journal of Institutional and Theoretical Economics, 140*, 7–17.

North, D. C. (1990). *Institutions, Institutional Change, and Economic Performance*. Cambridge, MA: Harvard University Press.

Obstfeld, M., & Rogoff, K. (1994). *The Intertemporal Approach to the Balance of Payments*. Boston. NBER Working Paper No. 4893.

Okina, K., & Shiratsuka, S. (2004). Policy Commitment and Expectation Formation: Japan's Experience under Zero Interest Rates. *North American Journal of Economics and Finance, 15* (1), 75–100.

Olson, M. (1982). *The Rise and Decline of Nations: Economic Growth, Stagflation, & Social Rigidities*. New Haven, CT: Yale University Press.

O'Rourke, K., & Eichengreen, B. (2010). What Do the New Data Tell Us? *VOXEU column*, 8 March 2010. Available at: https://cepr.org/voxeu/columns/what-do-new-data-tell-us.

Padoa-Schioppa, T. (2004). *Regulating Finance: Balancing Freedom and Risk*. Oxford: Oxford University Press.

Parkin, M. (1978). Central Bank Laws and Monetary Policies: A Preliminary Investigation. *Department of Economics, University of Western Ontario, Research Report 7804*.

Parkin, M. (2002). *Economics*. Boston, MA: Addison-Wesley, 6th edition.

Pattipeilohy, C., van den End, J. W., Tabbae, M., Frost, J., & de Haan, J. (2013). Unconventional Monetary Policy of the ECB during the Financial Crisis: An Assessment and New Evidence. *DNB Working Paper Series, May* (381).

Paulin, G. (2000). The Changing Face of Central Banking in the 1990s. *Bank of Canada Review* (Summer), 3–13.

Persson, T., & Tabellini, G. (1999). Political Economics and Macroeconomic Policy. In J. B. Taylor & M. Woodford (Eds.), *Handbook of Macroeconomics, Volume 1*. Amsterdam: Elsevier.

Phillips, A. W. (1950). Mechanical Models in Economic Dynamics. *Economica, 17*, 283–305.

Pill, H., & Reichlin, L. (2014). Exceptional Policies for Exceptional Times: The ECB's Response to the Rolling Crises of the Euro Area, and how it Has Brought Us Towards a new Bargain. *CEPR Discussion Paper* (No. 10193), 39.

Plosser, C. I. (2009). Ensuring Sound Monetary Policy in the Aftermath of Crisis. *Speech 24, Federal Reserve Bank of Philadelphia.*

Polo, M. (1930). *The Travels of Marco Polo (The Venetian).* New York: Liveright Publishing Corp.

Pooter, D., Desimone, R., Martin, R. F., & Pruitt, S. (2015). Cheap Talk and the Efficacy of the ECB' s Securities Market Programme: Did Bond Purchases Matter? *International Finance Discussion Papers* (1139).

Posen, A. (1998). Central Bank Independence and Disinflationary Credibility: A Missing Link? *Oxford Economic Papers, 50* (3), 335–359.

Reinhart, C. M. (2021). *Monetary Policy in an Era of High Debt.* Karl Brunner Distinguished Lecture. Zurich, Swiss National Bank. September 2021.

Reinhart, C. M., & Rogoff, K. S. (2002). *The Modern History of Exchange Rate Arrangements: A Reinterpretation.* Boston. *NBER Working Paper No. 8963.*

Reis, R. (2015). *Different Types of Central Bank Insolvency and the Central Role of Seignorage.* Boston. *NBER Working Paper No. 21226.*

Ricardo, D. (1824). *Plan for the Establishment of a National Bank.* London: John Murray.

Rieth, M., & Wittich, J. (2020). The Impact of ECB Policy on Structural Reform. *European Economic Review, 122,* 1–20.

Rodríguez, C., & Carrasco, C. A. (2014). ECB Policy Responses between 2007 and 2014: A Chronological Analysis and a Money Quantity Assessment of Their Effects. *FESSUD Working Paper, 65.*

Rogers, J. H., Scotti, C., & Wright, J. H. (2014). Evaluating Asset-Market Effects of Unconventional Monetary Policy: A Cross-Country Comparison. *No 1101, International Finance Discussion Papers, Board of Governors of the Federal Reserve System.*

Rogoff, K. (1985). The Optimal Degree of Commitment to an Intermediate Monetary Target. *The Quarterly Journal of Economics, 100* (4), 1169.

Rosa, C. (2012). How 'Unconventional' Are Large-Scale Asset Purchases? The Impact of Monetary Policy on Asset Prices. *FRB of New York Staff Report No. 560.*

Rose, A. K. (2007). A Stable International Monetary System Emerges: Inflation Targeting Is Bretton Woods, Reversed. *Journal of International Money and Finance, 26* (2007), 663–681.

Rossi, S. (2013). Post-crisis Challenges to Central Bank Independence. *Speech at the LBMA/LPPM Precious Metals Conference 2013, Rome, 30 September 2013.*

Sack, B. P. (2009). The Fed's Expanded Balance Sheet. *Remarks at the Money Marketeers of New York University, New York City.*

Sack, B. P. (2010). Reflections on the TALF and the Federal Reserve's Role as Liquidity Provider. *Remarks at the New York Association for Business Economics, New York, 9 June 2010.*

Saft, J. (2014). You Must Be Joking, Mr. Bernanke. *Reuters.* http://blogs.reuters.com/james-saft/2014/01/16/you-must-be-joking-mr-bernanke/

Samuelson, P. A., & Solow, R. M. (1960). Analytical Aspects of Anti-Inflation Policy. *American Economic Review, 50* (2), 177–194.

Sargent, T. J. (2017). The Ends of Four Big Inflations. In T. J. Sargent (Ed.), *Rational Expectations and Inflation*, 3rd ed. (Princeton, NJ, 2013; online ed., Princeton Scholarship Online, October 19, 2017).

Sargent, T. J., & N. Wallace (1981). Some Unpleasant Monetarist Arithmetic. *Federal Reserve Bank of Minneapolis Quarterly Review, 5* (3), 1–17.

Scheide, J. (1993). Preisniveaustabilität: Geldmengenregeln auch für unabhängige Notenbanken. *Zeitschrift für Wirtschaftspolitik, 42* (1–3), 97–121.

Schenkelberg, H., & Watzka, S. (2013). Real Effects of Quantitative Easing at the Zero Lower Bound: Structural VAR-based Evidence from Japan. *Journal of International Money and Finance, 33,* 327–357.

Schnabl, G. (2017). *The Impact of Japanese Monetary Policy Crisis Management on the Japanese Banking Sector. CESifo Working Paper (6440).*

Scholtes, B. (2019). *Staatliche Goldreserven – Wie Regierungen versuchen, aus Gold Geld zu machen. Deutschlandfunk (March 30, 2019).* www.deutschlandfunk.de/staatliche-goldreserven-wie-regierungen-versuchen-aus-gold.724.de.html?dram:article_id=445066

Schwartz, A. J. (1973). Secular Price Changes in Historical Perspective. *Journal of Money, Credit and Banking, 5* (February, Part II), 243–269.

Sengupta, R., & Tam, Y. (2008). The LIBOR-OIS spread as a summary indicator. *Monetary Trends, Issue Nov.*

Sheffrin, S. (1983). *Rational Expectations.* Cambridge: Cambridge University Press.

Shimizu, Y. (2019). Monetary Easing Policy and Stable Growth: A Theoretic Approach. *International Journal of Economic Policy Studies, 13,* 359–382.

Shirakawa, M. (2013). Central Banking: Before, During, and After the Crisis. *International Journal of Central Banking, 9* (SUPPL.1), 373–387.

Siklos, P. L. (2008). No Single Definition of Central Bank Independence Is Right for all Countries. *European Journal of Political Economy, 24* (4), 802–816.

Siklos, P. (2017). *Central Banks into the Breach – From Triumph to Crisis and the Road Ahead.* Oxford: Oxford University Press.

Simon, H. A. (1966). *Theories of Decision-Making in Economics and Behavioural Science*. New York: Springern.

Simons, H. C. (1936). Rules versus Authorities in Monetary Policy. *Journal of Political Economy*, *44* (1), 1–30.

Smith, A. (1776 [1981]). *An Inquiry into the Nature and Causes of the Wealth of Nations. Volume I*. Indianapolis: Liberty Fund.

Smith, V. C. (1936/1990). *The Rationale of Central Banking and the Free Banking Alternative*. Indianapolis: Liberty Press.

Stals, C. (1997). 'Mr. Stals Looks at the Effects of the Changing Financial Environment on Monetary Policy in South Africa Address by the Governor of the South African Reserve Bank,' Dr. C. Stals, at the Annual Dinner of the Pretoria branch of the Economic Society of South Africa held in Pretoria on 15/5/97.

Stark, J. (2020). Die EZB ist auf die schiefe Bahn geraten – Jürgen Stark im Gespräch. *Frankfurter Allgemeine Zeitung (FAZ)* (27 July 2020), www.faz.net/aktuell/ finanzen/was-juergen-stark-ueber-die-ezb-sagt-16876012.html?premium.

Steeley, J. M. (2015). The Side Effects of Quantitative Easing: Evidence from the UK Bond Market. *Journal of International Money and Finance*, *51*, 303–336.

Sterne, G. (1999). The Use of Explicit Targets for Monetary Policy: Practical Experience of 91 Economies in the 1990s. *Bank of England Quarterly Bulletin*, Q3 September (August), 272–281.

Steuer, W. (1997). Gibt es eine europäische Stabilitätskultur? *Wirtschaftsdienst*, *77* (2), 86–93.

Stiglitz, J. E. (1998). Central Banking in Democratic Society. *De Economist*, *146* (2), 199–226.

Summers, L. (1991). How Should Long-Term Monetary Policy Be Determined? *Journal of Money, Credit and Banking*, *23* (3), 625–631.

Summers, L. H. (2015). Demand Side Secular Stagnation. *American Economic Review: Papers and Proceedings*, *105* (5), 60–65.

Svensson, L. E. O. (1999). How Should Monetary Policy Be Conducted in an Era of Price Stability? *New Challenges for Monetary Policy*, 277–316.

Svensson, L. E. O., Houg, K., Haakon, O. A., & Steigum, E. (2002). *An Independent Review of Monetary Policy and Institutions in Norway*. Oslo: Centre for Monetary Economics at the Norwegian School of Management.

Szczerbowicz, U. (2015). The ECB Unconventional Monetary Policies: Have They Lowered Market Borrowing Costs for Banks and Governments? *International Journal of Central Banking*, *11* (4), 91–127.

Takahashi, W. (2013). Japanese Monetary Policy: Experience from the Lost Decades. *International Journal of Business*, *18* (4), 288–306.

Tappe, A. (2020). Former Fed Officials Slam Trump's Central Bank Pick and Urge Senate to Reject Her Nomination. *CNN Business*, https://edition.cnn.com/2020/08/21/economy/federal-reserve-judy-shelton-nomination/index.html (21 August, 2020).

Taylor, J. B. (1993). Discretion versus Policy Rules in Practice. *Carnegie-Rochester Conference Series on Public Policy, 39* (2), 195–214.

Taylor, J. B. (2000). Using Monetary Policy Rules in Emerging Market Economies. *75th Anniversary Conference, 'Stabilization and Monetary Policy: The International Experience'*, Bank of Mexico.

Taylor, J. B. (2009). *Getting Off Track: How Government Actions and Interventions Caused, Prolonged, and Worsened the Financial Crisis*. Stanford: Hoover Institution Press.

The Economist. (2020). Briefing: A New Era of Economics. *436* (9204), 13–16.

Tinbergen, J. (1952). *On the Theory of Economic Policy*. Amsterdam: North-Holland.

Trichet, J.-C. (2009). The ECB's Enhanced Credit Support. *CESifo Working Paper, 2833*.

Tucker, P. (2018). *Unelected Power*. Princeton, NJ: Princeton University Press.

Tullock, G., & McKenzie, R. B. (1985). *The New World of Economics*. Homewood, IL: Richard D. Irwin.

Ueda, K. (2005). The Bank of Japan's Struggle with the Zero Lower Bound on Nominal Interest Rates: Exercises in Expectations Management. *International Finance, Wiley Blackwell, 8* (2), 329–350, August.

Ueda, K. (2013). The Response of Asset Prices to Monetary Policy under Abenomics. *Asian Economic Policy Review, Japan Center for Economic Research, 8* (2), 252–269, December.

Ugai, H. (2007). Effects of the Quantitative Easing Policy: A Survey of Empirical Analyses. *Monetary and Economic Studies, 25* (1), 1–47.

Ulate, M. (2021). Going Negative at the Zero Lower Bound: The Effects of Negative Nominal Interest Rates. *American Economic Review, 111* (1), 1–40.

UNCTAD. (2020). *World Investment Report 2020*. Geneva: United Nations.

Valiante, D. (2015). The 'Visible Hand' of the ECB's Quantitative Easing. *CEPS Working Document* (407).

van't Klooster, J. (2018). Democracy and the European Central Bank's Emergency Powers. *Midwest Studies in Philosophy, 42*, 270–293.

Vaubel, R. (1986). A Public Choice Approach to International Organization. *Public Choice, 51* (1), 39–57.

Vayanos, D., & Vila, J.-L. (2009). A Preferred-Habitat Model of the Term Structure of Interest rates. *NBER Working Paper No. 15487*.

Végh, C. A. (1995). Stopping High Inflation: An Analytical Overview. In P. L. Siklos (Ed.), *Great Inflations of the 20th Century* (pp. 35–93). Cheltenham: Edward Elgar.

Vogel, E. (2016). Forward Looking Behavior in ECB Liquidity Auctions: Evidence from the Pre-Crisis Period. *Journal of International Money and Finance, 61,* 120–142.

Vollmer, U., & Bebenroth, R. (2012). The Financial Crisis in Japan: Causes and Policy Reactions by the Bank of Japan. *The European Journal of Comparative Economics, 9,* 51–77.

Vuletin, G., & Zhu, L. (2011). Replacing a 'Disobedient' Central Bank Governor with a 'Docile' One: A Novel Measure of Central Bank Independence and Its Effect on Inflation. *Journal of Money, Credit and Banking, 43* (6), 1185–1215.

Walsh, C. E. (1995). Optimal Contracts for Central Bankers. *American Economic Review, 85* (1), 150–167.

Weale, M., & Wieladek, T. (2016). What Are the Macroeconomic Effects of Asset Purchases? *Journal of Monetary Economics, 79,* 81–93.

Weymark, D. N. (2007). Inflation, Government Transfers, and Optimal Central Bank Independence. *European Economic Review, 51,* 297–315.

White, L. H. (1999). *The Theory of Monetary Institutions*. Malden and Oxford: Blackwell Publishers.

Willgerodt, H., Domsch, A., Hasse, R., & Merx, V. (1972). *Wege und Irrwege zur europäischen Währungsunion*. Freiburg: Rombach.

Woodford, M. (2003). *Interest and Prices: Foundations of a Theory of Monetary Policy*. Princeton: Princeton University Press.

Woodford, M. (2012). Methods of Policy Accommodation at the Interest-Rate Lower Bound. Paper presented at the Jackson Hole Symposium, 'The Changing Policy Landscape', 31 August to 1 September 2012, Jackson Hole, Wyoming.

World Bank. (2020). *Doing Business 2020.*

World Economic Forum. (2018). *The Global Competitiveness Report 2018.*

Wray, L. R. (2015). *Modern Money Theory: A Primer on Macroeconomics for Sovereign Monetary Systems*. Houndmills and New York. Palgrave Macmillan, 2nd volume.

Yellen, J. L. (2011). Commodity Prices, the Economic Outlook, and Monetary Policy. Paper delivered at The Economic Club of New York. New York. USA. Retrieved from www.federalreserve.gov/newsevents/speech/yellen20110411a.html.

Yellen, J. L. (2013). Challenges Confronting Monetary Policy. *Speech at the 2013 National Association for Business Economics Policy Conference, Washington, DC.*

Yellen, J. L. (2015). Normalizing Monetary Policy: Prospects and Perspectives. *Speech at 'The New Normal Monetary Policy,' A research conference sponsored by the Federal Reserve Bank of San Francisco, San Francisco, California.*

Yellen, J. L. (2016). The Outlook, Uncertainty, and Monetary Policy. *Speech at the Economic Club of New York, New York, New York.*

Index

Printed in the United States
by Baker & Taylor Publisher Services